"Dr. Pues[...] [...] the parent of a child [...] eader in the field. This [...] Down syndrome who read the successful stories of peers and to professionals who will gain knowledge and insight from the experts who have contributed to this important volume."

—**Mark L. Batshaw, M.D.**
Chief Academic Officer, Children's National Medical Center
Professor and Chair, Department of Pediatrics
and Associate Dean for Academic Affairs
The George Washington University
School of Medicine and Health Sciences

"Dr. Siegfried M. Pueschel has edited a terrific, engaging book, by and about adults with Down syndrome. We hear people with Down syndrome talk about their lives—school, work, friends, family, loves, living arrangements, hobbies, sports. They offer advice to the reader: focus on abilities and envision friends, partners, community living in their futures. These first-person essays from adults with Down syndrome are accompanied by informative chapters on issues of adult development: optimal health care, positive behavior support, self-esteem and sexuality, college and vocational support, community life and recreation, advocacy and services, well-being in aging. This is a book that will help families, professionals, and adults with Down syndrome themselves create supportive communities and celebratory lives."

—**Robin S. Chapman, Ph.D.**
Professor Emerita of Communicative Disorders
University of Wisconsin–Madison
Poet

"This book is a delightful collection. There are sixteen personal tales by inspired citizens, plus a dozen lessons that present the modern paradigm for adult life. It is a cultural victory."

—**Allen C. Crocker, M.D.**
Director, Down Syndrome Program
Children's Hospital Boston

Adults with
Down Syndrome

Adults with
Down Syndrome

edited by

Siegfried M. Pueschel, M.D., Ph.D., J.D., M.P.H.
Professor of Pediatrics
Brown University School of Medicine
Providence, Rhode Island

·P·A·U·L·H·
BROOKES
PUBLISHING Co. ®

Baltimore • London • Sydney

Paul H. Brookes Publishing Co.
Post Office Box 10624
Baltimore, Maryland 21285-0624

www.brookespublishing.com

Typeset by Auburn Associates, Inc., Baltimore, Maryland.
Manufactured in the United States of America by
Versa Press, Inc., East Peoria, Illinois.

Some of the stories in this book refer to real-life experiences. Many of the
individuals' names and other identifying features have been changed to protect individuals' identities. Stories involving real names and details are used
by permission.

Carolyn Hansen Bergeron retains copyright of her story, "The Special
Tomato," which appears on page 53.

Library of Congress Cataloging-in-Publication Data
Adults with down syndrome / edited by Siegfried M. Pueschel.
    p.   cm.
    Includes bibliographical references and index.
    ISBN-13: 978-1-55766-811-0 (pbk.)
    ISBN-10: 1-55766-811-6 (pbk.)
    1. Down syndrome.   2. Down syndrome—Patients—Biography.
    I. Pueschel, Siegfried M.   II. Title.
    RC571.A38 2006
    616.85'8842—dc22   2006008533

British Library Cataloguing in Publication data are available from the British
Library.

Contents

About the Editor

Siegfried M. Pueschel, M.D., Ph.D., J.D., M.P.H., studied medicine in Germany and graduated from the Medical Academy of Düsseldorf in 1960. He then pursued his postgraduate studies at Children's Hospital Boston and the Montreal Children's Hospital in Quebec, Canada. In 1967, he earned a master of public health degree from the Harvard School of Public Health in Boston. In 1985, Dr. Pueschel was awarded a doctoral degree in developmental psychology from the University of Rhode Island in Kingston, and in 1996, he was granted a Juris Doctor degree from the Southern New England School of Law in North Dartmouth, Massachusetts.

From 1967 to 1975, Dr. Pueschel worked at the Developmental Evaluation Clinic of Children's Hospital Boston. There, he became director of the first Down Syndrome Program and provided leadership to the PKU and Inborn Errors of Metabolism Program. In 1975, Dr. Pueschel was appointed Director of the Child Development Center at Rhode Island Hospital in Providence. He continued to pursue his interests in clinical activities, research, and training in the fields of developmental disabilities, biochemical genetics, and chromosome abnormalities, in particular Down syndrome. Dr. Pueschel has lectured both nationally and internationally. He has authored or co-authored 15 books and has written 250 scientific articles.

Dr. Pueschel is certified by the American Board of Pediatrics and is a diplomate of the American Board of Medical Genetics. His academic appointments include Lecturer in Pediatrics, Harvard Medical School, and Professor of Pediatrics, Brown University School of Medicine in Providence, Rhode Island.

About the Contributors

Angela Novak Amado, Ph.D., is Executive Director of the Human Services Research and Development Center and Research Associate at the Institute on Community Integration at the University of Minnesota. She has worked to support friendships between people with and without disabilities throughout the United States and several other countries and to empower communities to be fully inclusive.

Carolyn Hansen Bergeron lives in Dolgeville, New York, and works as an office assistant for her family's business. She also volunteers two mornings per week at a local elementary school and is training for her black belt in karate. In 2005, Ms. Bergeron became engaged to Sujeet S. Desai.

Chris Burke lives in New York and works as Goodwill Ambassador for the National Down Syndrome Society (NDSS). He is also Editor-in-Chief of the NDSS quarterly magazine, *UpBeat*. From 1989 to 1993, he played Charles "Corky" Thatcher on the television series *Life Goes On*.

Jennifer Cunningham lives in Worthington, Ohio. She attends the National Down Syndrome Congress (NDSC) Convention each year. She played Christa in the 2004 miniseries *Stephen King's Kingdom Hospital*.

Sujeet S. Desai lives in Rome, New York, and works for the New York Office on Mental Retardation and Developmental Disabilities (OMRDD). He is an accomplished violinist, pianist, and clarinetist. In 2005, he became engaged to Carolyn Hansen Bergeron.

Robert D. Dinerstein, J.D., is Professor of Law at American University, Washington College of Law. He teaches, writes, and speaks extensively on disability law issues, especially those related to people with intellectual disabilities. He is a former member of the President's Committee on Mental Retardation and a former president of the Legal Process and Advocacy division of the American Association on Mental

Retardation (AAMR). He was co-editor (with Stanley S. Herr and Joan L. O'Sullivan) of *A Guide to Consent* (AAMR, 1999).

Steven M. Eidelman, M.S.W., M.B.A., is Robert Edelsohn Professor at the University of Delaware. He has served in a number of high-profile positions at the local, state, and national levels, leading change efforts to include people with disabilities in their communities.

Ann M. Forts lives in Center Harbor, New Hampshire. She works as a motivational speaker and has started the Annie Forts UP Syndrome Fund (http://www.anniefortsupfund.org), which endeavors to raise $1,000,000 to assist people with Down syndrome.

Karen Elizabeth Gaffney lives in Portland, Oregon. She is the founder and chief speaker for the Karen Gaffney Foundation (http://www.karengaffneyfoundation.com), a nonprofit organization dedicated to making inclusion a reality for people with Down syndrome and other developmental disabilities.

Dave Hartzog volunteers for the trauma unit at the Medical University of South Carolina. A member of Redeemer Lutheran church, Mr. Hartzog is a greeter, lay reader, and Sunday School/ Vacation Bible School assistant. He enjoys helping out at home, cooking, reading, listening to music, going to the beach, and watching television.

Rose Iovannone, Ph.D., is Assistant Professor at the University of South Florida, Florida Mental Health Institute, Division of Applied Research and Educational Support. She is currently the Director of Evidence Based Strategies for Students with Severe Problem Behaviors (U.S. Department of Education grant) and co-principal investigator of the Professional Development in Autism Project—University of South Florida site. Dr. Iovannone consults with the Alabama Department of Mental Health/Mental Retardation in providing training and technical assistance in person-centered planning and positive behavior support for adults with Down syndrome.

Andrew Lee Jones lives in Kansas City, Missouri. He received his bachelor of arts degree in recreation from Graceland University in Iowa and now works as a fitness attendant for the YMCA of Kansas City. Mr. Jones lives independently in his own apartment.

Jason A. Kingsley lives in Hartsdale, New York. He works as the assistant cultural arts program coordinator for the Westchester Arc. Mr. Kingsley is also the co-author (with Mitchell Levitz) of *Count Us In: Growing Up with Down Syndrome* (Harcourt, 1994).

K. Charlie Lakin, Ph.D., is Director of the Research and Training Center on Community Living in the Institute on Community Integration at the University of Minnesota. He is the author of more than 200 books, book chapters, and journal articles on community living and public policy and is a frequent consultant to federal and state agencies. Among the recognitions for his work are appointments to the President's Committee on Mental Retardation, the Dybwad Humanitarian Award of the American Association on Mental Retardation, and the Outstanding Community Service Award of the University of Minnesota.

Katie Maly lives in Cincinnati, Ohio. She works in the mailroom at Great American Insurance Company and also as an office assistant at Cincinnati's Inclusion Network. Ms. Maly also serves on the board of the Down Syndrome Association of Greater Cincinnati. She would like to dedicate her chapter to the Inclusion Network and the Down Syndrome Association of Greater Cincinnati.

Meredith Leslie Martin lives in Neligh, Nebraska. She works part time as an office assistant at a local hospital and aspires to work there full time, with more patient-care responsibilities. She also works part time at a local grocery store.

Jeffery D. Mattson lives in Monarch Beach, California, and works at Pavilions supermarket in Laguna Beach as a courtesy clerk. In 2004, he made the keynote address at the Young Life All Staff Conference in Orlando, Florida.

Christine D. Maxwell lives in Evanston, Illinois. She attended National-Louis University's PACE program. She enjoys taking classes at the Evanston Art Center and the Evanston YMCA. Ms. Maxwell works as a ticket taker at Century Theatre.

Beverly A. Myers, M.D., is a graduate of medicine at McGill University. She trained in pediatrics at Montreal Children's Hospital and in psychiatry and child psychiatry at The Johns Hopkins Hospital. An expert in the psychiatric disorders of individuals with developmental disabilities, she has taught at Medical College of Wisconsin, The Johns Hopkins University (Kennedy Institute), and Brown University (Rhode Island Hospital Child Development Center). She has published numerous articles on the psychiatric disorders of individuals with developmental disabilities, particularly individuals with Down syndrome.

Jacob A. Neufeld, M.P.S.H., M.D., is Chair of the Division of Pediatric Rehabilitation and Associate Professor at Virginia Commonwealth

University. He holds joint appointments in the departments of neurology, pediatrics, and education. Dr. Neufeld is board certified in both pediatrics and physical medicine and rehabilitation. He completed his master of science degree in public health at the University of North Carolina, attended Wake Forest University School of Medicine, and completed residencies at Children's Hospital of Michigan and Rehabilitation Institute of Michigan at Wayne State University.

Courtney Pastorfield, PHN, is a registered nurse. She is the former manager of Healthy Athletes, a health promotion program for Special Olympics International.

Joel C. Peterson lives in Melrose, Massachusetts, where he works for Shaw's Supermarket. He recently graduated from Berkshire Hills Music Academy and performs music around the Boston area. Mr. Peterson also enjoys acting in community theater and dancing.

Mia Peterson (no relation to Joel C. Peterson) lives in Cincinnati, Ohio, and runs her own business, Aiming High. In this capacity, she gives presentations about different topics in self-determination and self-advocacy. Ms. Peterson enjoys sports and, in 2002, ran with the Winter Olympics torch through Cincinnati.

Nannie Sanchez volunteers with the Advocacy Resource Center, the Governor's Disability Committee, People First of Albuquerque, and other groups. Her passion is "working with people and politics." Ms. Sanchez is working on a book about her life.

Steven William Sauter lives in Canton, New York. He graduated from high school in 2004. His hobbies include acting, politics, swimming, baking, and biking. He hopes someday to work in an office and to do baking on the side.

Jim Schwier is a veteran volunteer with the YMCA. He was recently granted Landed Immigrant Status in Canada and travels extensively. He spends part of each year seeing family in California. Mr. Schwier enjoys going to movies, attending wine and cheese parties, making salads, exercising, and spending time on a university campus.

Karin Melberg Schwier is a writer in Canada with a focus on people with intellectual disabilities. Her most recent works include *Breaking Bread, Nourishing Connections* (co-authored with Erin Schwier Stewart; Paul H. Brookes Publishing Co., 2005) and *Sexuality: Your Sons and Daughters with Intellectual Disabilities* (co-authored with Dave Hinsburger; Paul H. Brookes Publishing Co., 2000). Ms. Melberg Schwier is the stepmother of Jim Schwier.

Pam Targett, M.Ed., is Program Director of Employment Services at Virginia Commonwealth University. She has been involved with the employment of people with significant disabilities since 1986. She oversees the supported employment program at Virginia Commonwealth University Rehabilitation Research and Training Center on Workplace Supports and Job Retention, which is directed by Dr. Paul Wehman. Her special interests include community-based vocational education and the transition of youth with severe disabilities to work.

Karen Taylor is a library/office assistant for an association for community living and for a public school. She lives in a group home, and rug hooking is her favorite hobby.

Steven J. Taylor, Ph.D., is Director of the Center on Human Policy, Professor of Cultural Foundations in Education, and Coordinator of Disability Studies at Syracuse University. He is also the co-director, along with Arlene Kanter, of the newly established Center on Human Policy, Law, and Disability Studies. Dr. Taylor specializes in qualitative research methods, the sociology of disability, disability studies, and disability policy.

Karen Toff lives in Bala Cynwyd, Pennsylvania, where she has lived independently for the past 9 years. She volunteers at Bryn Mawr Hospital and is a member of a young adult group called the Association for Developmental Disabilities, from which she received the "Member of the Year" award in 2004.

Stefanie Ward likes to cook, dance, and read and enjoys collecting stamps. She is involved in many sports through Special Olympics, including powerlifting. Ms. Ward recently finished school and is looking for full-time employment.

Paul Wehman, Ph.D., is Professor of Physical Medicine and Rehabilitation and Chairman of the Division of Rehabilitation Research at Virginia Commonwealth University (VCU). He is also Director of the VCU Rehabilitation Research and Training Center on Workplace Supports and Job Retention. Dr. Wehman is a long-time advocate for people with disabilities. His interests are employment and the transition from school to work.

Cate Weir, M.Ed., has worked with individuals with disabilities for more than 25 years. She worked for several years as Disability Support Coordinator at a community college and was the coordinator of two model demonstration projects on postsecondary education for students with significant disabilities at the University of New Hampshire.

Preface

The literature on Down syndrome has increased significantly since the 1970s. Before that time, only a few books and only a limited number of scientific articles were available on the subject. This has changed dramatically during the last 30 years, when we witnessed an exponential increase of written material on Down syndrome. A careful review of the ever-expanding literature reveals that most volumes deal with the young child with Down syndrome. In addition to biomedical information, guidelines for optimal medical care, and molecular genetic investigations, the literature pertaining to children and adolescents with Down syndrome has become replete with reports on early intervention, educational issues, behavioral concerns, and other topics.

Although this literature has been welcomed by both professionals and parents alike, there is little information available on the maturing person with Down syndrome. Only a few books discuss adolescent issues, transition from school to the world of work, supported employment, living options, and recreational opportunities.

The question then arises, Why is so little literature available on adults with Down syndrome? One of the answers to this question is that, in the decades prior to 1970, many individuals with Down syndrome did not survive early childhood, and the life expectancy was about one fourth of that observed today. In particular, children with severe congenital heart disease often succumbed during the first few years of life, and those who survived were rarely cared for adequately. Thus, not many people with Down syndrome grew up to become adults, and those who did often were placed in institutions.

The professional contributors to this book recognized the urgent need for a volume that would provide important information on the complex issues of adulthood in Down syndrome because many parents ask questions such as the following:

• Do our sons and daughters with Down syndrome have adequate educational, psychological, and vocational preparations so that they will be able to function well as adults?

- Are they in sufficient physical and mental health to allow them to perform optimally?

- What kind of living arrangements and job opportunities will be available in the community, and will they fulfill their needs?

- Will our young people with Down syndrome be able to engage in meaningful social relationships and perhaps be able to marry and have children of their own?

This book will provide answers to these questions. Most important, this book will give the reader up-to-date, comprehensive information on various aspects of the adult lives of people with Down syndrome.

A thorough literature review, the study of recent research data, and the personal experience of caring for numerous adults with Down syndrome permitted the professional contributors to concentrate on the most recent knowledge relating to this topic. Renowned scientists from the biomedical arena and the behavioral sciences as well as professionals from other fields describe succinctly the advances that have been made. These experts are uniquely qualified to discuss the progress that they have witnessed during the past decades with a sensitivity and clarity that is unmatched. For the most part, the contributors use a scholarly approach, yet they avoid as much as possible undue professional jargon that may preclude an understanding of a given topic by lay people. Their goal is to provide a text that will be read by professionals, including physicians, psychologists, educators, and other specialists involved in the care of people with Down syndrome, as well as by parents, caregivers, and other interested people.

Although the professional contributors to this book are highly proficient in their respective fields of work, this book also includes the life experiences of some "real experts," namely selected adults with Down syndrome. Their contributions are most meaningful because they go beyond both the scientific and clinical aspects relating to people with Down syndrome. These individuals provide us with insights into their daily lives, their thoughts and feelings, and their accomplishments as well as other concerns of adult life that are just not possible to be portrayed by many professionals. Although, for the most part, the essays were written by the respective authors, some of these individuals benefited from editorial assistance.

I interspersed the 16 short essays written by adults with Down syndrome throughout the book to illustrate the outstanding human qualities of the people with Down syndrome when they talk about their talents and skills as well as their frustrations and the challenges that lie ahead of them. These extraordinary individuals also speak for those people with Down syndrome who are not able to express themselves as eloquently as these individuals can, and their words signify that the dignity and worth of all individuals with Down syndrome should be acknowledged.

The primary objective of this book is to give a basic description of the many aspects of the adult lives of people with Down syndrome. The contributors and I believe that if the information in this book is applied in real life, most adults with Down syndrome will be able to live more fulfilling and happy lives; they will enjoy good physical and mental health, appropriate education, vocational and recreational pursuits as well as other positive life experiences in the community that should enhance their quality of life significantly so that they can become productive and contributing members of society.

Acknowledgments

I am foremost indebted to the innumerable people with Down syndrome I have had the privilege to care for during the past decades. These individuals taught me of their outstanding human qualities, their contribution to society, and their passion for life.

I would also like to express my gratitude to my son, Chris Pueschel, who was a true inspiration throughout his short life. Among the numerous important lessons he taught me, Chris instilled in me that the value of people with Down syndrome is intrinsically rooted in their very humanity and that there should be recognition of the dignity and worth of people with Down syndrome.

Adults with
Down Syndrome

1

■■■

Stars

MEREDITH LESLIE MARTIN

■■■

I was born a Wemmick, and so were you! Wemmicks are wooden people created by a woodworker named Eli. Each Wemmick is different. Some are beautiful. Some are smart, clever, or talented. Some are not. The Wemmicks spend their days running around putting stickers on each other. Those who do well get STARS. Those who make mistakes, fumble, or fail to excel get GRAY DOTS. Some Wemmicks are covered with STARS and feel great about themselves. Others find only GRAY DOTS for their efforts, so they do not feel good about themselves. Some even want to hide away or stop trying.

As Max Lucado (1997) writes in his book *You Are Special*, Punchinello learns that no one really needs stickers! He learns that the stickers only stick to those who let them stick. That is what it has been like growing up with Down syndrome. People have tried to put stickers on me. I have to admit I have felt pretty good about the STARS I have received, however the GRAY DOTS that have come, just because I was born with Down syndrome, are hard to live with.

My story started in April 1982. I was born in a small rural northeast Nebraska community. My parents didn't find out that I had Down syndrome until they started asking the doctor about some things they noticed about my development. Soon after the diagnosis of Down syndrome, the fun began! There was PT (physical therapy), speech therapy, early intervention services, doctor visits—you all know the routine!

Once it was time to start school, my parents had some work to do to start removing some of the GRAY DOTS. No one with Down syndrome had attended our school before. As it was, things worked out pretty well. I had a great resource teacher who taught me to read, and I love it. I struggled a bit more with math, but luckily I learned to use a calculator, so I can balance my checkbook. When I was in second grade, I made a career choice. I decided I wanted to become a nurse.

I had a few goofs in elementary school. Some folks were quick to reach out with more GRAY DOTS. After having long conversations with my parents about what I should have done and what I would try to do the next time, I told my parents that I was still learning. They quickly told me, "We are *all* still learning."

As I entered junior high school, it seemed that the GRAY DOTS from others my age were clinging pretty tightly. In order to fill my time and feel more appreciated, I began volunteering at the local nursing home and hospital. At school, I joined FCCLA (Family, Career and Community Leaders of America) and decided to compete in their annual speech contest. I received Top Gold for my speech "The Real Me—A Friend to Be" (about living with Down syndrome) and earned the right to compete at the state competition.

I continued to speak at these yearly meets throughout high school. It gave me the opportunity to tell others of my experiences and opinions about living with and meeting the challenges of a disability. It was a way for me to shed a few of those GRAY DOTS. One of the speeches centered on my motto "Aim High, Aim Far, Aim for the North Star." My "North Star" symbolized for me my independence.

My parents and I learned early on that we would meet with some challenges with health, educational, and social issues. We learned that those challenges offered a chance to bring about change and also build character. As I entered high school, I learned about self-advocacy and self-determination. Before that, I often felt that no one other than my family paid much attention to me or believed I was capable of doing things for myself or making decisions about my life.

I began to dream about my future and set my course toward my North Star. I became an active participant on my IEP (individualized education program) team. I learned to respect myself and the skills that I have. I learned that even though I was able to demonstrate skills beyond what many teachers and administrators believed, they were still hesitant to be creative in building an educational plan to truly meet my needs.

That is when we invited an advocate to become a member of my IEP team. This woman is a master at seeing potential in kids. She added a neutral slant of creativity and vision to my team. She was able to help create an individualized program that truly met my needs, rather than plugging me into an existing program that would not be practical or would be ineffective.

After my graduation from high school, I knew I wanted to go somewhere. After all, my classmates were moving on. I decided that I would move on, too. I decided to leave my parents' home and move to my own apartment. We were able to work out an 18–21 transition plan with the school. They agreed to provide an independent living instructor/job coach for a few hours each day. That, paired with my part-time independent employment, filled out my schedule nicely.

By living in my own apartment, I had to learn quickly just how to manage bills, shopping, cooking, cleaning, and all the other skills needed to live independently. It was one of the best moves I have made. I just love my independence.

My North Star was shining clearly. Yet, there was another big step that would help me move closer to my North Star. I wanted a driver's license. I had been "driving" my parents crazy about driving a red Mustang convertible for years. Well, I studied on my own, kept at my parents, hired a private driving instructor, and I am now a licensed driver! Having this license has allowed me a great deal more freedom to get to and from my jobs without having to have my parents provide transportation.

I am currently working part time at our hospital as an office assistant. It is not the same as being a nurse, but at least it is a start as I make plans to work closer to my goal of having more patient care responsibilities.

I also work at a grocery store part time. I do a number of different types of jobs there, including being a "sample lady." I am really a people person, so having jobs that allow me to meet and work with people helps fill some of my needs for friendships. My best friends from high school have graduated from college and are working away from home now. I have developed friendships with some of the people in my apartment complex. I am also an active member of my church and a member of the P.E.O. Sisterhood. I participate in a variety of exercise classes that meet weekly.

I have been dating a young man from a nearby community for several years. We enjoy dancing and listening to music when we get together. At this point in my life, I am not ready for a serious relationship with a man. I may want to get married some day. Time will tell.

Growing up with Down syndrome hasn't been all that bad. There are those who still want to attach GRAY DOTS. I do appreciate the STARS. I have tried to let neither of them influence me too much. GRAY DOTS or STARS, I have tried to focus on my own North Star. I have tried to live by the STAR philosophy. *S*—Surround yourself with positive, *S*upportive people. Find people who believe in you to be a part of your life and your IEP team. *T*—Take every opportunity possible to *T*each others about your disability. *A*—Always *A*dvocate for yourself. Let your dreams be known and then—*R*—*R*each for your North Star.

I have accomplished most everything I have set out to do. Although I am not there yet, and perhaps I will never actually reach my ultimate dream of becoming a nurse, I know that I don't ever want to quit trying. I will continue that journey, I will continue to learn, I will continue to advocate for myself and teach others of all the things people with disabilities can do if they are given some opportunities, given the needed support, and given a chance to reach for their North Star.

REFERENCE

Lucado, M., with Martinez, S. (Illus.). (1997). *You are special.* Wheaton, IL: Crossway Books.

2

...

My Adult Life Up to Now

JASON A. KINGSLEY

...

Hi-ho, I'm Jason Kingsley. I'm 30 years old, and I live on Chatterton Parkway in Hartsdale, New York, with two other roommates. One has worked 7 years at a pet store here in Hartsdale. The other roommate works at a law firm in Armonk, New York. He works in some of the law offices doing some office work.

We have been living in our house since 2 years ago. The house is a certified residence that Westchester ARC runs. We have 63 hours a week of staff supervision. The staff and the house manager observe us—how we live on our own, how we take care of our rooms, how we keep track of our meds, how we cook, and how we manage our money budgeting. We are doing pretty well up to now.

We sometimes are called The Three Musketeers, which means "all for one and one for all." Sometimes, that gets some of us in trouble. Some of the times, we disagree on different things and we don't all want to do the same thing. We are trying to find out ways to compromise and take turns to solve these problems. But somehow a lot of the ways of compromising don't work out at all.

There are some times we do need help working out our difficulties. We have a therapist that we talk to about our problems, and she gives us our techniques. She comes in once a week to help us to do some conflict resolution.

I also see my own therapist who helps me with my problems. He wants me to help myself to find some ways to solve my problems.

Some of the problems were I was having outbursts on my job. I was feeling depressed and angry because of my dad's death. It was very hard for me to adjust to it, and the truth is that I still haven't gotten adjusted to it. The outbursts were from my dad's death, and somehow I've been having a lot of problems accepting it.

My dad's death was a big blow for me, and because of that I gained a lot of weight. I had trouble sleeping, and, with the weight, it turns out I have sleep apnea. That does affect me focusing on the job, falling asleep on the job, and often being in a bad mood—on the job and off the job.

Now, I will be using a CPAP (continuous positive airway pressure) machine to see if that works to cure the sleep apnea. The doctors say it will diminish all those problems I just had. But I feel that I have many many doubts that it's going to work. But I'm going to try it, and I hope it will help. If it doesn't work, there is a kind of surgery where they take out the back of my tongue and the back of my throat to open up the airways towards the lungs. I hope we don't have to do that. I hope the CPAP will work, but I don't know what will happen if it doesn't.

In my leisure time, what I like to do is go out to the movies or to shows or concerts. My mom and I go out for something called "Lyrics and Lyricists." That is a series of concerts of composers and writers of music and lyrics. Each concert has the work of one lyricist, and people perform songs of that lyricist. We have been doing that for many years.

When I was growing up, I learned to listen to Broadway musicals, and I still like Broadway musicals even now. I know them all very well. My favorites are *Anything Goes, Carnival, Oliver,* and *Annie Get Your Gun.* Those are my favorites because I was working with them in the Drama Club in high school called Wig 'n' Whiskers.

Other than Broadway shows, I also played musical instruments and had lessons in them. My first instrument was the recorder. Then, when I was pretty good, I learned the violin and the piano for many years.

And I sing a lot, too. I sing many, many songs from many shows I love. Two of my biggest hit songs I love singing are "To Dream the Impossible Dream" and "If Ever I Would Leave You." The first one is from *Man of La Mancha,* and the other is from *Camelot.* I sing that in the car all the time.

One of the hit single songs I love is "Wind Beneath My Wings." Whenever my Mom and I hear that song, we have to stop what we are doing and dance together. No matter what. Sometimes, we hear that song in an elevator or in a supermarket. We always have to dance together no matter where we are if we hear that song, "Wind Beneath My Wings." Mom says I am the wind beneath her wings.

And I also love some of the songs that my dad loved to sing at his time, meaning songs of Nelson Eddy and Jeanette MacDonald.

Dad loved to sing "McNamara's Band" to me when I was going to sleep. He said that was his best lullaby. And I hope one day in the future that my Mom or I can make a CD of our classic songs of our family's past times.

A happy and sad memory is riding along in the convertible with my dad singing "Stout Hearted Men," and we also sang it at his memorial.

My dad was a fun-spirited guy. He made fun out of things that he taught me, like batting practice. The reason why we love batting practice is because my dad is into sports, as I am. He taught me to love sports.

There's two parts of Dad. One part was that he was the President of the Board of Westchester ARC, and we did a lot of charity drives and speeches. He founded the MBIA Invitational Golf and Tennis Tournament that raises money for Special Olympics and Westchester ARC.

The other side of Dad was the family that he also loved. He taught me to love the Chicago Cubs. So two of my favorite teams in baseball are the New York Yankees and the Chicago Cubs to honor my dad. My dad said that if the Cubs ever make the World Series that he will buy tickets for my brothers and me to watch the Cubs against the Yanks. Unfortunately, that has never happened since 1916. Every year, my dad would hope, but it would never happen.

And also I learned some other teams of baseball, but those teams were from my movies. Like the Cleveland Indians (that is from the movie *Major League*), the Chicago White Sox (in the movie of *Field of Dreams),* the Washington Senators (in the film called *Damn Yankees),* the Anaheim Angels (from *Angels in the Outfield),* and finally the Pittsburgh Pirates (from the 1950s version of *Angels in the Outfield,* black and white version).

As you can see, I love movies. I have a huge collection of videos. I have a complete set of Disney feature films up to now. There are some new films that I am waiting to get.

My roommates and I have "Movie Night" every night. We watch one of our videos. But Friday night is a special Movie Night because we send out for pizza or wedges for dinner. We have no staff coverage on Fridays. That's our favorite night of the week.

So, you can see my life is pretty good. I am working 2 days a week at a radio station doing a lot of media work on the radio. I hope I can turn it into a full-time job some day.

I hope to be married and live on my own some day, depending on how much supervision I still need after I master all my goals or most of my goals. Because some of them I can learn at a new place that I might be moving into. Those are my long-range goals.

... 3 ...

Optimal Health Care
and Medical Concerns

Siegfried M. Pueschel

GENERAL HEALTH MAINTENANCE

In the past, many individuals with Down syndrome were not afforded adequate medical care. Fortunately, this has changed significantly, and there have been major improvements in health care provision for people with developmental disabilities since the 1980s. Today, people are aware of the dignity and human rights of individuals with developmental disabilities, including those with Down syndrome; therefore, individuals with Down syndrome should be offered the same general health care and regular checkups as any other individual in the community. It is paramount that optimal health maintenance enhances the well-being of individuals with Down syndrome in all areas of human functioning.

Medical History and Physical Examination

During a medical visit, a person with Down syndrome will first be asked by the physician for his or her medical history to determine any significant changes in his or her physical or mental well-being. Next, the physician will conduct a "review of systems" by asking questions relating to vision; hearing; respiration; and cardiac, gastrointestinal, genitourinary, and neuromuscular functioning. At this time, he or she will also explore any other existing medical problems. Additional questions include nutrition and dietary issues; use of medications; sleep habits; vocational and recreational concerns; living arrangements; behavioral and psychiatric aspects; and social, environmental, and family circumstances. The physician will typically use guidelines for the health care of individuals with Down syndrome, as developed by the American Academy of Pediatrics (2001), the Down Syndrome

Medical Interest Group (Cohen, 1999), and an International Consortium that developed Guidelines for Optimal Medical Care of Persons with Down Syndrome (Pueschel et al., 1995).

Although in the past many physicians followed a paternalistic approach, they now more often realize the importance of communicating with the individual with Down syndrome. Specific questions should be addressed directly to the person, proper eye contact should be established, and simple, understandable language that is free of medical jargon should be used. If the person has significant intellectual disabilities and/or verbal communication is not feasible, then the accompanying parents or caregivers will need to be involved in order to obtain a pertinent medical history.

During subsequent complete physical and neurologic examinations, privacy should be taken into consideration and, of course, the person should be treated with kindness, respect, and dignity. In this way, a trusting relationship with the individual can be established, and the physician will usually be able to carry out the examination with full cooperation.

If the historical information and/or the physical examination reveal any specific concerns, these should be further investigated. For example, if blood is observed in the stool, a thorough gastrointestinal evaluation may be required. If the individual has been noted to snore and not breathe well during sleep, a sleep study should be arranged to rule out sleep apnea. For these and other specific medical issues, a professional from a subspecialty may need to be consulted.

Preventive Care

Although preventive health care for people with Down syndrome should be the same as for the general population, there are some specific issues of health supervision for individuals with Down syndrome that will be discussed in detail later in this chapter. Physicians need to review the immunization status of the individual, and, at an appropriate time, influenza, pneumococcal, hepatitis B, and other vaccines should be administered if indicated. Also, the adverse effects of smoking and alcohol consumption, prevention of accidents, and sexual abuse should be discussed at regular medical visits. Moreover, screening for increased cholesterol levels, hypertension, and osteoporosis should be conducted. Men should receive prostate and testicular cancer screening, and women should receive a Pap smear and breast examination. On an annual basis, individuals with Down syndrome should have vision and hearing screenings; thyroid function tests; determinations of zinc, selenium, and antiendomysial antibodies (the latter test will screen for celiac disease); and other tests as indicated. Appropriate dental hygiene should be discussed, and semiannual dental cleanings and examinations should be arranged. Other aspects of routine health care include periodic weight checks with the recommendation of a balanced diet with an adequate, but moderate, caloric intake (see section on nutrition) and regular exercise.

Approach to Comprehensive Health Care

Comprehensive health maintenance should focus on the whole person, including physical, mental, and social aspects. Health care for people with Down syndrome should be individualized, with an ultimate goal of keeping individuals with Down syndrome well adjusted and healthy, preventing illnesses and accidents, and emphasizing a healthy lifestyle. Successful health maintenance also requires the active participation of the individual as well as parents and/or caregivers. Whenever possible, adults with Down syndrome should take part in the decision-making process with regard to their health care.

NUTRITION

The following discussion of nutrition and dietary concerns is merely a brief overview. For more detailed information, see Guthrie Medlen (2002) and Pueschel (1999).

General Dietary Issues

Good nutrition and regular exercise are important among the many environmental and genetic factors that affect the pursuit of a healthy lifestyle. In order for both the body and the mind to function optimally, certain nutrients, including proteins, fats, carbohydrates, minerals, and vitamins, are required. These nutrients include the four basic food groups: 1) meat, fish, and eggs; 2) fruits and vegetables; 3) cereals and bread; and 4) milk and dairy products.

Information on proper nutrition for individuals with Down syndrome should be provided to parents or caregivers early on. Parents and caregivers should be told about the basic elements of a balanced diet. In general, three meals that are high in fiber (whole grain carbohydrates), contain meat or meat alternatives (e.g., fish, peanut butter), a variety of fruits and vegetables (in particular, those containing antioxidants), and small amounts of mostly unsaturated fats are recommended each day in addition to adequate fluid intake. Well-prepared meals that take into account these factors and are appropriate in caloric content should also be enjoyable. There is no reason why healthy eating cannot be pleasurable as well as nutritious.

Improper weight management and nutrition can lead to health problems, so it is very important to monitor the caloric intake, height, and weight of a person with Down syndrome. Regular physical activity should also be promoted to prevent obesity, one of many health risks associated with improper diet and lack of activity.

The Body Mass Index (BMI), which measures a person's height/weight ratio, is a good tool to indicate if an individual with Down syndrome is overweight. The BMI number is expressed as a person's weight in pounds divided by the square of the person's height in inches x 703. (Following the metric system, this calculation is: weight $(kg)/[height (m^2)]$.) Incidentally, this same calculation is accurate and can be used for both men and women. If a person's BMI falls between 20 and 25, the person is at the low-risk range for certain health problems. A BMI between 25 and 30 is considered overweight, and a BMI of more than 30 is considered obese. If the BMI of an individual is in either of these latter two categories, weight management is highly recommended (Guthrie Medlen, 2002).

Increased Weight Gain

During adolescence and into adulthood, many individuals with Down syndrome may become overweight. The adverse effects of obesity include diabetes mellitus, coronary artery disease, hypertension, and reduced life expectancy. If a person is significantly overweight, he or she may be less active, and in turn, this may affect his or her ability to participate in sports and recreational activities. A person's physical appearance is often an important factor in his or her social acceptability, so an overweight person also may have fewer opportunities for social interaction. Because obesity often carries a social stigma, it may affect the person's self-image.

Once a person with Down syndrome has become overweight, he or she will have a difficult time losing the excess weight. A behavior modification approach together with limited food intake, increased exercise, and cooperation of the individual and his or her parents or caregivers are the main elements of a successful weight reduction program.

Why are people with Down syndrome often overweight? Although there may be many answers to this question, such as increased food intake and a sedentary lifestyle, one of the answers relates to metabolic processes that take place when food is ingested. In this regard, the energy expenditure of individuals with Down syndrome is of paramount significance. Some investigators report that people with

Down syndrome have a markedly lower resting metabolic rate than other individuals (Allison et al., 1995; Luke, Roizen, Sutton, & Schoeller, 1994). It has also been noted that the energy expenditure of people with Down syndrome is significantly decreased (Chad, Jobling, & Frail, 1990). The decreased energy expenditure may be partially responsible for the observed weight gain in individuals with Down syndrome, and this needs to be taken into account when recommending an appropriate caloric intake of a balanced diet.

Megavitamins and Nutritional Supplements

Individuals with Down syndrome who get an adequate intake of nutrients through their normal diet will not need additional large supplements of vitamins and minerals. There are, however, some people who claim that adults with Down syndrome lack certain "nutrients," such as amino acids, vitamins, and minerals. They often claim that adults with Down syndrome will improve significantly when they are provided with such compounds. From the 1950s to the 1980s, Turkel (1975) recommended his U-series that included 49 compounds, such as vitamins, hormones, enzymes, and minerals. In 1981, Harrell, Capp, and Davis claimed that high doses of several vitamins and minerals improved intellectual function in individuals with Down syndrome; however, other investigators who attempted to replicate Turkel's and Harrell's programs did not find any benefit and reported that there was no enhanced cognitive function or neuromotor abilities in individuals with Down syndrome who followed either of these approaches (Pueschel, 1992).

In spite of these findings, many individuals with Down syndrome are provided with "nutritional supplements" such as Nutrivene-D, Hap-Caps, MSB Plus, Mirenex, and others. Although there are some anecdotal reports of the positive effects of these supplements and unsubstantiated claims of significant improvement of individuals with Down syndrome made by various manufacturers of these "nutritional supplements," there is no scientific evidence that individuals with Down syndrome benefit from such "therapy." Often, "nutritional supplements" contain large doses of vitamins, minerals, specific amino acids, and other compounds that are supposed to be beneficial but may have harmful side effects. Ani, Grantham-McGregor, and Muller (2000) have said that certain claims that nutritional supplements improve the outcome in people with Down syndrome have "left many health professionals confused and parents vulnerable to pressures to spend large amounts of money on these supplements whose benefits have not been proved" (p. 212). Also, Lejeune mentioned that "no claim of effective treatment has withstood scientific scrutiny" (1992, p. 661).

Zinc, Selenium, and Antioxidants

Among others, there are three specific metabolic concerns related to zinc, selenium, and antioxidants (Ani et al., 2000; Pueschel & Anneren, 1992). Several investigators have reported low *zinc* levels in many individuals with Down syndrome, and there have been a number of studies indicating that zinc supplementation will improve the health of these individuals. Although there are encouraging results from these studies that zinc supplementation will enhance the individual's immunity and thyroid function and may have other health benefits, there is a need for further rigorous controlled clinical studies.

Some individuals with Down syndrome have reduced *selenium* blood levels. Selenium is known to be an important cofactor in the glutathione peroxidase system and also has immunoregulatory functions. Therefore, if significantly low zinc and/or selenium blood levels are observed in individuals with Down syndrome, supplementation of these elements should be provided.

The oxygen metabolism in individuals with Down syndrome is affected due to the presence of increased oxidative stress. Because the gene for superoxide dismutase, an important enzyme within the body, is coded for on chromosome 21 and because there are three such chromosomes in individuals with Down syndrome, there is an overexpression of this enzyme. This increased enzyme activity results in free radicals responsible for enhanced cellular death and other negative effects. It has been suggested that the increased oxidative stress may lead to accelerated aging, decreased brain function, and perhaps Alzheimer disease.

Antioxidant therapy has a theoretical basis because the administration of *antioxidants* to tissue cultures has significantly reduced the harmful effects of oxidative stress and decreased the process of cell death. Yet, no long-term, well-controlled clinical studies have evaluated the supplementation of antioxidants in individuals with Down syndrome.

Synopsis

If people with Down syndrome have an intact gastrointestinal tract with normal physiologic and biochemical functions, if they are encouraged to exercise, and if they are provided with a balanced diet with an appropriate caloric intake that takes into consideration the energy metabolic concerns and nutritional aspects such as zinc, selenium, and antioxidants, their general health will be enhanced.

DERMATOLOGIC CONDITIONS

Individuals with Down syndrome experience similar skin conditions to those observed in the general population and some of these skin conditions are observed at an increased frequency.

Skin Infections

Infections or inflammations of the hair follicles (folliculitis) of the perigenital, thigh, and gluteal areas are often seen in adolescents and adults with Down syndrome, particularly in those who are overweight. These benign skin conditions can be treated best by regular sitz baths using antibacterial soap and subsequent frequent applications of antibiotic ointment (3–4 times daily). Most of the time, there will be significant improvement; however, in severe cases with formation of abscesses, a systemic antibiotic might need to be added to the treatment regimen.

Fungal infections of the toenails (onychomycosis) are also a common problem encountered by individuals with Down syndrome. Antifungal therapy should clear up the infection, although in some adults with Down syndrome, these fungal infections may be difficult to eradicate.

Xerosis

Xerosis is a very dry and rough skin condition that is rarely seen in very young children; however, by the age of 15 years, 70% of individuals with Down syndrome show mild to moderate symptoms of xerosis (Burton & Rook, 1986). Treatment options that may relieve some of the dryness of the skin are lubricating creams, emollients, moisturizers, and oils added to bath water. Similarly, thickening of the upper layers of the skin (hyperkeratosis), primarily on the feet and hands, is often encountered in adults with Down syndrome. Treatments vary depending on the type of hyperkeratosis (from corns to calluses), including home remedies to remove warts, skin peels, laser therapy, and cryosurgery.

Seborrheic Dermatitis

According to Carter and Jegasothy (1976), seborrheic dermatitis is noted in about one third of individuals with Down syndrome. These lesions are often located at the scalp, ears, skin folds, and eyebrows. Local treatment with special shampoos, topical steroid solutions, or ketoconazole cream will usually be effective. Atopic dermatitis (eczema) is usually treated with corticosteroid ointment or cream. It may be seen often in young children, but it is rarely observed in adults with Down syndrome.

Multiple Syringomas

Multiple syringomas are benign appendigeal tumors that are found in 20%–40% of individuals with Down syndrome. Syringomas are small yellowish papules often seen at the eyelids, at the upper part of the chest, and at the neck area (Moschella & Hurley, 1985). Although they can be removed surgically (usually with laser therapy), multiple syringomas are typically only operated on for cosmetic purposes.

Elastosis Perforans Serpiginosa

In elastosis perforans serpiginosa, thickened elastic fibers from the papillary dermis produce keratotic papules on the skin. These relatively rare skin lesions may be grouped or arranged in an annular (ring-shaped) pattern and most often occur at the face, on the arms, and at the nape of the neck. Although this benign skin condition may last for many years, it usually resolves without specific treatment (Benson & Scherbenske, 1992). Elastosis perforans serpiginosa can be removed by cryotherapy with liquid nitrogen, although this technique often leaves scars. A newer method using a flashlamp pulsed dye laser may prove to be an effective method (Kaufman, 2000).

Alopecia and Vitiligo

Alopecia areata and alopecia totalis are more often seen in people with Down syndrome than in the general population (Carter & Jegasothy, 1976). In alopecia areata, hair loss is noted in one or more areas of the scalp or other hairy areas of the body, whereas in alopecia totalis, all hair on the body is lost. The cause of the hair loss is not known, but it is most likely associated with autoimmune and genetic factors. Many individuals with alopecia areata may experience regrowth of hair within a year. Various therapeutic approaches have been suggested such as application of topical steroid ointments, injection of corticosteroids into the bald spots, minoxidil, and oral prednisone (Mitchell & Krull, 1984).

Vitiligo is a lack of pigment in some areas of the skin, which may occur in conjunction with alopecia. Treatment options include cortisone ointments and phototherapy. Other skin disorders that may be present in individuals with Down syndrome, such as scabies and psoriasis, usually do not occur at an increased frequency.

THYROID DISORDERS

Among several endocrinologic disorders observed in individuals with Down syndrome, thyroid abnormalities are of primary concern because of their high prevalence (Pueschel & Blaymore Bier, 1992) in this population. A voluminous literature pertaining to this topic has accumulated since the 1960s, and many reports have focused on various thyroid disorders including autoimmune problems, different forms of hypothyroidism, hyperthyroidism, and others.

Autoimmune Thyroiditis

Autoimmune thyroiditis is a condition in which the body develops antibodies against the person's own thyroid tissue, which can lead to a lack of thyroid hormone (hypothyroidism). Schindler (1989) reported that the incidence of autoimmune thyroiditis is about 30 times higher in individuals with Down syndrome than it is in the general population. People with Down syndrome may have an increased prevalence of autoimmune thyroiditis because of a triple gene dosage for specific receptors and/or because of an association between particular HLA antigens and autoimmune thyroiditis, viral infections, and others (Percy et al., 1990).

There is a significant positive correlation between antimicrosomal antibodies and increased thyroid-stimulating hormone as well as between decreased thyroxine levels and antimicrosomal antibodies (Pueschel & Pezzullo, 1985). These results indicate that individuals with Down syndrome who have hypothyroidism may have previously had Hashimoto thyroiditis. Treatment is limited to regular observation by a health care provider unless the condition results in hypothyroidism, in which case thyroid hormone is administered.

Hypothyroidism

Numerous investigators have emphasized that autoimmune processes are the main pathogenetic factors leading to hypothyroidism in individuals with Down syndrome (Pueschel & Blaymore Bier, 1992). An estimated 15%–50% of adults with Down syndrome have hypothyroidism, and in one study, abnormal thyroid function was found in 40.5% of 106 adults with Down syndrome (Dinani & Carpenter, 1990). Another study found that in 82 individuals with Down syndrome, 46% had abnormalities in one or more of the thyroid parameters (Murdoch, Ratcliffe, McLarty, Rodger, & Ratcliffe, 1977). Rooney and Walsh (1997) reported that the frequency of thyroid dysfunction increases with age. Also, other researchers reported a decline of thyroxine (T4) and triiodothyronine (T3) as individuals with Down syndrome advanced in age, indicating a decrease of thyroid function (Pueschel et al., 1991).

Establishing a clinical diagnosis of hypothyroidism may be difficult because the symptoms of hypothyroidism overlap with the observed findings in Down syndrome, particularly in the early stages of hypothyroidism. Later, symptoms may include lethargy, intolerance to cold, coarseness of voice, slowing of motor activity and intellectual functioning, dryness of skin, loss of hair, menstrual irregularities, slow heart rate, and swelling of the eyelids. It is paramount to identify individuals with hypothyroidism early because the lack of thyroid hormone will decrease cognitive function in individuals with Down syndrome (Pueschel et al., 1991).

In severe uncompensated hypothyroidism, thyroid-stimulating hormone will be significantly increased and thyroxine will be decreased. In compensated hypothyroidism, thyroxine will usually be normal or only slightly decreased, but the thyroid-stimulating hormone will be very high. It has been suggested that compensated hypothyroidism is more common in adults with Down syndrome who also have Alzheimer disease (Percy et al., 1990).

Some researchers think that zinc deficiency may be causatively related to subclinical hypothyroidism and that zinc supplementation will improve thyroid function in hypozincemic individuals with Down syndrome (Bucci et al., 1999). Other researchers have found a positive correlation between free thyroxine and selenium, suggesting that thyroid hypofunction is linked to low selenium levels and that selenium-containing proteins are involved in thyroid hormone synthesis (Kanavin, Aaseth, & Birketvedt, 2000).

Hyperthyroidism

Whereas hypothyroidism is common in Down syndrome, hyperthyroidism, the overproduction of thyroid hormone, is less often encountered. The prevalence of hyperthyroidism is 0.87%–2.5% in individuals with Down syndrome, and there have been reports of individuals with Down syndrome who have various degrees of hyperthyroidism (Pueschel & Blaymore Bier, 1992; Sustrova & Pueschel, 1998).

Testing for Thyroid Disorders

If a thyroid disorder is not recognized early, it may further compromise a person's intellectual functioning. Thyroid function tests, including thyroid-stimulating hormone, thyroxine, and others, if indicated, should be carried out at regular intervals and at least annually. When a person with Down syndrome is found to have hypo- or hyperthyroidism, prompt treatment should be forthcoming.

OPHTHALMOLOGY

As in other areas of investigation, many more studies on ocular problems have been carried out in children with Down syndrome than in adults, and there is only limited accurate information available on the latter population. Because there is little change in many ocular findings over time, the results of investigations performed during childhood are, for the most part, also relevant for adults. For example, hypotelorism (closely-spaced eyes), Brushfield spots (white speckles at the periphery of the iris), and often refractive errors will continue to be present in the mature person with Down syndrome.

In 1989, Caputo, Wagner, Reynolds, Guo, and Goel reviewed the prevalence of ocular features in people with Down syndrome and reported strabismus (inability of one eye to attain binocular vision with the other) in 65%, myopia (nearsightedness) in 22.5%, hyperopia (farsightedness) in 20.9%, and astigmatism in 22%. Among the various eye disorders that occur at an increased frequency in individuals with Down syndrome, the most important ones will be briefly discussed next.

Blepharitis

Blepharitis, an inflammation of the eyelid margin, sometimes covered with a crust, occurs in about 2%–47% of individuals with Down syndrome (Catalano, 1992). Mild blepharitis can be easily treated by wiping the eyelid margins daily using a clean washcloth or cotton swab dipped into baby shampoo. In the case of severe blepharitis accompanied by purulent discharge and conjunctivitis, an ophthalmic antibiotic ointment or drops should be prescribed and administered.

Strabismus

Strabismus is a vision problem in which the eyes are misaligned. Two common forms of strabismus are esotropia (inward turning of eyes) and exotropia (outward turning of the eyes). Esotropia in individuals with Down syndrome may be due to decreased fusional or visual resolution capacity or a failure to develop adequate accommodative convergence mechanism (Jaeger, 1980). Esotropia is more often seen than exotropia, and both may be associated with refractive errors.

Refractive Errors

Refractive errors are common in individuals with Down syndrome. The prevalence of high nearsightedness (myopia) has been estimated to be between 35% and 40%, and farsightedness (hyperopia) occurs in about 20% of individuals with Down syndrome (Jaeger, 1980). Correction of the refractive errors are usually accomplished in the same way as in other individuals who do not have Down syndrome, by prescribing appropriate glasses or contact lenses.

Amblyopia

Amblyopia (lazy eye) is defined as unilateral decreased visual acuity. Researchers have found between 12.5% and 22% of individuals with Down syndrome in their respective study cohorts to have amblyopia (Jaeger, 1980; Pueschel & Giesswein, 1993). Again, these individuals are in need of appropriate correction of their visual problem, which includes patching of "the good eye" and glasses to correct vision.

Keratoconus

Keratoconus, which affects the cornea of the eye, was rarely described in individuals with Down syndrome until the 1970s. This noninflammatory eye condition is characterized by progressive changes in the shape of the cornea. Today, keratoconus is recognized more frequently, and various investigators indicate that 5%–15% of people with Down syndrome have keratoconus (Schapiro & France, 1985). Proper treatment and follow-up should be offered. Treatment options include eyeglasses or contact lenses; corneal collagen crosslinking with riboflavin (C3-R), which increases collagen crosslinking to make the cornea stronger; the placement of Intacs, small plastic rings that are surgically placed in the cornea to flatten the central area of the cornea; and corneal transplants.

Cataracts

Although cataracts are found in approximately 3% of all newborns with Down syndrome, the percentage of adults with Down syndrome who have cataracts is nearly 13% (National Institute of Child Health and Human Development, 2005; Smith, 2001). Cataracts are cloudy areas on the lens of the eye that block the passage of light. They are most often gray, flake, or punctate opacities with a predilection for the peripheral cortex and the anterior and posterior polar areas of the lens

(Jaeger, 1980). Senile cataracts, a gradual thickening of the lens, occur in people with Down syndrome at a younger age, possibly due to the accelerated aging process in individuals with Down syndrome. If cataracts severely affect the person's vision, cataract surgery can be performed to restore vision.

Synopsis

There is an increased prevalence of several ocular disorders in individuals with Down syndrome that could lead to significant disability if not attended to appropriately. Cataracts and acute keratoconus continue to be principal causes of visual loss, and high refractive errors and strabismus may be functionally debilitating. Treatments for all of these disorders are available; therefore, individuals with Down syndrome should have regular follow-up visits with an ophthalmologist.

EAR, NOSE, AND THROAT CONCERNS

Auditory and ear, nose, and throat concerns are often encountered in children with Down syndrome but less frequently in adults. Many children with Down syndrome are known to have recurrent ear infections, fluid accumulations in the middle ear, hearing loss, and other ear problems that are rarely seen in adults with Down syndrome. The treatment of most of the auditory and ear, nose, and throat problems in adults with Down syndrome does not differ in that ear infections will be treated with antibiotics if indicated, and severe hearing impairments will often necessitate hearing aids. If the tonsils are very large and cause airway narrowing, then tonsillectomy will need to be performed.

Structural Variations

Anatomic variations in adults with Down syndrome are similar to those observed in children with Down syndrome (Pueschel, 1984). The external ear is structured differently and relatively small. The most prominent finding is the overfolding of the upper part of the ear (helix), absent or attached earlobes, and projecting ears. There are also structural abnormalities of the ossicles (the bony structures that reside in the middle ear) (Balkany, Mischke, Downs, & Jafek, 1979).

The nose of the very young child with Down syndrome is usually smaller than average and the nasal bridge is depressed. As the individual matures, his or her nose appears normal in structure, although the nasal passage may be narrow.

The oral cavity of individuals with Down syndrome is frequently small; therefore, the tongue may appear large. However, an abnormally large tongue (macroglossia) is usually not present. The palate is often narrow and may be high and/or short due to the smaller than average bony structures. The small oral cavity and the relatively large tongue may lead to mouth breathing and tongue protrusion in some individuals with Down syndrome (Dahle & Baldwin, 1992).

Also, structural variations are noted in the back of the throat (pharyngeal area). The pharynx is usually narrow, and sometimes enlarged tonsils and adenoids are present. Together with other factors, these altered anatomic structures may contribute to the increased prevalence of sleep apnea in individuals with Down syndrome (see section on pulmonary issues). Sclerotic mastoid bones, abnormalities of the tympanic membranes and the middle ear ossicles, and inner ear problems may also be present. Most of the time, treatment options for structural variations are not available. Adenoidectomy and tonsillectomy are usually recommended for sleep apnea.

Infections

Individuals with Down syndrome may occasionally have ear infections, sinusitis, pharyngitis, allergies, and other conditions of the upper respiratory tract. If infections are identified, prompt appropriate treatment should be initiated.

Hearing Impairments

Adults with Down syndrome, particularly those with premature aging, may show a high-frequency sensorineural hearing impairment, which consists of a hearing loss of high tones (presbycusis). When Buchanan (1990) examined 255 individuals with Down syndrome, he found that these individuals had an earlier onset of presbycusis than people without disabilities.

ORAL HEALTH ISSUES

Oral health concerns include appropriate dental and orthodontic care; dental hygiene; and prevention of dental caries and gum disease (gingivitis and periodontitis). Both the upper and lower jaws (maxilla and mandible) are smaller in individuals with Down syndrome, who sometimes have an underbite. As mentioned above, the palate is usually narrow, high, and short, and the oral cavity is smaller than average. Individuals often experience faulty contact between the upper and lower teeth (malocclusion), due to abnormal cranial structures, underbite, crossbite, and other factors. Therefore, in addition to regular dental care, some individuals with Down syndrome will also need orthodontic intervention, such as palate expansion, braces, and other procedures.

Dental Caries

The question has been raised as to whether individuals with Down syndrome have a higher frequency of dental caries (cavities). Some studies do not report any differences in the rate of dental caries between individuals with and without Down syndrome; however, other studies indicate a lower rate of dental caries in individuals with Down syndrome. Many theories have been proposed to explain the decreased dental caries rate in people with Down syndrome such as lower consumption of sweets, reduced number of teeth, late eruption of teeth, chemical effects, and environmental factors (Vigild, 1992). The presence of dental caries should lead to routine dental treatment.

Gingivitis and Periodontitis

Most important is the increased prevalence of gum disease, including gingivitis, an inflammation of the gums, and periodontitis, a condition where, in addition to the inflammation, the inner layer of the gum and bone pull away from the teeth and form pockets. If not attended to, tooth loss is common. Although some reports indicate that all people with Down syndrome will eventually develop these gum problems, frequent and appropriate dental hygiene will most often prevent gingivitis and periodontitis. Many individuals with Down syndrome who had been institutionalized in the past may not have been provided with routine dental care (Vigild, 1992). In addition, those people who did not practice proper dental hygiene often present with marked gum disease and loss of teeth. Other aspects may contribute to periodontal disease, such as nutritional, genetic, immunologic, and bacteriologic factors as well as tooth morphology, bruxism, and lack of masticatory function.

Because it is apparent that many individuals with Down syndrome are at an increased risk to develop gum disease, meticulous dental hygiene should be pursued. Moreover, regular dental checkups, frequent cleanings by dental hygienists, proper toothbrushing, flossing, and use an effective mouthwash will prevent dental and gum problems and will contribute to optimal oral health of individuals with Down syndrome.

CARDIAC ISSUES

Congenital Heart Disease

Congenital heart disease in children with Down syndrome has been studied extensively; however, there is limited information available with regard to cardiac concerns in adults with this disorder (Marino & Pueschel, 1996). Most likely, this is due to the fact that before the emergence of cardiac surgery, many infants with Down syndrome who had significant congenital heart disease succumbed during early childhood. Cardiac surgery has only become widely available since the 1970s, and more sophisticated diagnostic techniques as well as compassionate and rational medical care have been introduced.

Structural Anomalies

Individuals with Down syndrome often have structural abnormalities of the heart, even in the absence of significant congenital heart disease (Marino & Pueschel, 1996). In the center of the heart, there are structural deviations that involve the heart valves and the part (ventricular septum) that divides the left and right heart chambers. The membranous ventricular septum is often enlarged, and the commissure between the anterior and medial leaflets of the tricuspid valve is commonly absent in individuals with Down syndrome (Rosenquist, Sweeney, & McAllister, 1974). Also, the atrioventricular valves do not insert at the same level at the ventricular septum as they do in individuals without Down syndrome (Ammirati et al., 1991). The clinical significance of these and other minor structural differences in people with Down syndrome are not known. Although there is a "cardiovascular phenotype," or set of observable physical characteristics involving the heart and the blood vessels from a cardiovascular point of view, most adults with Down syndrome who do not have congenital heart disease function fairly well.

In addition to the previously mentioned structural cardiac manifestations in people with Down syndrome, studies have found a significant increase of mitral valve prolapse in adults with Down syndrome when compared with adults without Down syndrome (Barnett, Friedman, & Kastner, 1988; Goldhaber, Brown, & St. John Sutton, 1987; Pueschel & Werner, 1994). These reports indicated that about 44%–57% of individuals with Down syndrome have mitral valve prolapse, which is caused by a "bulging out" of the mitral valve during systole. Some individuals with Down syndrome and mitral valve prolapse also have tricuspid valve prolapse (20%); aortic regurgitation, where the aortic valve fails to close properly (11%–14%); and other minor mitral valve abnormalities.

The increased prevalence of mitral valve prolapse and aortic regurgitation may have important clinical implications. Several researchers have recommended antibiotic prophylaxis before dental procedures and any form of surgical intervention because they say there is an increased risk that these individuals may develop endocarditis, an inflammation of the lining of the valves of the heart (Barnett et al., 1988; Goldhaber, Brown, Robertson, Rubin, & St. John Sutton, 1988). There are, however, other cardiologists who disagree and do not advise antibiotic prophylaxis in uncomplicated mitral valve prolapse in individuals with Down syndrome.

The majority of individuals with Down syndrome who have mitral valve prolapse will not have any symptoms and will be able to participate in various sports activities without harmful effects. If a person with Down syndrome displays an alteration in the rhythm of the heart, loss of consciousness, a leakage between the left upper and lower chambers of the heart, chest pain, or specific electrocardiographic abnormalities, then that person should be followed by a cardiologist and refrain from participating in sports activities.

Lipids and Lipoproteins

There are no significant differences between people with and without Down syndrome with regard to total cholesterol and LDL cholesterol (Pueschel, Craig, & Haddow, 1992). Triglyceride levels, however, are significantly higher, and serum HDL cholesterol, apo AI, and HDL cholesterol to total cholesterol ratio are significantly lower in individuals with Down syndrome. The latter are all associated with an increased risk for coronary artery disease, although previous studies did not report such increased risk (Murdoch, Rodger, & Rao, 1972). If cholesterol levels and certain lipids are increased, a low cholesterol diet is recommended. If cholesterol levels are significantly increased, medications may be prescribed.

Synopsis

It is important to realize that an ever-increasing population with Down syndrome who were born with congenital heart disease are reaching adulthood. Thus, cardiologists have to become aware of the natural history of uncorrected, palliated, and corrected congenital heart disease. Individuals with Down syndrome who were born prior to the cardiac surgery era and who may now be inoperable may have significant pulmonary artery hypertension. Others who underwent successful cardiac surgery in early childhood may have residual defects such as mitral insufficiency. There are many individuals, however, who postoperatively do not have any sequelae. All three patient populations require follow-up care by a team of cardiologists who are familiar with the many aspects of congenital heart disease in adults. Numerous Adult Congenital Heart Disease Clinics that are in operation provide comprehensive, coordinated medical care for this population.

PULMONARY ISSUES

Respiratory problems in individuals with Down syndrome are more frequently observed during early childhood. In particular, infants with Down syndrome who have congenital heart disease and pulmonary artery hypertension are at an increased risk to succumb to lower respiratory infections. In addition, children with compromised immune systems contract infections more often, including pneumonia, bronchitis, upper respiratory infections, and others.

As individuals with Down syndrome mature, respiratory infections are usually less common, although Howenstine (1992) maintained that lower respiratory infections continue to cause significant morbidity and mortality in adults with Down syndrome. The signs and symptoms as well as the treatment of respiratory infections in individuals with Down syndrome parallel those of the general population and include antibiotics, other medications, and ventilatory assistance, if indicated.

Structural Anomalies

Individuals with Down syndrome often have structural pulmonary abnormalities. The lungs of people with Down syndrome are different both in gross appearance and on histologic examination. Gross appearance shows a uniform porous pattern instead of the velvety appearance of the "normal" lung; however, this does not usually affect the person's breathing and lung functions (Cooney, Wentworth, & Thurlbeck, 1988).

Pulmonary Artery Hypertension

Pulmonary artery hypertension, or increased blood pressure in the vessels of the lungs, is frequently observed in individuals with Down syndrome, and it is most often noted in conjunction with congenital heart disease. In order to prevent longstanding pulmonary artery hypertension, most children with significant congenital heart disease will undergo cardiac surgery in early life; however, as mentioned previously, there are some adults with Down syndrome who have not had cardiac surgery, and they often have severe pulmonary artery hypertension. They may have episodes of bluish-pale skin due to lack of oxygen in the blood (cyanosis). They also may fatigue easily and be less active than if they did not have pulmonary artery hypertension. The current treatment of pulmonary artery hypertension includes supplemental oxygen; calcium channel blockers; and other newer, recently marketed medications as indicated by the given circumstances.

Individuals with Down syndrome and chronic pulmonary hypertension, frequent infections, pulmonary overperfusion, and lung injury from existing or previous cardiac defects are at a high risk of developing high altitude pulmonary edema when traveling to even moderate altitudes (Durmovicz, 2001). Because of this possibility, it is recommended that individuals with Down syndrome with these conditions avoid traveling to places that are more than 1,500–2,000 m (4,921–6,561 ft) above sea level. If they do travel to these places, however, they should be aware of the symptoms of high altitude pulmonary edema, including shortness of breath, dyspnea, persistent cough with frothy sputum, cyanosis, headaches, and lethargy. If diagnosed early, high altitude pulmonary edema can be treated effectively.

Sleep Apnea

The most frequent respiratory problem in individuals with Down syndrome concerns obstructive sleep apnea that is manifested by partially blocked inspiratory airflow from the upper airway to the lungs. Sleep apnea is a condition that occurs when a person regularly stops breathing for 10 seconds or longer during sleep. From 60% to 80% of individuals with Down syndrome experience sleep apnea (Howenstine, 1992). In addition to apneic episodes, individuals with sleep apnea are restless sleepers; assume unusual positions during sleep; snore frequently; have difficulty waking in the morning; and often present with daytime somnolence and behavioral changes.

Obstruction of the airway is suspected if a person does not breathe comfortably and is primarily a mouth breather. Then, the airway of the person with sleep apnea will need to be evaluated with focus on nasal patency, size of tonsils and adenoids, and the position of the tongue in relation to the hypopharynx. The best way to document and quantify sleep apnea is the polysomnogram, a study that usually records nasal and oral air flow, pulse rate, electrocardiographic pattern, thoracic and abdominal impedance, oximetry, and end-tidal carbon dioxide to determine whether a person does or does not have sleep apnea. Ordinarily, these studies are carried out in a sleep laboratory with a surrounding that is conducive to a normal sleep pattern.

There are various treatment modalities available, such as positioning during sleep; continuous positive airway pressure (CPAP); and surgical interventions including tonsillectomy and adenoidectomy, uvulopala-topharyngoplasty (excess tissue in the throat is removed), and in extreme circumstances, tracheostomy. Moreover, if a person is significantly over-weight, a reduced caloric intake and an exercise program are usually rec-ommended. If obstructive sleep apnea is not treated properly, significant complications may ensue, including oxygen deprivation of the central nervous system and other vital organs, pulmonary artery hypertension, cor pulmonale, and heart failure. Because sleep apnea is an important pulmonary concern with potentially serious health consequences, it should be identified and treated appropriately.

GASTROINTESTINAL DISORDERS

Gastrointestinal disorders in Down syndrome are primarily observed in the early neonatal period. There is a high prevalence of congenital anomalies such as

- Esophageal atresia and fistula—abnormalities of the esophagus

- Pyloric stenosis—narrowing of the stomach outlet, interfering with food's ability to enter the intestine

- Duodenal atresia—partial or complete blockage of the upper part of the small intestine

- Hirschsprung disease—lack of nerves of part of the colon

- Anal atresia—no anal opening

Most of these conditions are usually corrected with surgery as soon as they are diagnosed (Pueschel, 1999).

Esophageal Dysfunction

Gastrointestinal concerns can occur during both childhood and adult-hood. Esophageal dysfunction, such as abnormal esophageal peristalsis and gastroesophageal reflux have been reported (Hillemeier, Buchin, & Gryboski, 1982). In a prospective evaluation of esophageal function in individuals with Down syndrome, an increased prevalence of esoph-ageal motor problems, in particular a rare disorder characterized by fail-ure of the ring-shaped muscle at the bottom of the esophagus to relax (achalasia), have been found (Zarate, Mearin, Hidalgo, & Malagelada, 2001). Zantac and other medications may be prescribed for gastro-esophageal reflux. Other treatment options may include surgery.

Intestinal Absorption

Reports of suspected protein and fat-soluble vitamin malabsorption in people with Down syndrome have appeared sporadically in the medical literature (Abalan et al., 1990); however, a study of vitamin A absorption in individuals with Down syndrome and control subjects failed to document a significant difference between these two groups (Pueschel, Hillemeier, et al., 1990). Other investigators studied xylose absorption and found that 90% of individuals with Down syndrome excreted xylose below the normal range; their findings, however, never have been duplicated (Williams et al., 1985). In general, individuals with Down syndrome have no significant difficulties with absorption except when they have celiac disease or other severe gastrointestinal disorders.

Celiac Disease

Celiac disease occurs more often in people with Down syndrome than in the general population (Pueschel et al., 1999). It is characterized by a lifelong intolerance to gluten, a protein in flour. Individuals with celiac disease may be asymptomatic, or they may have symptoms such as poor weight gain and failure to thrive, a distended abdomen, diarrhea, irritability, and personality changes. Screening for celiac disease is usually done by testing for certain antibodies, including IgA and IgG gliadin antibodies, but more often for antiendomysial antibodies and/or tissue transglutaminase antibodies. If the latter tests are positive, then a small bowel biopsy is usually recommended. The final diagnosis of celiac disease is made when the small bowel biopsy shows villus atrophy and increased lymphocyte accumulation in the wall of the bowel.

Once the diagnosis of celiac disease has been established, a strict gluten-free diet should be instituted. If diagnosed promptly and treated appropriately, individuals with Down syndrome will recover well, if they had symptoms, and they also will avoid future complications. If osteoporosis is present, calcium and vitamin D are administered.

Synopsis

In general, most adults with Down syndrome have a normally functioning gastrointestinal tract. If individuals are diagnosed with a specific gastrointestinal disorder, then the ensuing treatment will be similar as for the general population. Of importance is that individuals with Down syndrome have a relatively low caloric intake and a balanced diet with adequate nutrients and antioxidants as outlined in the section on nutrition.

GENITOURINARY FACTORS

There is limited information available on renal disorders in adults with Down syndrome. Previous reports (Benda, 1969; Naeye, 1967) have indicated that the kidneys of individuals with Down syndrome are small. Also, Ariel, Wells, Landing, and Singer (1991) reported that the kidney weight is reduced in adults with Down syndrome. In addition, a significant number of people with Down syndrome have renal hypoplasia, which is defined as less than two thirds of the normal combined weight of the kidneys.

Microscopic studies reveal numerous abnormalities in the filtering units (glomeruli) of the kidneys in individuals with Down syndrome. Despite changes in the kidneys, the vast majority of individuals with Down syndrome appear to have normal kidney function (Ariel & Shvil, 1992; Lo, Brown, Fivuch, Neu, & Racusem, 1998). Regular monitoring (creatinine and urinalysis) is recommended.

Kidney Dialysis and Transplants

There have been sporadic reports in the medical literature describing individuals with Down syndrome who required dialysis and/or renal transplantation (Baqi, Tejani, & Sullivan, 1998). In the past, most of these individuals were not considered to be eligible for kidney dialysis and/or transplantation. Today, there should be no discrimination because of the presence of a developmental disability. For ethical and moral reasons, the same criteria for these procedures that are used for the general population should also apply for people with Down syndrome.

Male Genitalia

Men with Down syndrome are more likely than men without Down syndrome to have hypospadias, a condition where the development of the penal shaft is abnormal (Lang, Van Dyke, Heide, & Lowe, 1987). Usually surgical repair of the hypospadias is carried out by a urologist during early childhood. Although some previous authors had mentioned underdeveloped sex organs (hypogenitalism) in men with Down syndrome, others have noted the size of both testes and penis to be within the "normal" range (Pueschel, Orson, Boylan, & Pezzullo, 1985). Also, studies concerning specific pituitary and testicular hormones that influence secondary sex organs revealed that follicle-stimulating and luteinizing hormones as well as testosterone levels in men with Down syndrome were comparable to those found in men without disabilities. Thus, the latter investigations of biologic parameters and specific hormone levels in maturing men with Down syndrome are similar to normative data obtained from the literature.

Although men with Down syndrome have been reported to have erections and ejaculations, there are many unanswered questions relating to libido, sexual function, sperm production, and fertility in these individuals. Whereas previously it was felt that all men with Down syndrome were infertile because of reduced sperm count and spermatogenic arrest, a report by Sheridan, Llerena, Matkins, Debenham, Cawood, and Bobrow (1989) indicated that a person with Down syndrome had fathered a child, which is the first confirmed paternity in a man with Down syndrome. Therefore, it is possible that men with Down syndrome, when given the opportunity to become sexually active, could reproduce.

Testicular Tumors

Of great concern is the increased prevalence of testicular tumors in individuals with Down syndrome. Most of these testicular tumors are seminomas (radiosensitive tumors) (Kamidono, Takada, Ishigami, Furumoto, & Urano, 1985; Sasagawa et al., 1986). Because of the increased frequency of testicular tumors, it is paramount that primary care physicians conduct regular examinations of the testes. If a testicular tumor is identified early, and if appropriate surgical and medical therapies are carried out, there is often a favorable outcome.

Female Genitalia

In the past, it was generally felt that women with Down syndrome did not need routine reproductive and gynecologic care, and often physicians were not willing or inadequately trained to provide such services (Elkins, 1992). Fortunately, there have been significant improvements in the gynecologic service provision of women with Down syndrome.

Menstrual Periods

Although there are some reports in the medical literature describing precocious sexual maturation in girls with Down syndrome, the majority of women with Down syndrome start menstruating between the ages of 9 and 15 years, with the average onset of the first menstrual cycle in girls with Down syndrome at 12 years, 6 months. The majority of women with Down syndrome have regular menstrual cycles and do not require help with menstrual hygiene (Scola & Pueschel, 1992).

Gynecologic Examination

Ordinarily, the first gynecologic examination of a woman with Down syndrome is initiated when menstrual problems become apparent. There may be irregular menstrual periods, dysmenorrhea, sexual abuse, or other gynecologic issues. The initial gynecologic office visit may be stressful for women with Down syndrome; therefore, the patients should be prepared appropriately. Visual aids that depict the procedures to be carried out and/or anatomically correct dolls can be used to prepare women for gynecologic checkups. If a patient is extremely anxious, the pelvic examination could be postponed.

Following the preparation of the examination, the gynecologic examination itself should be performed in the least fearful and threatening way. The professional might want to start with a breast examination. Gentleness and trust may be established with patience. Usually, the pelvic examination can be carried out with good cooperation. If the patient cannot relax or is combative, sedation may be administered.

Sometimes the pelvic examination cannot be performed with traditional techniques. In this instance, transabdominal ultrasonography can be done to provide important information. Although an annual gynecologic examination is part of routine health care for women with Down syndrome, it is probably not necessary to obtain a Pap smear in sexually nonactive females at yearly intervals (Elkins, 1992).

Menorrhagia

Women with Down syndrome often have various menstrual-related problems. For instance, prolonged or excessive uterine bleeding (menorrhagia) is quite common in women with Down syndrome. It can be treated medically with nonsteroidal anti-inflammatory medications or low doses of oral contraceptives, synthetic androgens, gonadotropic-releasing hormone agonists, progestins, or Depo-Provera. Surgical treatment in more severe cases includes dilatation and curettage of the uterus or hysterectomy, as a last resort, when all other methods fail to control the excessive or prolonged bleeding (Elkins, 1992).

Premenstrual Syndrome

Women with Down syndrome also encounter premenstrual syndrome. Premenstrual syndrome is characterized by any combination of the following during the days prior to each menstrual period: bloating, irritability, depression, weight gain, headaches, and cramping. For mild symptoms, nonsteroidal pain medications, mild diuretics, or a low dose of oral contraceptives can be administered. If premenstrual symptoms are severe, which is rare in women with Down syndrome, Depo-Provera has been used successfully in conjunction with counseling to provide an explanation of premenstrual syndrome (Elkins, 1992).

Amenorrhea

Primary amenorrhea, or lack of menstrual periods, is not common in women with Down syndrome; however, secondary amenorrhea, the discontinuation of menstruation, is more often observed. There are various causes for secondary amenorrhea, including thyroid disorders, polycystic ovary syndrome, physiologic ovarian cysts, prolactinomas, and other significant medical disorders, as well as pregnancy (Lawson & Elkins, 1997). A thorough evaluation should be carried out and the specific underlying problem should be treated appropriately.

Reproductive Issues

The question often arises as to whether women with Down syndrome are fertile and whether they will be able to bear children. There are numerous accounts of women with Down syndrome having given birth, so parental concerns about unwanted pregnancies in women with Down syndrome are indeed legitimate, in particular because Scola and Pueschel's (1992) investigation on ovulation found that almost all young women with Down syndrome in their study ovulated (Rani, Jyothi, Reddy, & Reddy, 1990). In Pueschel and Scola's (1988) survey, more than 50% of the parents wanted their daughters to have contraceptives or sterilization. In order to prevent unintended pregnancies, young women with Down syndrome should have appropriate counseling and, if necessary, they should be provided with an individualized contraceptive method. Gynecologic counseling and care must always take the woman's wishes and parental concerns into consideration, as well as legal guidelines and ethical issues.

MUSCULOSKELETAL DISORDERS

Ligamentous Laxity

There are several musculoskeletal concerns in individuals with Down syndrome. Many of these muscle and joint problems are due to the general ligamentous laxity, or loose-jointedness. Various theories have been proposed to explain the cause of ligamentous laxity, but the most recent reports indicate that fetal heart collagen is encoded by two genes mapped to the "Down syndrome region" of chromosome 21 (Duff, Williamson, & Richards, 1990). These two genes encode for two chains of collagen type VI molecule during fetal heart development. It is hypothesized that ligamentous collagen of the musculoskeletal system is either encoded for by the same genes or by other genes on chromosome 21, which in triple dosage may result in ligamentous laxity.

Atlantoaxial Instability

Atlantoaxial instability in individuals with Down syndrome, first described by Spitzer, Rabinowich, and Wybar (1961), has been investigated extensively during the past 40 years. About 15% of individuals with Down syndrome have atlantoaxial instability, where the distance between atlas and axis (also called dens or odontoid process) in the cervical spine is 5 mm or more (Pueschel & Scola, 1987). The other 85% of individuals with Down syndrome have "normal" radiologic findings (no atlantoaxial instability).

Individuals with the asymptomatic form of atlantoaxial instability should avoid certain sports activities such as gymnastics, diving, butterfly stroke in swimming, high jump, pentathlon, alpine skiing, and others as described by the Special Olympics. There is an increased risk for these people to injure their neck and to become neurologically symptomatic. Individuals with asymptomatic atlantoaxial instability need close follow-up and should undergo neurologic examinations at least annually but more often if symptoms become apparent. Should neurologic symptoms emerge, then further studies such as computerized tomography (CT scan) or magnetic resonance imaging (MRI) may be necessary. Individuals with Down syndrome who have significant neurologic symptoms usually will need surgical stabilization of the upper cervical spine.

It is of paramount importance to identify those people who are at increased risk before they develop serious neurologic signs. Questions may arise such as whether there is a need to obtain x-rays of the neck, when x-rays should be taken, and how many times x-rays should be repeated. Some professionals feel that radiographic screening for atlantoaxial instability is not indicated because asymptomatic atlantoaxial instability has not been proven to be a significant risk factor, that the expense of screening is of concern, and that it would be more important to obtain "good medical histories as well as physical and neurologic examinations in individuals with Down syndrome" (American Academy of Pediatrics, 1995). Others, however, emphasize the need for obtaining radiographs of the cervical spines of individuals with Down syndrome because it would be unwise and medico-legally incorrect to wait until significant neurologic symptoms and spinal cord damage become evident (Pueschel, 1998). There are other compelling reasons to obtain cervical spine radiographs of people with Down syndrome either to rule out or to identify the presence of atlantoaxial instability.

The first x-ray is usually taken when the person with Down syndrome is about 3 years of age. The next x-ray should be obtained before playing sports regularly or when entering Special Olympics activities. Another x-ray of the cervical spine is recommended by some professionals during adolescence. Of course, if there should be specific neurologic symptoms or neck discomfort, then the physician should not hesitate to take a radiograph of the cervical spine at once and pursue other studies as indicated. The primary goal is to prevent irreversible spinal cord injury that could be very debilitating.

Other Cervical Spine Concerns

Other cervical spine problems concern skeletal anomalies of the neck area, occipitoatlantal instability, and degenerative changes. Only a few investigations have been performed in these areas. A number of people with Down syndrome have been found to have cervical spine anomalies involving the first two neck bones, and it has been suggested that this may be a contributing factor to the pathogenesis of atlantoaxial instability (Pueschel, Scola, Tupper, & Pezzullo, 1990). In addition, it has been noted that 8%–37% of people with Down syndrome have occipitoatlantal instability. In the latter condition, there is increased movement between the base of the skull and the atlas that could potentially lead to spinal cord compression. Degenerative changes of the cervical spine that could exaggerate preexisting atlantoaxial instability and may cause significant discomfort are more often observed in older people with Down syndrome (Pueschel & Solga, 1992).

Patella and Hip Problems

Patella subluxation, a condition where the knee cap is out of place, may be encountered by individuals with Down syndrome. Scoliosis, hip dysplasia, and hip dislocation may also be experienced. At times, when hip dislocation was previously not appropriately treated, degenerative changes at the hip joint may require hip replacement.

Synopsis

The majority of individuals with Down syndrome have an intact musculoskeletal system. Physicians, however, should be aware that people with Down syndrome may have various orthopedic concerns. Important musculoskeletal problems include loose ligaments between the first two neck bones, the atlas and the axis (atlantoaxial instability); an instability between the first neck bone and the base of the skull (occipitoatlantal instability); degenerative changes; and other conditions related to cervical spine concerns. It is well known that cervical spine pathology may have life-threatening consequences, and chronic disabilities of the hip, knee, and other joints may affect an individual's physical activity. Adults with Down syndrome who do have such musculoskeletal disorders should be provided with optimal medical and orthopedic care and, if indicated, surgical intervention should be pursued.

NEUROLOGIC ASPECTS

General Central Nervous System Involvement

The central nervous system is one of the components of the human body that is most affected in individuals with Down syndrome. Limited intellectual function and neurologic impairments are most likely the result of many factors, including structural, neurophysiologic, and neurobiochemical abnormalities. The brain not only governs cognition, but it is also responsible for motor performance, language abilities, executive and sensory functions, behavioral aspects, and other factors.

Structural Abnormalities

The brains of individuals with Down syndrome are significantly smaller than those of age-equivalent individuals without the disorder (Kemper, 1991; Wisniewski, 1990). In addition, the brainstem, cerebellum, and other central nervous system structures have been found to be smaller than those in people who do not have Down syndrome (Sylvester, 1983). There are fewer neurons in various areas of the brain of a person with Down syndrome versus the brain of an individual without Down syndrome (Kemper, 1988; Wisniewski, Laure-Kamionowska, Connell, & Wen, 1986). In addition, there are abnormalities in the organization of the neurons of the motor cortex as well as reduced development of dendritic branching and limited dendritic spine production in adults with Down syndrome (Marin-Padilla, 1976). Although postsynaptic spines on basal dendrites slowly increase during childhood, they rapidly decrease during adulthood (Takashima, Iida, Mito, & Arima, 1994). The overexpression of gene products in the central nervous systems of individuals with Down syndrome may be related to these individuals' predisposition to dendritic hypogenesis, a condition where the branches (dendrites) that are attached to nerve fibers are underdeveloped.

Apoptosis

Since 1995, many investigators have studied neuronal death (apoptosis) in individuals with Down syndrome (Nagy, 1999; Sawa, 1999; Seidl, Fang-Kircher, Bidmon, Cairns, & Lubec, 1999). The accumulating literature on this subject indicates that most neuronal death is due to apoptotic mechanisms that may be part of the pathogenesis of mental retardation and precocious dementia in individuals with Down syndrome. It has been suggested that several genes are involved in this process (Bennett et al., 1998; Muller et al., 1998; Sawa, 1999).

Neurotransmitters

Neurotransmitters (e.g., noradrenaline, dopamine) are chemicals that transmit information from one brain cell to another. In individuals with Down syndrome, several abnormalities of neurotransmitters have been described, most often a diminished activity of neurotransmitter function. Many researchers have studied neurotransmitter functions in individuals with Down syndrome. Adults with Down syndrome have a deficiency in the cholinergic system (McCoy & Enns, 1986; Mann, Yates, & Marcyniuk, 1985). There is less acetyl cholinesterase (an enzyme involved in specific neurotransmitters) activity in the temporal cortex and less noradrenaline and dopamine in the hypothalamus and the mamillary body of people with presenile and senile Alzheimer-type dementia and Down syndrome (Yates et al., 1983). One group of investigators noted that other neurotransmitters such as glutamic acid and γ-aminobutyric acid were reduced in certain areas of the brain (the hippocampus and temporal cortex) in individuals with Down syndrome (Reynolds & Warner, 1988). Reynolds and Godridge (1985) also reported that noradrenaline and 5-hydroxytryptamine are diminished in cortical brain tissue in adults with Down syndrome.

Seizures

Seizure disorders are more common in individuals with Down syndrome than in the general population (Pueschel, Louis, & McKnight, 1991). About 26.5% of adults with Down syndrome will have seizures at a mean age of onset of 36.8 years, and there is a strong association between the occurrence of Alzheimer disease and seizures (Puri, Ho, & Singh, 2001). Another group of researchers noted that the late onset of seizures in people with Down syndrome is an indicator of a dementing process (Prasher & Corbett, 1993). In addition, Lott and Lai (1982) found that 53% of individuals with Down syndrome and a clinical diagnosis of Alzheimer disease have epileptic seizures.

Alzheimer Disease

The association of Alzheimer disease and Down syndrome has been discussed in the medical literature since the 1940s (Jervis, 1948). Neuropathologic and clinical evidence clearly point to a link between Down syndrome and Alzheimer disease (Lai, 1992). Although most adults with Down syndrome 40 years and older have the neuropathologic changes of Alzheimer disease, including loss of neurons, neurofibrillary tangles, and senile plaques, only a limited number of these individuals develop clinical signs of dementia (Malamud, 1972; Oliver, & Holland, 1986). Because individuals with Down syndrome have an extra chromosome, they have a dose-dependent increase in the production of the amyloid precursor protein, which eventually leads to deposits in the brain tissue. Schapiro, Haxby, and Grady (1992), who studied the nature of mental retardation and dementia, noted that older adults with Down syndrome and no dementia showed a distinctive pattern of age-related impairments. Older patients with Down syndrome and dementia had identical patterns of abnormal glucose metabolism as patients with Alzheimer disease using positron emission tomography. Zigman, Schupf, Lubin, and Silverman (1987) reported premature regression in adults with Down syndrome whose adaptive competence declined with increasing age; however, age-related impairments associated with Down syndrome were observed only in individuals older than 50 years.

During the past decade, apolipoprotein E ε4 has been studied in the development of Alzheimer disease in the general population and in individuals with Down syndrome. There are several therapeutic interventions available today and numerous research activities are being pursued to find preventive, ameliorative, and curative treatments (Lott, & Head, 2001). For example, acetylcholinesterase inhibitors (e.g., donepezil) have shown some improvements in individuals with Down syndrome and Alzheimer disease. Antioxidant therapy is another possible promising treatment approach. Sano et al. (1997) reported a slowing of deterioration in activities of daily living in individuals with Alzheimer disease using either vitamin E or selegiline (Eldepryl). According to Lott and Head (2001), it is suggested that a combination of acetylcholinesterase inhibitors, antioxidants, anti-inflammatory medications, and perhaps others may prevent or slow down the dementing process in people with Down syndrome.

Synopsis

Individuals with Down syndrome experience many structural and functional neurologic concerns as a result of the overexpression of specific genes and gene interrelations. Novel brain imaging techniques as well as innovative neuropsychological and neurophysiologic approaches should be employed to provide a better understanding of central nervous system abnormalities in adults with Down syndrome.

SUMMARY

Individuals with Down syndrome experience many medical concerns at a higher frequency than people without Down syndrome; however, the majority of individuals with Down syndrome enjoy good health. Adults with Down syndrome should be examined regularly by their physicians and/or specialists and undergo certain radiologic and laboratory tests. If they are provided with optimal medical and dental services to foster their well-being in all areas of human functioning, then they will enjoy an enhanced quality of life, will function more effectively, and will make a substantial contribution to society.

REFERENCES

Abalan, F., Jouan, A., Weerts, M.T., Solles, C., Brus, J., & Sauneron, M.F. (1990). A study of digestive absorption in four cases of Down syndrome: Down syndrome, malnutrition, malabsorption, and Alzheimer's disease. *Medical Hypotheses, 31*, 35–38.

Allison, D.B., Gomez, J.E., Heshka, S., Babbitt, R.L., Geliebter, A., Kreibich, K., et al. (1995). Decreased resting metabolism rate among persons with Down syndrome. *International Journal of Obesity, 19*, 858–861.

American Academy of Pediatrics. (2001). Health supervision for children with Down syndrome. *Pediatrics, 107*, 442–449.

American Academy of Pediatrics, Committee on Sports Medicine. (1995). Atlantoaxial instability in Down syndrome: Subject review. *Pediatrics, 96*, 151–154.

Ammirati, A., Marino, B., Annicchiarico, M., Ferrazza, A., Affinito, V., & Ragonese, P. (1991). Sindrome di Down senza cardiopatia cengenita: E'realmente normale l'anatomia ecocardiografica? *Giornale Italiano di Cardiologia, 21*, 55–59.

Ani, C., Grantham-McGregor, S., & Muller, D. (2000). Nutritional supplementation in Down syndrome: Theoretical considerations and current status. *Developmental Medicine & Child Neurology, 42,* 207–213.

Ariel, I., & Shvil, Y. (1992). Genitourinary system. In S.M. Pueschel & J.K. Pueschel (Eds.), *Biomedical concerns in persons with Down syndrome* (pp. 133–138). Baltimore: Paul H. Brookes Publishing Co.

Ariel, I., Wells, T.R., Landing, B.H., & Singer, D.B. (1991). The urinary system in Down syndrome: A study of 124 autopsy cases. *Pediatric Pathology, 11,* 879–888.

Balkany, T.J., Mischke, R.E., Downs, M.P., & Jafek, B.W. (1979). Ossicular abnormalities in Down's syndrome. *Otolaryngology—Head & Neck Surgery, 87,* 372–384.

Baqi, N., Tejani, A., & Sullivan, E.K. (1998). Renal transplantation in Down syndrome: A report of the North American Pediatric Renal Transplant Cooperative Study. *Pediatric Transplantation, 2,* 211–215.

Barnett, M.L., Friedman, D., & Kastner, T. (1988). The prevalence of mitral valve prolapse in patients with Down's syndrome: Implications for dental management. *Oral Surgery, Oral Medicine and Oral Pathology, 66,* 445–447.

Benda, C.E. (1969). *Down's syndrome: Mongolism and its management.* New York: Grune & Stratton.

Bennett, M., MacDonald, K., Chan, S.W., Luzio, J.P., Simari, R., & Weissberg, P. (1998). Cell surface trafficking of Fas: A rapid mechanism of p53-mediated apoptosis. *Science, 282,* 290–297.

Benson, P.M., & Scherbenske, J.M. (1992). Dermatologic findings. In S.M. Pueschel & J.K. Pueschel (Eds.), *Biomedical concerns in persons with Down syndrome* (pp. 209–215). Baltimore: Paul H. Brookes Publishing Co.

Bucci, I., Napolitano, G., Giuliani, C., Lio, S., Minnucci, A., Giacomo, F., et al. (1999). Zinc sulfate supplementation improves thyroid function in hypozincemic Down children. *Biological Trace Element Research, 67,* 257–268.

Buchanan, L.H. (1990). Early onset of presbycusis in Down syndrome. *Scandinavian Audiology, 19,* 103–110.

Burton, J.L., & Rook, A. (1986). Genetics in dermatology. In A. Rook, F.J.G. Ebling, D.S. Wilkinson, R.H. Champion, & J.L. Burton (Eds.), *Textbook of dermatology* (p. 115). Oxford: Blackwell.

Caputo, A.R., Wagner, R.S., Reynolds, D.R., Guo, S.Q., & Goel, A.K. (1989). Down syndrome: Clinical review of ocular features. *Clinical Pediatrics, 28,* 355–358.

Carter, D.M., & Jegasothy, B.V. (1976). Alopecia and Down's syndrome. *Archives of Dermatology, 112,* 1397–1399.

Catalano, R.A. (1992). Ophthalmologic concerns. In S.M. Pueschel & J.K. Pueschel (Eds.), *Biomedical concerns in persons with Down syndrome* (pp. 59–68). Baltimore: Paul H. Brookes Publishing Co.

Chad, K., Jobling, A., & Frail, H. (1990). Metabolic rate: A factor in developing obesity in children with Down syndrome. *American Journal on Mental Retardation, 95,* 228–235.

Cohen, W.I. (for the Down Syndrome Medical Interest Group). (1999). Health care guidelines for individuals with Down syndrome. *Down Syndrome Quarterly, 4,* 1–16.

Cooney, T.P., Wentworth, P.J., & Thurlbeck, W.M. (1988). Diminished radial count is found only postnatally in Down's syndrome. *Pediatric Pulmonology, 5,* 204–209.

Dahle, A.J., & Baldwin, R.L. (1992). Audiologic and otolaryngologic concerns. In S.M. Pueschel & J.K. Pueschel (Eds.), *Biomedical concerns in persons with Down syndrome* (pp. 69–80). Baltimore: Paul H. Brookes Publishing Co.

Dinani, S., & Carpenter, S. (1990). Down syndrome and thyroid disorder. *Journal of Mental Deficiency Research, 34,* 187–193.

Duff, K., Williamson, R., & Richards, S.J. (1990). Expression of genes encoding two chains of the collagen type VI molecule during human fetal heart development. *International Journal of Cardiology, 27,* 128–129.

Durmovicz, A.G. (2001). Pulmonary edema in six children with Down syndrome during travel to moderate altitudes. *Pediatrics, 108,* 443–447.

Elkins, T.E. (1992). Gynecologic care. In S.M. Pueschel & J.K. Pueschel (Eds.), *Biomedical concerns in persons with Down syndrome* (pp. 139–146). Baltimore: Paul H. Brookes Publishing Co.

Goldhaber, S.Z., Brown, W.D., Robertson, N., Rubin, H., & St. John Sutton, N.G. (1988). Aortic regurgitation and mitral valve prolapse with Down's syndrome: A case-controlled study. *Journal of Mental Deficiency Research, 32,* 333–336.

Goldhaber, S.Z., Brown, W.D., & St. John Sutton, N.G. (1987). High frequency of mitral valve prolapse and aortic regurgitation among asymptomatic adults with Down's syndrome. *Journal of the American Medical Association, 258,* 1793–1799.

Guthrie Medlen, J.E. (2002). *The Down syndrome nutrition book.* Kensington, MD: Woodbine House.

Hillemeier, C., Buchin, P.J., & Gryboski, J. (1982). Esophageal dysfunction in Down's syndrome. *Journal of Pediatric Gastroenterology and Nutrition, 1,* 101–104.

Howenstine, M.S. (1992). Pulmonary concerns. In S.M. Pueschel & J.K. Pueschel (Eds.), *Biomedical concerns in persons with Down syndrome* (pp. 105–118). Baltimore: Paul H. Brookes Publishing Co.

Jaeger, E.A. (1980). Ocular findings in Down's syndrome. *Transactions of the American Ophthalmologic Society, 158,* 808–845.

Jervis, G.A. (1948). Early senile dementia in mongoloid idiocy. *American Journal of Mental Deficiency, 105,* 102–106.

Kamidono, S., Takada, K., Ishigami, J., Furumoto, M., & Urano, Y. (1985). Giant seminoma of undescended testes in Down syndrome. *Urology, 25,* 637–640.

Kanavin, O.J., Aaseth, J., & Birketvedt, G.S. (2000). Thyroid hypofunction in Down syndrome: Is it related to oxidative stress? *Biology of Trace Elements Research, 78,* 35–42.

Kaufman, A.J. (2000). Treatment of elastosis perforans serpiginosa with the flashlamp pulsed dye laser. *Dermatologic Surgery, 11,* 1060–1062.

Kemper, T.L. (1988). Neuropathology of Down syndrome. In L. Nadel (Ed.), *The psychobiology of Down syndrome* (pp. 269–289). Cambridge, MA: MIT Press.

Kemper, T.L. (1991). Down syndrome. In A. Peters & E.G. Jones (Eds.), *Cerebral cortex* (pp. 511–526). New York: Plenum.

Lai, F. (1992). Alzheimer disease. In S.M. Pueschel & J.K. Pueschel (Eds.), *Biomedical concerns in persons with Down syndrome* (pp. 175–196). Baltimore: Paul H. Brookes Publishing Co.

Lang, D.J., Van Dyke, D.C., Heide, F., & Lowe, P.L. (1987). Hypospadias and urethral abnormalities in Down syndrome. *Clinical Pediatrics, 26,* 40–42.

Lawson, J.D., & Elkins, T.E. (1997). Gynecologic concerns. In S.M. Pueschel & J.K. Pueschel (Eds.), *Biomedical concerns in persons with Down syndrome* (pp. 39–46). Baltimore: Paul H. Brookes Publishing Co.

Lejeune, J. (1992). The pathogenesis of mental retardation in trisomy 21. *Monatsschrift Kinderheilkunde, 139,* 655–661.

Lo, A., Brown, A.G., Fivuch, B.A., Neu, A.M., & Racusem, L.C. (1998). Renal disease in Down syndrome: Autopsy study with emphasis on glomerular lesions. *American Journal of Kidney Diseases, 31,* 329–335.

Lott, I.T., & Head, E. (2001). Down syndrome and Alzheimer's disease: A link between development and aging. *Mental Retardation and Developmental Disability Research Reviews, 7,* 172–178.

Lott, I.T., & Lai, F. (1982). Dementia in Down's syndrome: Observations from a neurology clinic. *Applied Research in Mental Retardation, 3,* 233–239.

Luke, A., Roizen, N.J., Sutton, M., & Schoeller, D.A. (1994). Energy expenditure in children with Down syndrome: Correcting metabolic rate for movement. *Journal of Pediatrics, 125,* 829–838.

Malamud, N. (1972). Neuropathology of organic brain syndromes associated with aging. In C. Gaitz (Ed.), *Aging and the brain* (pp. 63–87). New York: Plenum.

Mann, D.M.A., Yates, P.O., Marcyniuk, B. (1985). Pathological evidence for neurotransmitter deficits in Down's syndrome of middle age. *Journal of Mental Deficiency Research, 29,* 125–135.

Marino, B., & Pueschel, S.M. (1996). *Heart disease in persons with Down syndrome.* Baltimore: Paul H. Brookes Publishing Co.

Marin-Padilla, M. (1976). Pyramidal cell abnormalities in the motor cortex of a child with Down syndrome: A Golgi study. *Journal of Comparative Neurology, 167,* 63–82.

McCoy, E.E., & Enns, L. (1986). Current status of neurotransmitter abnormalities in Down syndrome. In C.J. Epstein (Ed.), *The neurobiology of Down syndrome* (pp. 73–87). New York: Raven Press.

Mitchell, A.J., & Krull, E.A. (1984). Alopecia areata: Pathogenesis and treatment. *Journal of the American Academy of Dermatology, 11,* 763–775.

Moschella, S.L., & Hurley, H.J. (1985). *Dermatology* (2nd ed.). Philadelphia: W.B. Saunders.

Muller, M., Wilder, S., Bannasch, D., Israeli, D., Lehlbach, K., Li-Weber, M., et al. (1998). p53 activates the CD95 (APO-1/FAS) gene in response to DNA damage by anticancer drugs. *Journal of Experimental Medicine, 188,* 2033–2045.

Murdoch, J.C., Ratcliffe, W.A., McLarty, J.C., Rodger, J.C., & Ratcliffe, J.G. (1977). Thyroid function in adults with Down syndrome. *Journal of Clinical Endocrinology and Metabolism, 44,* 153–158.

Murdoch, J.C., Rodger, C.J., & Rao, S.S. (1972). Down's syndrome: An atheroma-free model? *British Medical Journal, ii,* 226–228.

Naeye, R.L. (1967). Prenatal organ and cellular growth with various chromosomal disorders. *Biology of the Neonate, 11,* 248–260.

Nagy, Z. (1999). Mechanisms of neuronal death in Down's syndrome. *Journal of Neural Transmission Supplement, 57,* 233–245.

National Institute of Child Health and Human Development. (2005). *Facts about Down syndrome.* Retrieved August 10, 2005, from http://www.nichd. nih.gov/publications/pubs/downsyndrome/down.htm

Oliver, C., & Holland, A.J. (1986). Down's syndrome and Alzheimer's disease: A review. *Psychological Medicine, 16,* 307–322.

Percy, M.E., Dalton, A.J., Markowitz, V.D., Crapper-McLachlan, D.R., Gera, E., Hummel, J., et al. (1990). Autoimmune thyroiditis associated with mild "subclinical" hypothyroidism in adults with Down syndrome: A comparison of patients with and without manifestations of Alzheimer's disease. *American Journal of Medical Genetics, 36,* 148–154.

Prasher, V.P., & Corbett, J.A. (1993). Onset of seizures as a poor indicator of longevity in people with Down syndrome and dementia. *International Journal of Geriatric Psychiatry, 8,* 923–927.

Pueschel, S.M. (1984). *A study of the young child with Down syndrome.* New York: Human Science Press.

Pueschel, S.M. (1992). General health care and therapeutic approaches. In S.M. Pueschel & J.K. Pueschel (Eds.), *Biomedical concerns in persons with Down syndrome* (pp. 289–300). Baltimore: Paul H. Brookes Publishing Co.

Pueschel, S.M. (1998). Should children with Down syndrome be screened for atlantoaxial instability? *Archives of Pediatrics and Adolescent Medicine, 125,* 123–125.

Pueschel, S.M. (1999). Gastrointestinal concerns and nutritional issues in persons with Down syndrome. *Down Syndrome Quarterly, 4,* 1–11.

Pueschel, S.M., & Anneren, G. (1992). Metabolic and biochemical concerns. In S.M. Pueschel & J.K. Pueschel (Eds.), *Biomedical concerns in persons with Down syndrome* (pp. 273–287). Baltimore: Paul H. Brookes Publishing Co.

Pueschel, S.M., Anneren, G., Durlach, R., Flores, J., Sustrova, M., & Verma, I.C. (1995). Guidelines for optimal medical care for persons with Down syndrome. *Acta Paediatrica, 84,* 823–827.

Pueschel, S.M., & Blaymore Bier, J. (1992). Endocrinologic aspects. In S.M. Pueschel & J.K. Pueschel (Eds.), *Biomedical concerns in persons with Down syndrome* (pp. 259–272). Baltimore: Paul H. Brookes Publishing Co.

Pueschel, S.M., Craig, W.Y., & Haddow, J.E. (1992). Lipids and lipoproteins in persons with Down syndrome. *Journal of Mental Deficiency Research, 25,* 365–369.

Pueschel, S.M., & Giesswein, S. (1993). Ocular disorders in children with Down syndrome. *Down Syndrome: Research and Practice, 1,* 129–132.

Pueschel, S.M., Hillemeier, C., Caldwell, M., Senft, K., Mevs, C., & Pezzullo, J.C. (1990). Vitamin A gastrointestinal absorption in persons with Down's syndrome. *Journal of Mental Deficiency Research, 34,* 264–275.

Pueschel, S.M., Jackson, I.M.D., Giesswein, P., Dean, M.K., & Pezzullo, J.C. (1991). Thyroid function in Down syndrome. *Research in Developmental Disabilities, 12,* 287–296.

Pueschel, S.M., Louis, S., & McKnight, P. (1991). Seizure disorders in Down syndrome. *Archives of Neurology, 48,* 318–320.

Pueschel, S.M., Orson, J.M., Boylan, J.M., & Pezzullo, J.C. (1985). Adolescent development of males with Down syndrome. *American Journal of Diseases of Children, 139,* 236–238.

Pueschel, S.M., & Pezzullo, J.C. (1985). Thyroid dysfunction in Down syndrome. *American Journal of Diseases in Children, 139,* 636–639.

Pueschel, S.M., Romano, C., Failla, P., Barone, C., Pettinato, R., Castellano Chioda, A., et al. (1999). A prevalence study of celiac disease in persons with Down syndrome residing in the United States of America. *Acta Paediatrica, 88,* 953–956.

Pueschel, S.M., & Scola, F.H. (1987). Atlantoaxial instability in individuals with Down syndrome: Epidemiologic, radiographic, and clinical studies. *Pediatrics, 80,* 555–560.

Pueschel, S.M., & Scola, F.H. (1988). Parent's perception of social and sexual functions in adolescents with Down syndrome. *Journal of Mental Deficiency Research, 32,* 215–218.

Pueschel, S.M., Scola, F.H., Tupper, T.B., & Pezzullo, J.C. (1990). Skeletal anomalies of the upper cervical spine in children with Down syndrome. *Journal of Pediatric Orthopedics, 10,* 607–611.

Pueschel, S.M., & Solga, P.M. (1992). Musculoskeletal disorders. In S.M. Pueschel & J.K. Pueschel (Eds.), *Biomedical concerns in persons with Down syndrome* (pp. 139–146). Baltimore: Paul H. Brookes Publishing Co.

Pueschel, S.M., & Werner, J.C. (1994). Mitral valve prolapse in persons with Down syndrome. *Research in Developmental Disability, 15,* 91–97.

Puri, B.K., Ho, K.W., & Singh, I. (2001). Age of seizure onset in adults with Down syndrome. *International Journal of Clinical Practice, 55,* 442–444.

Rani, A.S., Jyothi, A., Reddy, P.P., & Reddy, O.S. (1990). Reproduction in Down's syndrome. *International Journal of Gynecology and Obstetrics, 31,* 81–86.

Reynolds, G.P., & Godridge, H. (1985). Alzheimer-like brain monoamine deficits in adults with Down's syndrome. *The Lancet, 2,* 1368–1369.

Reynolds, G.P., & Warner, C.E.J. (1988). Amino acid neurotransmitter deficit in adult Down's syndrome brain tissue. *Neuroscience Letter, 94,* 224–227.

Rooney, S., & Walsh, E. (1997). Prevalence of abnormal thyroid function tests in a Down syndrome population. *Irish Journal of Medical Science, 166,* 80–82.

Rosenquist, G., Sweeney, L.J., & McAllister, H.A. (1974). Relationship of the tricuspid valve to the membranous ventricular septum in Down's syndrome without endocardial cushion defect: Study of 28 specimens, 14 with a ventricular septal defect. *American Heart Journal, 90,* 458–462.

Sano, M., Ernesto, C., Thomas, R., et al. (1997). A controlled trial of selegiline, alpha-tocopherol, or both as treatment for Alzheimer's disease. *New England Journal of Medicine, 336,* 1216–1222.

Sasagawa, I., Kazama, T., Umeda, K., Kohno, T., Katayama, T., & Miva, A. (1986). Down's syndrome associated with seminoma. *Urologia Internationales, 41,* 238–240.

Sawa, A. (1999). Neuronal cell death in Down's syndrome. *Journal of Neural Transmission Supplement, 57,* 87–97.

Schapiro, M.B., & France, T.D. (1985). The ocular features of Down's syndrome. *American Journal of Ophthalmology, 66,* 659–663.

Schapiro, M.B., Haxby, J.V., & Grady, C.L. (1992). Nature of mental retardation and dementia in Down syndrome: Study with PET, CT, and neuropsychology. *Neurobiology of Aging, 13,* 723–734.

Schindler, S. (1989). Hypothyroidism in a child with Down syndrome. *Hospital Practice, 24,* 231–232.

Schmid, F. (1976). *Das Mongolismus-Syndrom.* Munsterdorf: Hansen and Hansen.

Scola, P.S., & Pueschel, S.M. (1992). Menstrual cycles and basal body temperature curves in women with Down syndrome. *Obstetrics and Gynecology, 79,* 91–94.

Seidl, R., Fang-Kircher, S., Bidmon, B., Cairns, N., & Lubec, G. (1999). Apoptosis-associated proteins p53 and APO-1/FAS (CD95) in brains of adult patients with Down's syndrome. *Neuroscience Letters, 260,* 9–12.

Seward, J.B. (1996). Long-term follow-up care of persons with Down syndrome and congenital heart disease. In B. Marino & S.M. Pueschel (Eds.), *Heart disease in persons with Down syndrome* (pp. 136–148). Baltimore: Paul H. Brookes Publishing Co.

Sheridan, R., Llerena, J., Jr., Matkins, S., Debenham, P., Cawood, A., & Bobrow, M. (1989). Fertility in a male with trisomy 21. *Journal of Medical Genetics, 26*(5), 294–298.

Smith, D.S. (2001) Health care management of adults with Down syndrome. *American Family Physician, 6,* 1031–1044.

Spitzer, R., Rabinowich, J.Y., & Wybar, K.C. (1961). A study of abnormalities of the skull, teeth, and lenses in mongolism. *Canadian Medical Association Journal, 84,* 567–572.

Sustrova, M., & Pueschel, S.M. (1998). Hyperthyroidism in children with Down syndrome. *Down Syndrome Quarterly, 3,* 1–4.

Sylvester, P.E. (1983). The hippocampus in Down's syndrome. *Journal of Mental Deficiency Research, 27,* 227–236.

Takashima, S., Iida, K., Mito, T., & Arima, M. (1994). Dendritic and histochemical development and aging in patients with Down's syndrome. *Journal of Intellectual Disability Research, 38,* 265–273.

Turkel, H. (1975). Medical amelioration of Down's syndrome incorporating the orthomolecular approach. *Journal of Orthomolecular Psychiatry, 4,* 102–115.

Vigild, M. (1992). Oral health conditions. In S.M. Pueschel & J.K. Pueschel (Eds.), *Biomedical concerns in persons with Down syndrome* (pp. 81–89). Baltimore: Paul H. Brookes Publishing Co.

Williams, C.A., Quinn, H., Wright, E.C., Sylvester, P.E., Gosling, P.J.H., & Dickerson, J.W.T. (1985). Xylose absorption in Down's syndrome. *Journal of Mental Deficiency Research, 29,* 173–177.

Wisniewski, K.E. (1990). Down syndrome children often have brain with maturation delay, retardation of growth, and cortical dysgenesis. *American Journal of Medical Genetics, Supplement 7,* 274–281.

Wisniewski, K.E., Laure-Kamionowska, M., Connell, F., & Wen, G.Y. (1986). Neuronal density and synaptogenesis in the postnatal stage of brain maturation in Down syndrome. In C.J. Epstein (Ed.), *The neurobiology of Down's syndrome* (pp. 29–44). New York: Raven Press.

Yates, C.M., Simpson, J., Gordon, A., Maloney, A.F.J., Allison, Y., Ritchie, I.M., et al. (1983). Catecholamines and cholinergic enzymes in pre-senile and senile Alzheimer-type dementia in Down's syndrome. *Brain Research, 280,* 119–126.

Zarate, N., Mearin, F., Hidalgo, A., & Malagelada, J.R. (2001). Prospective evaluation of esophageal motor function in Down's syndrome. *American Journal of Gastroenterology, 96,* 1718–1724.

Zigman, W.B., Schupf, N., Lubin, R.A., & Silverman, W.P. (1987). Premature regression of adults with Down syndrome. *American Journal of Mental Deficiency, 92,* 161–168.

4

■■■

Life Experiences

JENNIFER CUNNINGHAM

■ ■ ■

When I first went to elementary school, I did not have a lot of friends. Then, I met friends in elementary school. I joined Brownies and Girl Scouts. I started doing Early Bird gymnastics. I liked elementary school. When I left, they voted me into the hall of fame. I was the first student in the hall of fame. I also started Special Olympics in gymnastics.

When I was in third grade, my school district made me change schools. I was away from my friends and made new friends. I met my best friend at the new school. But my new school was far away. I went to a different school than the kids in my neighborhood. I didn't do Girl Scouts any more. But I did do Special Olympics gymnastics at my old school.

When I was in middle school, my school district sent me to a different school. I was far away from my house. I was not with any of my friends in elementary school. I didn't know anyone. My Special Olympics gymnastics coach told me to try out for the gymnastics team. So I did. I made the team. Only 4 girls made the cartwheel on the balance beam, and I was one of them. In middle school, our teacher was sick a lot. Other than gymnastics, we didn't do much in middle school. We didn't spend a lot of time with students outside the special education classroom.

In high school, I was back with the students I knew in elementary school. But the special education classrooms were down in the corner. We did not spend a lot of time with the high school kids. I tried out for gymnastics again and made the team. The girls on the team were my friends. I still did Special Olympics gymnastics. I wanted to go to the regular Olympics, but that did not happen.

I went to the Ohio Special Olympics every year, and I competed on the high school team. I did not do very well on the high school team, but in little districts, I got tenth all around and came in third on the bars. That was good. I went to school in the morning and after school went to gymnastics until 7:00 and then went home and ate dinner and did homework and went to bed. I wanted to go to Special Olympics International, but they did not pick me. Then, I went to Special Olympics International two times at Hartford, Connecticut, and again at North Carolina.

I did not have a date to the dances. I did not have a date to the prom. My dad and I went to my senior prom, and he took me out for dinner. I did not have a boyfriend in school. My friend and I went to the homecoming dance.

I wanted to be in drama, but I was told I had to do stagecraft first. And then I took a class. And it took me 2 years before I was allowed to be in drama. I was in *Skin of Our Teeth* and *Just Like Old Times*.

I ran the Olympic Torch for the Atlanta games. I had my picture taken. I took a class in reading. There were just two of us. We did the Stevenson reading, and we went to the church once a week for class. Then, I took a class at college. My mom drove me to class, and it was in communication. I had to write papers. I got a *C*. And I went to Cincinnati to be with the Advocacy Press. I was a reporter for the newsletter.

Every year, I joined the teen group or young adult group later, and I met my boyfriend. We went out, and he drives. We got engaged to be married. We have been engaged for 4 years now. We don't do young adult group because they have a waiting list.

I go to the National Down Syndrome Congress Convention every year. Sometimes I speak at the convention. I have a lot of fun. One year, they asked if anyone wanted to do acting. I signed up, but they didn't call me. Then, one day they called me to audition for a movie. I did the audition in the living room, and I got the part in *Kingdom Hospital*.

I had to go to Vancouver, Canada, to film the show. I had to live in Canada for 8 months. Sometimes, I was by myself. It was a lot of fun in Canada. We went to see a lot of things.

I liked working on the movie. I met all the actors—Bruce Davison, Diane Ladd, Andrew McCarthy, and Ed Begley, Jr. We had fun on the set. They had food all the time. We went a lot of places. I met Stephen King and Wayne Newton. I had an apartment and my own computer and my own money. I met my costar Brandon Bauer. His mom died in

Canada while we were filming the show. That was very sad. He was very sad. He lives in California.

I like the National Down Syndrome Congress conventions. I take my friends. This year, I am taking two friends. We are going to Minneapolis with my mom and stepfather. I do not have a job yet. I worked at Krogers for 7 years, but now I am trying to get a job in an office. I have a meeting with the Bureau of Vocational Rehabilitation (BVR) to see if they can help me get a job in an office.

5

■■■

My Life as a Special Tomato

CAROLYN HANSEN BERGERON

■■■

In my daily life, I volunteer at my local school two mornings a week helping in the pre-K and first grades. I also help out at our family business two afternoons a week filing, doing computer work, and assisting in any way I can. On the other days, I get together with my home waiver aide. We exercise together at the gym, volunteer where we pack grocery boxes for those who are in need, and work on independent skills. She assists me with money management, household skills, and studying for my learner's permit, plus maintaining my comprehension skills. We also do fun things like taking sign language, going to movies, planning parties, and going on trips.

Another exercise that I do is karate two to three times a week. This helps me with one of my challenges, which is maintaining physical fitness. Now, I have my first-degree brown belt and will hopefully be receiving my black belt in the spring of 2005.

One concern I have as a young adult with Down syndrome is what will be my living arrangement in the future. Now, I am living with my parents and feel blessed that they want me around. In December 2003, I found out that my dad was diagnosed with chronic lymphocytic leukemia. This made me realize that life is full of challenges and that I need to be flexible and prepared when they happen. I would like to move out one day, but at this point I want very much to be with my dad until he gets better. I know myself well enough that when I do move out, I will need some assistance wherever I am living. My ultimate dream would be to meet "Mr. Right" and get married.

A second concern is having more close friends to hang out with. I e-mail some of my friends from the National Down Syndrome Congress Conference but they do not live near me. I had not found anyone in my area who communicates on the same level as I do and felt lonely, trying to focus on the good times with family and other friends, such as my home waiver friend/aide. I am so happy to share that I now have a close friend nearby and look forward to being with him as often as possible. He also has Down syndrome and understands where I am coming from. I also was an attendant in a wedding for one of my preschool friends this summer and had a wonderful time, especially dancing at the reception!

I did not realize that I had Down syndrome until I was in sixth grade. All of my life, I have been trying to be a positive person but felt frustrated. I noticed some of the students were teasing me. I was thinking I knew that I did not do anything to them and thought I was just another human being. I did not understand why they were making fun of me. I also felt like I had a heart of stone because I did not want to pout in front of them, showing my weak spot. I waited until I got home to let my feelings out with the unconditional love of my parents.

I asked my parents about the teasing. They said I have what is called Down syndrome. I felt a bit relieved knowing now why the students would tease me and was determined to have a positive attitude even when others would hurt my feelings.

Now, I would like to share some embarrassing moments when I was young. I was hugging too much so my parents said the keyword *honey jar* to remind me. I also let my tongue hang out and my parents said another keyword, *Carrie T,* to remind me as well. Also, I have always talked with my pretend friends. It feels like I am role-playing when I feel lonely. It adds a dramatic flair to my life! I learned to do it privately at home! My mom said that a psychologist told her when I was 10 years old that I was practicing my social skills with my pretend friends but needed to learn to do it appropriately.

I guess my biggest accomplishment was getting through school and a 2-year college. I worked very hard but could not have succeeded without the support of my teachers, friends, and family. My English and speech classes especially helped me to make presentations locally and nationally as an ambassador for those of us with Down syndrome and their families. I also wrote the following "Tomato Story" for an English assignment, which was published in several magazines and books.

THE SPECIAL TOMATO

My dad and mom had four children. The first three children were healthy and regular people. I came along, a baby with a difference, Down syndrome. I had a hole in my heart, a rip in my heart valve, jaundice, a big tongue, and a wobbly head. As I got older, I also realized that I am a slow learner.

One day, it was bothering me that I was having a hard time doing my schoolwork. I told my dad about this problem, and he shared a story about when he was out in his garden picking tomatoes the year I was born. Every year, my dad grows a garden and loves to plant tomatoes. At harvest time, there were Beefsteak tomatoes on a bush. When he saw a differently shaped tomato, it got his attention. It had a large, smooth, bright red enlarged side that made my dad want to pick it up and study the bump because it was so unique and looked appetizing. At supper, that tomato was just as juicy as the others.

Even though I'm different like the tomato as a person with Down syndrome, my family and friends love me even more and want to help me when I need it. My dad tells me that even though I have more difficulty learning than my brother and sisters, my lovable and outgoing personality and strong character make me just as special as they are. I guess I am the special "tomato" on the Bergeron bush!

This story is also on my website: http://www.carriebergeron.org along with ordering note cards and posters. The artwork is by Michael Johnson, another young adult with Down syndrome!

My goals, as I said before, are having more close friends and finding a soul mate (could be my present boyfriend!). Those would be two wonderful accomplishments for the future. However, I do feel so fortunate to have a busy schedule and to be able to work 5 days a week. I am so blessed to have a wonderful life and to be able to share it with my loved ones!

■■■ 6 ■■■

Are Psychiatric Disorders of Concern in Adults with Down Syndrome?

Siegfried M. Pueschel and Beverly A. Myers

When John Langdon Down (1866) described some of the features of individuals with Down syndrome, he did not mention any specific psychiatric or behavioral signs or symptoms. He only remarked, in passing, that individuals with Down syndrome "have considerable power of imitation even bordering on mimics." And he continued to say, "they are humorous, and a lively sense of the ridiculous often colors their mimicry."

During the middle of the 20th century, there was a persistent notion that individuals with Down syndrome exhibit characteristic temperament and behavior traits (Benda, 1969; Domino, 1965; Menolascino, 1965; Tredgold & Soddy, 1956). Many authors described people with Down syndrome as good-tempered, affectionate, and placid individuals, having a cheerful and happy disposition. Other behavioral characteristics that have been reported include stubborn, sullen, withdrawn, and defiant. However, as early as 1953, Blacketer-Simmonds noted that the observed behaviors in people with Down syndrome did not fit a stereotype and were by no means homogeneous. Subsequently, there have been many other investigators who have emphasized that this old stereotype is incorrect and indicated that individuals with Down syndrome have the same range of personality, behavioral, and mental attributes as people without Down syndrome.

EPIDEMIOLOGIC STUDIES

With regard to psychiatric disorders in individuals with Down syndrome, there were only a few sporadic publications in the medical literature during the first half of the 20th century (Biewald, 1940; Bradway, 1939; Rollins, 1946). Then, in the 1950s and 1960s scientists started to report more often on psychiatric issues in individuals with Down syndrome (Haberlandt, 1966; Menolascino, 1965; Neville, 1959). Since 1980, an increasing literature on psychiatric disorders in individuals with Down syndrome has accumulated. Some of these publications focused on the entire spectrum of psychiatric conditions (Collacott, Cooper, & McGrother, 1992; Lund, 1988; Myers & Pueschel, 1991).

In a survey of psychiatric morbidity, Lund (1988) compared 44 adults who had Down syndrome with 58 individuals with intellectual disabilities of other etiologies and reported that 11 of 44 (25%) individuals with Down syndrome had psychiatric disorders. Myers and Pueschel (1991) examined 497 children and adults with Down syndrome in the state of Rhode Island and found the overall frequency of psychiatric disorders to be 22%. Whereas the younger population with Down syndrome often displayed disruptive behaviors, anxiety disorders, and repetitive behaviors, individuals 20 years and older frequently exhibited major depressive symptoms, bipolar disorders, dementia, and others. The prevalence of psychiatric disorders in this study of individuals 20 years and older was 25.6%, which is very similar to Lund's (1988) survey as noted previously. Another large-scale study was carried out by Collacott et al. (1992) involving 378 individuals with Down syndrome and a comparison group. The authors noted that people with Down syndrome more often had major depression and dementia than people with other intellectual disabilities.

DEPRESSION

Among the various psychiatric disorders, major depressions and dysthymic disorders (i.e., minor depressions) are the most frequently observed in the adult population; 5.5%–11.3% of young adults with Down syndrome were found to have major depression compared with 4.3% of young adults with other intellectual disabilities (Collacott et al., 1992; Myers & Pueschel, 1995). McGuire and Chicoine (1996) followed a large cohort of individuals with Down syndrome in their Adult Down Syndrome Center and observed that 40 of 272 people with Down syndrome had depressive disorders. Of these 40 individuals, 16 carried the diagnosis of major depression, 14 had major depression together with comorbid conditions, and 10 were diagnosed with mood disorders associated with general medical conditions such as hypothyroidism. Many other reports have appeared in the medical literature, including case studies and reviews, that contributed to the increasing knowledge of depression in individuals with Down syndrome.

Diagnosis

The question often arises how the diagnosis of depression in individuals with Down syndrome is made because many people with Down syndrome have significant intellectual limitations. Although the criteria of the *Diagnostic and Statistical Manual of Mental Disorders, Fourth Edition, Text Revision* (DSM-IV-TR; American Psychiatric Association, 2000) are the hallmark that assist in establishing the diagnosis of depression, adaptations may have to be made in diagnosing depression in individuals with Down syndrome for a number of reasons. It is often difficult to directly obtain an accurate history from adults with Down syndrome, and it is also difficult to determine their feelings, perceptions, and thoughts. Parents or other caregivers of a person with Down syndrome can often provide observations of the person's mood, thoughts, and behavior so that a diagnosis of major depression can be made by using modifications of the DSM-IV-TR criteria.

In making the diagnosis of depression in individuals with Down syndrome, one has to take into consideration the influence of intellectual disabilities. Certain behaviors that may appear abnormal considering the person's chronological age may be appropriate in relation to a younger mental age. Also, individuals with intellectual disabilities may present with significant psychiatric symptoms that cannot be ignored because standardized criteria have not been met. Moreover, the diagnosis of depression may be missed because it may be assumed that the presenting symptoms are just part of the "Down syndrome condition" or the signs and symptoms may be misinterpreted as part of Alzheimer disease.

Crying, irritability or agitation, loss of interest or pleasure and social withdrawal, poor appetite and weight loss, sleep impairment, reduced concentration, fatigue, and lack of energy can be observed in individuals with Down syndrome who are depressed (Myers, 1998). Depression is often indirectly expressed by aggressive acting out and/or somatic complaints. In addition, withdrawal and somatic complaints are often experienced concurrently with increased dependency, irritability, and disturbances of vegetative function.

A host of medical conditions—Alzheimer dementia; complicated and uncomplicated grief; sleep apnea; certain infections; tooth abscesses; lack of appetite; and cardiovascular, respiratory, gastrointestinal, endocrine, and immunologic disorders—may cause symptoms that mimic those of depression (Khan, Osinowo, & Pary, 2002; Pary, Loschen, & Tomkowiak, 1996). In addition, comorbid disorders, including Alzheimer disease, hypothyroidism, vitamin B_{12} deficiency, various behavior disorders, obsessive-compulsive symptoms, anxiety problems, and anorexia nervosa are often encountered in association with depression (McGuire & Chicoine, 1996). These and other concerns should be taken into consideration in the differential diagnosis of depression.

The question has been raised as to why there is an observed increased prevalence of depression in individuals with Down syndrome. Although there is no one specific answer to this question, researchers speculate that genetic factors, possibly specific genes located on chromosome 21 or genes from other chromosomes that work in concert with genes on chromosome 21, may play a part. In addition, neurochemical impairments and dementia may induce depression (Geldmacher et al., 1997). The possibility of low serotonin function in the neurotransmitters of individuals with Down syndrome and depression has not been established (Gedye, 1991).

Environmental stressors may also contribute to depression. For example, an episode of depression may be triggered by a loss, or it may be the consequence of a change in the individual's life circumstance that is experienced or perceived as a threatening stressor. "Higher-functioning" individuals with Down syndrome who live in an inclusive society may become depressed when they realize their limitations and perceive themselves as "different." Of course, these reasons are not inclusive, and there can be many reasons why individuals with Down syndrome exhibit depressive behaviors. In addition, a person with Down syndrome who experiences depression may have numerous episodes of depression for different reasons in different stages of his or her life.

Prognosis

Only a few studies have pursued long-term follow-up in individuals with Down syndrome with regard to the prognosis for depression. Cooper and Collacott (1994) described 42 subjects with Down syndrome who had a history of depression. Among this group, 8 individuals had 22 sustained recurrent episodes of depression. Thirty-four individuals had experienced only one episode of depression, and 18 of them had been followed for at least 5 years without recurrence.

If adults with Down syndrome have their first episode of depression at an older age (beyond 40–50 years) and this episode is of short duration, then they are at an increased risk to have a recurrence of depression. The short-term prognosis for depression in adults with Down syndrome is relatively guarded according to some researchers, who noted some improvement but that the majority of depressed individuals remained symptomatic (Prasher & Hall, 1996). Other follow-up studies revealed that relapse of depression is associated with short-term duration of depressive episodes and the absence of compromising life events prior to the first episode, which suggests the presence of a biological origin of depression (Cooper, & Collacott, 1994).

Treatment

Although a person's quality of life is impaired when he or she is severely depressed, treatment for depression can help a person return to his or her predepressed level of functioning and mindset. Once a diagnosis of depression is made, it is important to start therapy as soon as possible. The treatment plan should be individualized, and close follow-up services should be provided. Treatment components primarily involve specific medications, environmental strategies implemented with family and/or caregiver assistance, cognitive-behavioral intervention by a trained psychologist, and general counseling. With optimal psychotropic medications and adequate environmental supports, hospitalization can be avoided.

The pharmacologic treatment of depression previously included tricyclic antidepressants and monoamine oxidase inhibitors that are often associated with significant side effects. With the introduction of newer medications (selective serotonergic reuptake inhibitors), the treatment of depression in the general population, as well as in individuals with Down syndrome, has become more effective and has fewer side effects. Selective serotonergic reuptake inhibitors include fluoxetine (Prozac, Sarafem), sertaline (Zoloft), paroxetine (Paxil, Pexeva), and fluvoxamine (Luvox).

There are few reports available on the treatment of depression in individuals with Down syndrome, but some investigators found that the serotonergic reuptake inhibitors have a beneficial effect in the treatment of depression (Cooper & Collacott, 1994; Myers, 1998; Pary et al., 1996). Geldmacher et al. (1997) pointed out that some of the individuals who display aggression, social withdrawal, and compulsive behaviors improved significantly when serotonergic reuptake inhibitors were administered.

If individuals with Down syndrome are resistant to specific treatments for depression, then the diagnosis of depression and prior treatment adequacy need to be reconsidered (Khan et al., 2002). Another antidepressant should be administered or a combination of several antidepressants should be used. In addition, antipsychotic medications such as risperidone (Risperdal), quetiapine (Seroquel), and olanzapine (Zyprexa) may help treat hidden psychotic symptoms.

Also, electroconvulsive therapy has been employed in the past for the treatment of severe depression in individuals with Down syndrome (Lazarus, Jaffe, & Dubin, 1990; Warren, Holroyd, & Folstein,

1990). Although it is never the first line of treatment, its use may be safely considered in situations when individuals did not respond to intensive pharmacologic approaches.

As mentioned previously, the treatment for depression consists primarily of providing specific medications. If the depression is due to environmental circumstances, then the stressors in the environment need to be removed if possible. Some individuals with mild intellectual disabilities may be helped at times with cognitive-behavioral intervention focusing on the positive aspects of life and ignoring negative influences. General counseling can also be provided to individuals with mild impairments. Physicians and caregivers can explain the circumstances leading to depression and offer support and assistance. Often, a combination of these treatment approaches is employed.

Suicidal Ideation

Although suicidal thoughts and behaviors are highly related to depression in people in the general population, expressions of suicidal ideation, death, and self-deprivation are uncommon features of depression in individuals with Down syndrome (Khan et al., 2002). People with Down syndrome have a significantly lower prevalence of suicidal ideation than other individuals (Pary, Strauss, & White, 1997); however, suicidal ideation may be overlooked and might occur more often than documented in the literature because people with Down syndrome are reluctant to report any negative experiences. These factors may be obstacles in determining the true occurrence of suicidal thoughts (Myers, 1998).

BIPOLAR DISORDERS

Bipolar disorders, which include periods of significant depression and episodes of mania, may also occur in people who have been diagnosed with depression. Mania is characterized by an elevated mood, inflated self-esteem, excessive talking, flight of ideas, distractibility, increased activity or agitation, buying sprees, and/or sexual indiscretion. Sometimes, a manic episode may appear years after the first presentation of depression, then changing the diagnosis from unipolar depression to bipolar disorder. This new diagnosis necessitates the addition of mood stabilizers and/or antipsychotic medications.

In the 1980s and 1990s, there was a debate whether bipolar disorder ever occurred in individuals with Down syndrome. Also, the frequency of bipolar disorders in Down syndrome has been difficult to ascertain because, prior to 1980, bipolar and unipolar disorders were combined and referred to as affective disorders. Since 1985, several publications have reported that mania may occur in individuals with Down syndrome (Collacott et al., 1992; Cooper & Collacott, 1993). Bipolar disorder has been identified in 0.5% of individuals with Down syndrome. It has been suggested that the predisposition to depression and relative protection from mania occurs in people with Down syndrome possibly as a result of reduced serotonergic and noradrenergic function in their central nervous system. Individuals with bipolar disorders are usually treated with lithium (Eskalith, Lithobid), carbamazepine (Carbatrol, Epitol, Tegretol), valproic acid (Depakene), risperidone (Risperdal), quetiapine (Seroquel), and other medications if indicated.

OTHER PSYCHIATRIC DISORDERS

In addition to major depression and bipolar disorder, there are a number of other psychiatric ailments that have been observed in people with Down syndrome. Myers and Pueschel (1991) provided an overview of the various psychiatric conditions in a population of 497 individuals with Down syndrome. Some of these disorders are primarily noted during childhood and adolescence, such as conduct and oppositional behaviors, adjustment problems, elimination disorders, and repetitive and stereotypic behaviors—these will not be discussed in this chapter. This chapter also will not detail schizophrenia, personality disorders, and chronic psychosis because they are rarely seen in Down syndrome (Myers, 1992). Obsessive-compulsive disorder, anorexia nervosa, autism spectrum disorders, attention deficit hyperactivity disorder, and dementia are more often observed in adults with Down syndrome and are discussed next.

Obsessive-Compulsive Disorder

People with Down syndrome may also have obsessive-compulsive disorder, a disorder in which a person exhibits persistent obsessions or repetitive thoughts and compulsions or recurrent unusual behaviors. Although obsessive-compulsive disorder occurs in 1.2%–2.4% of the general population, it only occurs in 0.6% of adults with Down syndrome (Lewis, 1996).

The appropriate treatment for obsessive-compulsive disorder includes behavioral approaches (i.e., directing compulsive tendencies into positive actions) and/or selective serotonergic reuptake inhibitors. DeVeaugh-Geiss, Landau, and Katz (1989) conducted a double blind study using clomipramine (Anafranil) versus a placebo and demonstrated the efficacy of serotonergic antidepressant therapy in obsessive-compulsive disorder.

Obsessive slowness is a distinct form of obsessive-compulsive disorder that can be seen in individuals with Down syndrome (Charlot, Fox, & Friedlander, 2002; Pary, 1994). It is rarer in the general population than it is in people with Down syndrome. Individuals who are diagnosed with obsessive-compulsive disorder and who exhibit obsessive slowness may spend hours on end with routine daily living tasks that significantly interfere with regular functioning. Their obsessive slowness can sometimes be the result of interfering ritualistic actions, including touching, hoarding, hesitancy, freezing, and problems with initiating movements.

Obsessive slowness frequently begins during late adolescence and the early 20s. It appears that obsessive slowness occurs along a continuum. For some, it may be just important to follow a "routine" with a relatively low anxiety component; however, for others with a high level of anxiety, obsessive slowness may affect their lives to a point where it seriously interferes with their normal daily functioning. Most individuals with Down syndrome and obsessive slowness display some form of perfectionism and fastidiousness.

A behavioral therapeutic approach is usually of some benefit (Charlot et al., 2002). The majority of individuals with obsessive slowness respond moderately well to selective serotonin reuptake inhibitor drugs such as fluoxetine (Prozac, Sarafem), sertaline (Zoloft), and paroxetine (Paxil, Pexeva).

The "groove" is a milder form of obsessive slowness (McGuire, 1999). The groove may be a methodical and meticulous morning routine of dressing and grooming, making order in the bedroom, and doing daily activities where thoughts and action tend to follow a well-worn path. Grooves can give an important sense of structure in daily routines; however, when grooves become a maladaptive rut that interferes with important functioning of daily living, appropriate treatment, including counseling and/or medications such as fluoxetine (Prozac) and fluvoxamine (Luvox), are often needed.

Anorexia Nervosa

Anorexia nervosa is not uncommon in the general population, but it is rarely observed in individuals with Down syndrome (Cottrell & Crisp, 1984; Fox, Karan, & Rotatori, 1981; Holt, 1988; Morgan, 1989; Szymanski, 1984). Symptoms of people with Down syndrome who have anorexia nervosa include decreased food intake, marked weight loss, withdrawal, depression, amenorrhea, and behavioral regression.

Intense fear of becoming obese, a primary symptom in anorexia nervosa, may be difficult to elicit in individuals with Down syndrome. Anorexia may present itself as one way a person can control his or her body. The treatment of choice for this condition is intensive therapy in conjunction with environmental changes and serotonergic antidepressants (Rader, Specht, & Reister, 1989; Raitasuo, Virtanen, & Raitasuo, 1998).

Autism Spectrum Disorder

Autism, autism spectrum disorder, or pervasive developmental disorder is usually diagnosed during the first few years of life. Most studies have been carried out during childhood and adolescence; however, ordinarily youngsters with autism survive into adulthood. It has been suggested that autism spectrum disorder occurs more often in individuals with Down syndrome than in the general population (Collacott et al., 1992), but Myers and Pueschel's (1991) study did not reveal an increased prevalence of autism spectrum disorder in Down syndrome.

The symptoms of autism spectrum disorder include impaired social relationships, limited communication abilities, and repetitive behaviors. Although there have been suggestions of hereditary and prenatal influences, the etiology of autism is unknown. No effective treatment is available at the present time. Early behavioral intervention, language stimulation, and appropriate social interaction are usually recommended. Modern communication devices can often facilitate social engagements. Some individuals with Down syndrome and autism spectrum disorder may exhibit secondary symptoms such as aggressive behavior and self-injurious behavior. Specific treatment is then indicated, including behavioral and/or psychopharmacologic interventions.

Attention Deficit Hyperactivity Disorder

Similar to autism spectrum disorder, attention deficit hyperactivity disorder is primarily encountered in childhood and adolescence, yet many individuals continue to have symptoms of this disorder during their adult years, perhaps in a somewhat modified way. The symptoms of attention deficit hyperactivity disorder usually include short attention span, hyperactivity, impulsivity, and distractibility. Attention deficit hyperactivity disorder does not occur more frequently in individuals with Down syndrome than in the general population. In addition to the traditional treatment approaches with dextroamphetamine (Dexedrine), amphetamine & dextroamphetamine (Adderall), and methylphenidate

(Concerta, Metadate CD, Methylin, Ritalin), there are a number of newer, long-acting, and more effective medications available.

Dementia

The decline of intellectual and social functioning in some individuals with Down syndrome that ultimately leads to the diagnosis of Alzheimer disease usually appears in adults older than 50 years of age. If young people with Down syndrome during their 20s and 30s exhibit functional decline, it is highly unlikely that they have Alzheimer disease. They more likely either have a major depression that can be treated or a central nervous system disorder. There is an association between depression and dementia in people with Down syndrome that is not present in individuals with other intellectual disabilities. It has been suggested that individuals with Down syndrome who are depressed are at increased risk for a later decline in intellectual and adaptive functioning (see section on Alzheimer disease in Chapter 3) (Burt, Loveland, & Lewis, 1992). The co-occurrence of depression and dementia in people with Down syndrome can be treated with antidepressants, but the dementia will remain.

SUMMARY

This chapter focuses on the more frequently encountered psychiatric problems in adults with Down syndrome. A number of psychiatric disorders can be identified in people with Down syndrome; therefore, it is paramount that in the course of optimal medical and psychiatric care of adults with Down syndrome, attention be paid to changes in functioning such as affect, behavior, cognition, and daily living circumstances. When significant signs and symptoms in these and other realms of functioning are noted, it is important that the individual receives a comprehensive assessment, that an accurate diagnosis is established, and that appropriate rehabilitation and intervention services are provided, including the administration of disorder-specific medications, environmental and behavioral interventions, social support, and coordinated follow-up care. If individuals with psychiatric disorders receive such services, their overall functioning and their quality of life will improve significantly.

REFERENCES

American Psychiatric Association. (2000). *Diagnostic and statistical manual of mental disorders* (4th ed., text revision). Washington, DC: Author.
Benda, C.E. (1969). *Down's syndrome: Mongolism and its management.* New York: Grune & Stratton.

Biewald, E.M. (1940). *Beitrag zur erforschung der psyche der aelteren mongoloiden.* Dissertation, University of Erlangen, Germany.

Blacketer-Simmonds, D.A. (1953). An investigation into the supposed differences existing between mongols and other mentally defective subjects with regard to certain psychological traits. *Journal of Mental Science, 90,* 702–719.

Bradway, K.P. (1939). Hysterical mutism in mongol imbecile. *Journal for Abnormal Social Psychology, 31,* 458–463.

Burt, D.B., Loveland, K.A., & Lewis, K.R. (1992). Depression and the onset of dementia in adults with mental retardation. *American Journal on Mental Retardation, 96,* 502–511.

Charlot, L., Fox, S., & Friedlander, R. (2002). Obsessional slowness in Down's syndrome. *Journal of Intellectual Disability Research, 46,* 517–524.

Collacott, R.A., Cooper, S.A., & McGrother, C. (1992). Differential rates of psychiatric disorders in adults with Down's syndrome, compared to other mentally handicapped adults. *British Journal of Psychiatry, 161,* 671–674.

Cooper, S.A., & Collacott, R.A. (1993). Prognosis of depression in Down's syndrome. *Journal of Nervous and Mental Diseases, 181,* 204–205.

Cooper, S.A., & Collacott, R.A. (1994). Relapse of depression in people with Down's syndrome. *British Journal of Developmental Disabilities, 78,* 32–37.

Cottrell, D.J., & Crisp, A.H. (1984). Anorexia nervosa in Down's syndrome— A case report. *British Journal of Psychiatry, 145,* 195–196.

DeVeaugh-Geiss, J., Landau, P., & Katz, R. (1989). Preliminary results from a multicenter trial of cloripramine in obsessive-compulsive disorder. *Psychopharmacologic Bulletin, 25,* 36–40.

Domino, G. (1965). Personality traits in institutionalized mongoloids. *American Journal of Mental Deficiency, 69,* 568–570.

Down, J.L. (1866). Observations on an ethnic classification of idiots, London Hospital. *Clinical Lectures and Reports, 3,* 259–262.

Fox, R., Karan, O.C., & Rotatori, A.F. (1981). Regression including anorexia nervosa in a Down's syndrome adult: A seven-year follow-up. *Journal of Behavior Therapy and Experimental Psychiatry, 12,* 351–354.

Gedye, A. (1991). Serotonergic treatment for aggression in a Down's syndrome adult showing signs of Alzheimer's disease. *Journal of Mental Deficiency Research, 35,* 247–258.

Geldmacher, D.S., Lerner, A.J., Voci, J.M., Noelkler, E.A., Sompler, Z.L.C., & Whitehouse, P.J. (1997). Treatment of functional decline in adults with Down syndrome using selective serotonin-reuptake inhibitor drugs. *Journal of Geriatric Psychiatry and Neurology, 10,* 99–104.

Haberlandt, W.F. (1966). The chromosomal pathology as a contribution to a genetically oriented psychiatry. *Nervenarzt, 37,* 45–51.

Holt, G.M. (1988). Down syndrome and eating disorders. *British Journal of Psychiatry, 152,* 847–848.

Khan, S., Osinowo, T., & Pary, R.J. (2002). Down syndrome and major depressive disorder: A review. *Mental Health Aspects of Developmental Disabilities, 5,* 46–52.

Lazarus, A., Jaffe, R.L., & Dubin, W.R. (1990). Electroconvulsive therapy and major depression in Down's syndrome. *Journal of Clinical Psychiatry, 51,* 422–425.

Lewis, M. (1996). *Child and adolescent psychiatry: A comprehensive textbook.* Philadelphia: Lippincott, Williams & Wilkins.

Lund, J. (1988). Psychiatric aspects of Down's syndrome. *Acta Psychiatrica Scandinavia, 78,* 369–374.

McGuire, D. (1999, November). The groove. *Newsletter of the National Association for Down Syndrome, 1,* 6.

McGuire, D.E., & Chicoine, B.A. (1996). Depressive disorders in adults with Down syndrome. *Habilitative Mental Healthcare Newsletter, 15,* 1–7.

Menolascino, F.J. (1965). Psychiatric aspects of mongolism. *American Journal of Mental Deficiency, 69,* 553–560.

Morgan, J.R. (1989). A case of Down's syndrome, insulinoma, and anorexia. *Journal of Mental Deficiency Research, 33,* 185–187.

Myers, B.A. (1992). Psychiatric disorders. In S.M. Pueschel & J.K. Pueschel (Eds.), *Biomedical concerns in persons with Down syndrome* (pp. 197–208). Baltimore: Paul H. Brookes Publishing Co.

Myers, B.A. (1998). Major depression in persons with moderate to profound mental retardation: Clinical presentation and case illustrations. *Mental Health Aspects of Developmental Disabilities, 1,* 3.

Myers, B.A., & Pueschel, S.M. (1991). Psychiatric disorders in a population with Down syndrome. *Journal of Nervous and Mental Disease, 179,* 609–613.

Myers, B.A., & Pueschel, S.M. (1995). Major depression in a small group of adults with Down syndrome. *Research in Developmental Disabilities, 16,* 285–299.

Neville, J. (1959). Paranoid schizophrenia in a mongoloid defective: Some theoretical considerations derived from an unusual case. *Journal of Medical Science, 105,* 445–447.

Pary, R.J. (1994). Down syndrome update: Obsessional slowness. *Habilitative Mental Healthcare Newsletter, 13,* 49–50.

Pary, R.J., Loschen, E.L., & Tomkowiak, S.B. (1996). Mood disorders in Down syndrome. *Seminar in Clinical Neuropsychiatry, 1,* 148–153.

Pary, R.J., Strauss, D., & White, J.F. (1997). A population survey of suicide attempts in persons with and without Down syndrome. *Down Syndrome Quarterly, 2,* 12–13.

Prasher, V.P., & Hall, W. (1996). Short-term prognosis of depression in adults with Down's syndrome: Association with thyroid status and effects on adaptive behavior. *Journal of Intellectual Disability Research, 40,* 32–38.

Rader, K., Specht, F., & Reister, M. (1989). [Anorexia nervosa in Down syndrome]. *Praxis Kinderpsychologie und Kinderpsychiatrie, 9,* 343–346.

Raitasuo, S., Virtanen, H., & Raitasuo, J. (1998). Anorexia nervosa, major depression, and obsessive-compulsive disorder in a Down's syndrome patient. *International Journal for Eating Disorders, 23,* 10–19.

Rollins, H.R. (1946). Personality in mongolism with special reference to the incidence of catatonic psychosis. *American Journal of Mental Deficiency, 51,* 219–221.

Szymanski, L.S. (1984). Depression and anorexia nervosa of persons with Down syndrome. *American Journal on Mental Deficiency, 89,* 246–251.

Tredgold, A.F., & Soddy, K. (1956). *Textbook of mental deficiency*. Philadelphia: Lippincott, Williams & Wilkins.

Warren, A.C., Holroyd, S., & Folstein, M.P. (1990). Major depression in Down's syndrome. *British Journal of Psychiatry, 155,* 202–295.

Positive Behavior Support Process for Adults with Down Syndrome and Challenging Behavior

Rose Iovannone

Adults with Down syndrome often have challenging behaviors. Many behavior traits have been attributed to people with Down syndrome, including being good-tempered, affectionate, placid, cheerful, stubborn, sullen, withdrawn, and defiant, but the range of behavior problems in this population is as variable as it is in any other group of people (Cohen, Nadel, & Madwick, 2002; Pueschel, Bernier, & Pezzullo, 1991). There have been reports, however, of a higher incidence of behavior problems in people with Down syndrome when compared with the general population (Coe et al., 1999). Specifically, externalizing behaviors such as not attending to tasks or activities, being oppositional, and showing inflexibility and rigidity in complying with requests occur more frequently (Dykens, Shah, Sagun, Beck, & King, 2002).

Much research has been devoted to the relationship between problem behavior and other health conditions common in individuals with Down syndrome, such as sleep apnea, anemia, gastroesophageal reflex, constipation, and premature aging problems (i.e., early-onset Alzheimer disease) (Patterson, 2002; Carr, 2002). There is a lack of literature devoted to addressing behavior problems using a systematic process that can be applied across different environments and with different people.

Historically, problem behaviors exhibited by individuals with disabilities, including Down syndrome, have resulted in segregated, separate settings, including separate work environments (e.g., sheltered workshops or day programs), separate living environments (e.g., group homes and other assembled group facilities), and artificial social and leisure opportunities (e.g., groups consisting of and formed for people with disabilities) (Carr et al., 2002; Sailor, 1996). Moreover, problem behaviors limit the activities available within segregated settings. For example, inappropriate behaviors may prevent individuals with Down syndrome from obtaining competitive employment outside of a day program, significantly affecting their ability to earn higher wages and gain future employment opportunities. This chapter describes positive behavior support, a systematic approach that can help individuals with Down syndrome overcome behavior problems.

POSITIVE BEHAVIOR SUPPORT

Positive behavior support is a process based on applied science (e.g., applied behavior analysis principles) that uses educational and environmental redesign to enhance the quality of life of a person with behavior problems and anyone who supports the person. It aims to decrease the overall occurrence of the problem behavior (Carr et al., 2002). This process can be used effectively with the majority of externalizing behavior problems exhibited by individuals with Down syndrome, such as oppositionality, inattention, and noncompliance. Positive behavior support places emphasis on improving quality of life, treating people with dignity, encouraging socially valid goals, and modifying events in the environment to ameliorate problem behavior; therefore, it is a valid process to use with individuals with Down syndrome who have problem behavior.

Prior to positive behavior support, traditional behavioral interventions focused on applying consequences after behaviors were exhibited to stop or extinguish future behaviors or to increase alternative behaviors. For example, interventions may have included time-out (isolating in room); removal of preferred or reinforcing items (taking away television); giving tokens or points for appropriate, alternative behaviors; or ignoring any problem behavior until appropriate behaviors were displayed. Although these contingency management procedures are appropriate and valid, the broader process of positive behavior support has now become the standard approach to problem behavior management and support (Carr et al., 2002).

A vast amount of research shows the effectiveness of the positive behavior support process in addressing problem behaviors (Carr, Levin, McConnachie, Carlson, Kemp, & Smith, 1994; Horner et al., 1996; Koegel, Koegel, & Dunlap, 1996). Even though many behavioral treatment approaches use similar strategies, the uniqueness of positive behavior support lies in the embedding of several characteristics that define the process, including across-the-board lifestyle change, lifetime perspective, environmental and social validity, multicomponent interventions, and emphasis on prevention.

Positive behavior support goes beyond traditional behavioral interventions in that it focuses on a broader context in determining treatments and supports and in evaluating success (Edmonson & Turnbull, 2002). Whereas traditional behavior or treatment plans focus on changing the individual, positive behavior support explores the environmental factors that are routinely associated with the presentation of aberrant behavior and responses or consequences that maintain the occurrence of behavior. This information allows an understanding of the purpose or function of the behavior. A multicomponent support plan is developed to render problem behavior irrelevant, ineffective, and inefficient. Providing antecedent interventions to rearrange the environmental factors prevents the problem behavior so that it becomes irrelevant. Providing the teaching of new skills or replacement behaviors that obtain the same favorable outcome as the problem behavior results in aberrant behavior becoming inefficient. Coaching relevant people in the person's environment to reinforce the new desired replacement behavior ensures that environment ensures that the new desired replacement behavior is repeated and the old behavior becomes ineffective (Edmonson & Turnbull, 2002; O'Neill et al., 1997).

Positive behavior support evolved from several sources, including 1) applied behavior analysis, 2) the normalization/inclusion movement, and 3) person-centered values. Applied behavior analysis is a set of principles that explain how behaviors are learned and what motivates people to continue to perform the behaviors, even when the behaviors are problematic. Behavior analysis principles include the procedures of shaping, fading, chaining, prompting, and reinforcing positive behavior.

Positive behavior support's philosophy is that all people, including people with Down syndrome, should have the same access to settings, activities, living arrangements, and work options as do others. This notion of normalization aims to help individuals achieve respect from others by having socially valid and respected roles (Wolfensberger, 1983). That is, they hold competitive jobs that match their abilities and preferences and they live in a setting of their choice whether it be their family's home, an apartment with a roommate of their choosing, or a house that they own.

Person-centered planning is a process that elicits a person's values, vision, and opportunities. It allows behavioral interventions to be driven by the individual's specific short-term and long-term goals and needs rather than the available resources and programs provided by specific agencies, systems (including family systems), or institutions. This process empowers people with Down syndrome by providing them with opportunities to self-determine the environments and systems in which they live, work, and socialize (Kincaid, 1996). The primary goal of positive behavior support, then, is to enhance the person with Down syndrome's quality of life as well as the quality of life of all relevant stakeholders (e.g., parents, employers, residential staff, day program staff, friends) (Carr et al., 2002).

This chapter describes the 5-step systematic process of positive behavior support: 1) setting goals through person-centered planning; 2) gathering information; 3) developing a hypothesis; 4) designing a support plan; and 5) implementing, evaluating, and monitoring the plan (Hieneman, Nolan, Presley, DeTuro, Gayler, & Dunlap, 1999).

SETTING GOALS THROUGH PERSON-CENTERED PLANNING

The first step of the positive behavior support process is to identify the goals for intervention. This activity involves having a team of vested stakeholders (e.g., family, friends, support providers, employers, staff in group home) collect information that creates a profile of the person, including his or her preferences, opportunities to make choices, and behaviors that earn and lose respect. The person should be encouraged to provide others with a description of how he or she would like to live his or her life. This is an essential step, particularly for adults with Down syndrome, because many of these individuals are living lives in which they have little, if any, control over what happens on a day-to-day basis (Carr et al., 2002).

Depending on the person's level of receptive and expressive language, direct questions could be asked of the person, such as, "What do you like to do the most?" or "What things are most important to you?" Confirmation questions could be used if the person with Down syndrome has difficulty articulating information, causing other people to interpret and provide the information. For example, asking the person questions such as, "Is that correct? Do you like to go to Kentucky Fried Chicken and get a bucket of wings?" can facilitate accurate interpretation of information provided by others. For an individual who has trouble understanding or speaking, questions can be presented in pictorial or video forms, with the person with Down syndrome selecting pictures or video segments of his or her desired activities, places, and people.

Many occurrences of problem behaviors seen in individuals with Down syndrome are indicators of the person's dissatisfaction with his or her current lifestyle (Lohrmann-O'Roarke & Gomez, 2001). Having an enhanced quality of life involves empowering the person to have a voice in how his or her life is to be lived, including where he or she works and resides, with whom he or she interacts, and in which activities he or she participates (Bambara, Cole, & Koger, 1998; Wehmeyer & Schwartz, 1997). In addition, many behavior problems exhibited by adults with Down syndrome are directly associated with an environment that provides them with few meaningful activities. Problem behavior can be a way of communicating dissatisfaction and is often a person's attempt to have some control over the situation.

Often, people with Down syndrome are told what to do, who to do it with, where to do it, when to do it, and how to do it (Carr et al., 2002). Person-centered planning should be used with individuals with Down syndrome to help them determine how their lives should be lived (Kincaid, 1996; O'Brien, Mount, & O'Brien, 1991; Smull & Harrison, 1992; Vandercook, York, & Forest, 1989). The process allows a person with Down syndrome to be the primary director in his or her life by getting a supportive team (e.g., family members, employers, friends, community contacts) to change policies in the systems and by developing environments that reduce the negative influences affecting the person (Bambara et al., 1998; Carr et al., 2002; Wehmeyer & Schwartz, 1997).

Person-centered planning provides a foundation in which an individual with disabilities has the power to set his or her intervention goals and self-determine the direction of his or her life while a team of relevant stakeholders who are committed to carrying out the plan help the individual achieve the long-term goals that have been set. It is an important first step in the positive behavior support process because it establishes both short-term and long-term goals that move beyond merely eliminating the aberrant behavior. Person-centered planning provides a map that helps a team develop interventions that will teach new, socially valid behaviors in order to enhance the likelihood of the person achieving his or her goals and preferred lifestyle.

Person-centered planning approaches differ from traditional program-centered planning approaches (e.g., behavioral treatment planning meetings, case-study clinical meetings) that tend to develop action steps or solutions that are constrained by perceived program parameters and by limited resources available within the agencies (Carr et al., 2002). Because the person-centered planning process focuses on the person's strengths, rather than his or her impairments and problems, and uses a team approach, creative solutions can be developed to move the person toward his or her vision (Clark & Hieneman, 1999; Eber, 1996; VanDenBerg & Grealish, 1998). The process involves a collaborative team that designs services and supports dictated by the person's individual needs, resulting in behavior support plans that highlight the context of normalization and focus on providing meaningful activities that are preferred by the individual (Carr et al., 2002).

Several processes can be used for person-centered planning: Life Style Planning (O'Brien, 1987), Personal Futures Planning (Mount, 1987), Making Action Plans (MAPs; Forest & Lusthaus, 1987), the

Framework for Accomplishment/Personal Profile (O'Brien et al., 1991), and Essential Lifestyle Planning (Smull & Harrison, 1992). The processes share common features, including

1.   Forming a team of people who are interested in the person with Down syndrome and who will commit to supporting the person

2.   Having the person with Down syndrome be in control of the process

3.   Identifying the person's vision of his or her preferred lifestyle

4.   Using available resources that are natural or within the community to achieve goals

5.   Embedding the person's preferences in his or her life activities and providing opportunities to make choices

6.   Promoting multiple stakeholders and agencies to collaborate in supporting the person

All of the processes are similar in that a facilitator, using group graphic techniques, takes a team through a series of themes or questions (also called *frames*), which provide a profile of the focus individual and result in action plan steps to achieve goals. Figure 7.1 shows an example of a frame completed from a person-centered planning process. The use of visual graphic frames during the person-centered planning process helps to develop a broad understanding of the person with Down syndrome and his or her life. The processes differ mainly on the format of the visual presentation of information (e.g., graphics, color coding, words), the amount of focus on different areas (e.g., friendships, circle of support), and the sequence of the process (starting from the goal and going backward to get to the vision or starting with the vision and going forward to get to goals).

When preparing for a person-centered plan for an adult with Down syndrome, it is important to make sure that the person is actively participating and leading the team in developing the plan for his or her life. Allowing this person to lead the team can be hard for a team to do, especially when the individual may have difficulty with expressive or receptive communication skills. It becomes very easy for a well-intentioned team member to misinterpret the communication signals sent by the person with Down syndrome or to inaccurately report what he or she thinks the person wants or prefers.

Several strategies can be used to help minimize these difficulties. For example, before the day of the person-centered plan, providing the person with a script of questions and statements he or she can

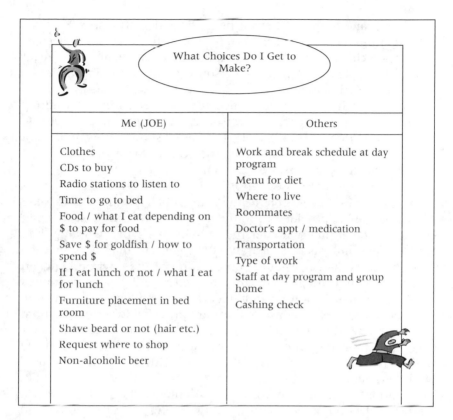

Figure 7.1. Sample choices frame from a person-centered plan.

make during the process is helpful, along with having someone who is trusted prompt and coach the person at the appropriate times. For individuals who use communicative devices or picture/visual schedules, having appropriate phrases programmed into the device or the appropriate written text or pictures prepared prior to the meeting is essential. The person should be asked who he or she wants to be on the team, and he or she should also be allowed to say who should not be on the team.

During the planning activities, the person with Down syndrome should be put in a leadership position (e.g., calling the meeting to order and recognizing people as they speak). Because this process is one that focuses on validating the life and the choices of the individual, it is important that others see the person in a leadership role. Providing the person with information before the meeting in a format that is comprehensible so that he or she understands what will be taking place is another way of ensuring participation (Holburn & Vietze, 2002; Lohrmann-O'Roarke & Gomez, 2001). If the person has communication challenges, it is important to include someone on the team who will be able to interpret the person's responses so that the information obtained is accurate.

Indicators have been developed to assist teams in determining whether effective practices in person-centered planning are being implemented (Smith et al., 2004). Figure 7.2 shows an example of a person-centered planning checklist that can be used to ensure that effective, quality practices are being implemented.

Checklists to help assess positive living environments for adults with disabilities have been developed (Albin, Horner, & O'Neill, 1994). Figure 7.3 provides a positive environment checklist that can be used to determine whether the individual's living, working, and leisure environments are pleasant. Responses to questions in each area should be based on direct observation of the environment, on review of written program documents and records, or on responses obtained from questioning individuals involved in supporting the focus person. Three response options are provided for each question: *yes, no,* and *unclear.* The term *support provider* applies to family members, educators, and others who provide support and services in the setting. The term *people* refers to the people with disabilities who live, work, or attend school in the setting.

Scoring the completed positive environment checklist is simply a matter of determining which questions received a *yes* response and which received *no* or *unclear* responses. *No* responses indicate areas or issues that should be addressed to create a more positive environment. *Unclear* responses indicate the need for further analysis, perhaps by extended observation or by questioning a larger number of support providers.

Lohrmann-O'Rourke and Gomez (2001) have developed a systematic assessment of preferences that allows individuals with limited communication to express their opinions to person-centered planning teams with less likelihood of misinterpretation. The steps in the preference assessment include 1) having the person select options from different domains to sample; 2) providing opportunities for the person to try the options within a natural context; and 3) determining the person's preferences by observing his or her responses while performing the activities. The authors use a layered assessment method that allows major life domains to be broken into natural segments. For example, the living domain breaks into three segments: the neighborhood, living arrangements, and physical structure.

The person is provided different options of neighborhoods to sample. This can be done either by taking the person to different neigh-

Location	Item
	1. Ensuring the involvement of the person with Down syndrome
	The planning is coordinated by the person under consideration or his or her designated individual.
	The planning is undertaken with the involvement of the person's circle of support.
	The plan is approved in writing by the person or his or her designee.
	2. Understanding the person's preferences
	The plan contains a description of the individual's preferred lifestyle, including
	a. Type of living setting
	b. With whom he or she wants to live
	c. What work or other valued activity the person wants to do
	d. With whom the person wants to socialize
	e. What social, leisure, religious, or other activities to participate in
	3. Ensuring opportunities for choice
	The plan describes how opportunities for choice will be provided, including
	a. Permitting the person to indicate preferences among choices using preferred means of communication
	b. Providing necessary support and training to allow the person to be able to indicate his or her preferences
	c. Assisting the person in understanding the negative consequences of choices and any risks associated with choices
	4. Connecting actions to preferred lifestyles
	The plan describes the services needed to assist the person to achieve his or her preferred lifestyle, including
	a. Activities
	b. Training
	c. Materials
	d. Equipment
	e. Assistive technology
	The plan describes (when necessary) any limitations due to imminent danger to the person's health, safety, or welfare based on an assessment of the following:
	a. The person's history of decision making
	b. The possible short- and long-term consequences of a poor decision

(continued)

Figure 7.2. Person-centered planning checklist. *Instructions:* For each item listed, identify the page(s) or location(s) in the person-centered plan where that item can be found or where the item is demonstrated. (From Smith, C., Hine, K., Costlow, T., Freeman, R., Zarcone, J., Tieghi-Benet, M., & Kimbrough, P. [2004]. *Person-centered planning quality indicators checklist.* Lawrence: University of Kansas; reprinted by permission.)

Figure 7.2. *(continued)*

	c. The possible short- and long-term consequence of a provider limiting the choices of the person
	d. The safeguards available to protect the person's safety and rights in each context of choices
	The plan prioritizes and structures services to achieve the person's preferred lifestyle.
	The plan contributes to the continuous movement toward the preferred lifestyle.
	5. Continuous evaluation of the plan The plan is reviewed regularly and revised taking into account the following:
	a. Changes in the person's preferred lifestyle
	b. Achievement of goals or skills outlined in the plan
	c. Any determination that any service or support is unresponsive

borhoods to observe or by providing the person with pictures of two different neighborhoods to see which one he or she would prefer. Other methods include showing the individual videos or objects that will allow him or her to discriminate between the options and make choices.

After deciding the type of neighborhood preferred by the individual, the team would then determine living arrangements (e.g., living alone, with a roommate, or with a group of people). Sampling would again be provided and reactions observed to help the team make a final decision. This systematic process would be completed for each segment of all domains.

Indicators that assist teams in determining whether effective practices in person-centered planning are being implemented have been developed (Smith et al., 2004). Since an underlying value of positive behavior support is that interventions should enhance the person's abilities and access to desirable life circumstances, it is important to include supports and practices that will generate the desired results (a change in behavior) and simultaneous improvement in the person's quality of life (Carr et al., 2002).

A person-centered plan can achieve powerful outcomes in quality-of-life indicators for individuals with Down syndrome by making small environmental changes. Joe's story demonstrates how a team took information obtained from a person-centered plan for Joe and made small changes that had a large impact on Joe's life.

1. Physical setting

Is the physical setting clean, well lighted, and odor free?	yes	no	unclear
Is temperature regulation in the setting adequate?	yes	no	unclear
Is the physical setting visually pleasant and appealing?	yes	no	unclear
Does the arrangement of the setting promote easy access for all individuals within the setting?	yes	no	unclear
Is the setting arranged in a manner that facilitates needed support and supervision?	yes	no	unclear
Does the setting contain or provide interesting, age-appropriate items and materials for people to use?	yes	no	unclear
Is the setting located and structured in a manner that promotes and facilitates physical integration into the "regular" community?	yes	no	unclear

2. Social setting

Is the number of people in this setting appropriate for its physical size and purpose?	yes	no	unclear
Are the people who share this setting compatible in terms of age, gender, and support needs?	yes	no	unclear
Do the people who share this setting get along with each other?	yes	no	unclear
Is the support provider ratio in this setting adequate to meet the support needs of all the people here at all times?	yes	no	unclear
Do support providers actively work to develop and maintain a positive rapport and relationship with the people here?	yes	no	unclear
Do support providers promote and facilitate opportunities for social integration with people who are not paid to provide services?	yes	no	unclear

3. Activities and instruction

Do people in this setting regularly participate (whether independent, supported, or partial participation) in activities and tasks that are useful and meaningful to their daily lives?	yes	no	unclear
Do people participate in a variety of different activities?	yes	no	unclear
Do people participate in a variety of different activities that occur in a regular community settings outside of the home, school, and workplace?	yes	no	unclear
Do people in this setting receive instruction on activities and skills that are useful and meaningful to their daily lives?	yes	no	unclear
Is the instruction that people receive individualized to meet specific learner needs?	yes	no	unclear
Are people's personal preferences taken into account when determining the activities and tasks in which they participate and receive training?	yes	no	unclear

(continued)

Figure 7.3. Positive environment checklist. (From Albin, R.W., Horner, R.H., & O'Neill, R.E. [1994]. *Proactive behavioral support: Structuring and assessing environments.* Eugene: University of Oregon, Research and Training Center on Positive Behavioral Support, Specialized Training Program; adapted by permission.)

Figure 7.3. *(continued)*

4. Scheduling and predictability			
Is there a system or strategy used to identify what people in this setting should be doing and when?	yes	no	unclear
Is there a means to determine whether things that should be occurring actually do occur?	yes	no	unclear
Do people in this setting have a way of knowing or predicting what they will be doing and when?	yes	no	unclear
Do support providers prepare people in this setting in advance for changes in typical schedules or routines?	yes	no	unclear
Do people in this setting have opportunities to exercise choice in terms of what they will do, when, and with whom and what rewards they will receive?	yes	no	unclear
5. Communication			
Do people in this setting have acceptable means to communicate basic messages (e.g., requests, comments, rejections) to support providers or others in the setting?	yes	no	unclear
Do support providers promote and reward communication?	yes	no	unclear
Are effective, efficient communication strategies being used by or taught to the people in this setting?	yes	no	unclear
Are support providers familiar with the receptive language levels and skills of the people in this setting?	yes	no	unclear
Do support providers have acceptable means to communicate basic messages to the people in this setting?	yes	no	unclear

■ ■ ■　Joe is 37 years old and has Down syndrome. He has lived with his parents for most of his life until the recent death of his dad. His mom is in her 70s and, with the death of Joe's father, has had problems meeting Joe's needs, especially because Joe has problem behaviors. There is no other family to help support Joe, so Mom is considering different options for living arrangements for Joe.　■ ■ ■

Joe has been attending a day program in the community for some years but has not been enthusiastic about going to the program in recent months, especially since his dad died. Mom is reporting that Joe doesn't seem to want to wake up and get going for the day. The day program staff has adopted the person-centered planning approach as a strategy to help set goals for the people working in day programs so that they can improve their employment options and earning capacity.

The facilitator who took the team, including Joe's day program staff and his mother, through the person-centered planning activities asked Joe what was one thing that would make him want to get up in the morning. The facilitator modeled a response by saying that she really enjoyed a chai latte every morning. Joe responded by saying he loved coffee, missed having it with his dad in the morning, and would want to be able to have a coffee maker in his room so that he could have a cup in the morning.

Mom and Joe decided together that he could purchase a coffee maker to stay in his room, with some rules for safety and cleanliness. The team also discussed ways they could have a coffee maker available in the day program for Joe and others to get and take coffee back to their work areas.

This strategy took some creative thinking on how to change some of the policies instituted such as not having food or drink in the work area. The team understood, however, that this small action would go a long way toward making life more pleasant for Joe, both at home and at work. It also provides Joe with more independence.

Person-centered planning is an important first step toward understanding and intervening with challenging behavior. The action steps taken to help individuals achieve an enviable life for themselves can prevent a multitude of problem behaviors.

GATHERING INFORMATION

During the information-gathering step, a functional behavior assessment is conducted to help a team understand the situations that trigger occurrences of challenging behavior (antecedents) and the responses from others that maintain a person's challenging behavior (consequences). The functional behavior assessment process has its roots in behavioral theory (operant learning and applied behavior analysis) in the notion that all behavior is learned and is affected by the conditions in the person's environment, including events that seem to trigger or predict the problem behavior occurring (e.g., asking the person to stop watching television, a preferred activity, or go shopping with his or her parents, a nonpreferred activity) and the events or reactions that follow the person's behavior (e.g., letting the person continue to watch television rather than making him or her do the nonpreferred activity) (Benson & Havercamp, 1999).

Behavioral theory helps explain why problem behavior continues even when families and others try intervention strategies to change or stop the behavior. The family may believe that denying the person the opportunity of going in the car and shopping will result in a behavior change the next time the same situation presents itself, but instead, if the preferred outcome was to watch television and not go in the car, the behavior is reinforced and most likely will repeat.

Learned behaviors typically have two purposes. A person may be 1) trying to escape or avoid a situation or activity, a person, or an object, or 2) trying to get or obtain a specific activity or situation, a person, or an object. The situations that trigger behaviors, also called *antecedents*, can happen right before or up to several hours before the behavior occurs. Some examples of immediate antecedents include asking the person to do something he or she does not want to do, paying attention to another person, or denying the person access to a desired activity or object.

Antecedents that do not immediately precede problem behavior, also called *setting events*, are situations that "set the stage" for behaviors to happen. The possibility of setting events leading to challenging behavior is extremely important to explore, specifically with adults with Down syndrome. Events such as residence changes, conflicts with other people, family bereavements and relationships, medication changes, sleep deprivation, and injury or illness can be factors that contribute to challenging behaviors (Owen et al., 2004). Sleep deprivation may be a common setting event for adults with Down syndrome due to the increased prevalence of sleep apnea.

Consequences are the events and responses that follow problem behavior and provide others with some insight into why the behavior continues to occur. Typical responses to problem behavior include coaxing (e.g., "Come on! You can do this!"), ignoring, taking away preferred items or activities, reprimands (e.g., "You know better than that!"), and redirects ("You need to make your bed now").

To make the collection of the antecedents and consequences surrounding problem behavior in a functional behavior assessment as consistent and accurate as possible, behavior should be clearly defined (operationalized). This lets everyone who will be collecting data agree that the behavior of interest actually occurred. Merely describing the person's behavior as "stubborn" or "oppositional" may not result in consistent data collection because the behaviors can look very different depending on the data collector's perception and his or her tolerance for problem behavior. Accurate and consistent data can result in a higher chance of designing interventions that will be effective.

The people who will collect information about the behavior are determined at this step. People who know the individual well and are often present when problem behavior occurs should be asked to collect information. This can include family members (e.g., caregivers, siblings), friends, neighbors, employers, and day program staff.

In recent years, the collection of functional behavior assessment data has become more pragmatic and feasible, so practitioners in natural environments can more easily collect information (Carr et al., 2002; Desrochers, Hile, & Williams-Moscley, 1997). One way to collect this information in a systematic method is by using an antecedent-behavior-consequence (A-B-C) card as shown in Figure 7.4. This card lists the most common antecedents (Column 1) that happen before problem behavior and the most common consequences (Column 3) that happen after the problem behavior. Clear descriptions of the specific problem behaviors on which the information is being collected are written on the card in the middle column. Although the antecedents and consequences listed on the template card are the most common, the card can be customized for each focus individual by listing the

Individual: Joe	Date/time: 2/14 9:30	Activity: ⟨Assigned work task⟩ Break Meal time Recreational/ leisure time	Observer: Florence Smith— Day Program Supervisor

Antecedents:
☐ Demand/request
☐ Alone (no attention)
☐ Alone (no apparent task or assignment given
☐ Attention given to others
☐ Transition
☐ Specific person
_____
☐ Nonpreferred activity
☐ Had to stop preferred activity
☐ Difficult task/ activity
☒ Working for more than _5_ minutes on an activity
☐ Told "no"
☐ Other _____
		Challenging behavior:
		Describe briefly in specific terms
		☒ *Pushes work materials away; puts head down in hands; does not respond to instructions or questions from others*
		☐ *Throws materials off table onto floor or toward others; screams loudly*
			Consequences:
			☐ Verbal redirect
			☐ Physical redirect
			☐ Ignored
			☐ Activity/materials/ task taken away
			☐ Another task presented
			☒ Removed from setting
			☐ Calming/soothing
			  ☐ Verbal
			  ☐ Physical
			  ☐ Both
			☐ Physical restraint
			☐ Others' remarks/laughs
			☐ Help/assistance given
			☐ Other _____

Figure 7.4. Functional behavior assessment (antecedent-behavior-consequence) data collection card (front).

behaviors that are being targeted for data collection and by including the specific antecedents and consequences most commonly used. The card is used by all of the individuals who will be gathering information.

The A-B-C card is simple in its use. Each time the person with Down syndrome exhibits one of the behaviors delineated on the A-B-C card, the information collector present merely checks the specific behavior that occurred along with the antecedents and the consequences that were related to the behavior. The data collector can also indicate the purpose he or she thinks the behavior served (escape or obtain). Figure 7.5 shows the reverse of the A-B-C card, on which information on setting events can be collected.

Setting events:

☐ Medical/physical condition   ☐ Parties/social gatherings

☐ Hunger/thirst   ☐ Medication

☐ Fatigue   ☐ Staff change (transition)

☐ Sleep patterns   ☐ Eating routines/diet

☐ Weather conditions   ☐ Preferred staff member
                                        moved/changed jobs

☐ Sensory events (e.g., lights, noise) ☐ Change in schedule or routine
                                        (home/work)

☐ Temperature   ☐ Change in residence

☐ Fight/conflict with family,   ☐ Staff, co-workers
  day program

☐ Other (specify) _____

_____

Notes/comments/unusual events: *None noted* _____

_____

_____

_____

_____

_____

_____

_____

_____

_____

_____

Figure 7.5. Functional behavior assessment (antecedent-behavior-consequence) data collection card (back).

Descriptive assessments similar to these have been used with both agencies and families and have a high degree of acceptability and success. The cards allow people involved in the life of a person with Down syndrome who has behavior problems to check for relevant antecedents and consequences that are associated with each behavior event. The information collected from the A-B-C cards is used to explore whether there are repeated events or patterns that are associated with the problem behavior.

For example, if 10 A-B-C cards were collected on a specific behavior, and 7 of the cards showed that asking the person to do something (a demand) happened right before the behavior and 5 of the cards showed that the result was a delay or removal of the demand, an informed statement can be formed about the possible purpose of the person's behavior. Furthermore, the A-B-C cards can provide additional information about the behavior, including the time of day, the specific settings or people involved, and details about specific activities. The additional information can help in the design of more effective interventions.

Indirect methods, such as interviews and rating scales, can also be used to collect functional behavior assessment information. Indirect methods that do not require direct observation of the person with Down syndrome can provide information on antecedents, consequences, and setting events in a time-efficient manner. The important consideration is what type of functional behavior assessment tools would be feasible and acceptable for people to use in order to collect the essential information that will provide an understanding of the events predicting the behavior and the consequences maintaining the behavior.

■ ■ ■   Joe's team agreed that Joe's problem behavior of noncompliance during day program activities needed to be targeted. The noncompliance resulted in a loss of income for Joe and disruptions to the work schedule. Team members agreed that Joe had skills that might allow him to be promoted or be employed in a competitive job; however, they believed that as long as Joe exhibited problem behaviors, he would not be able to move from his current job position. The noncompliance was carefully defined as Joe shaking his head back and forth, saying "no" loudly, or folding his arms and bowing his head down.   ■ ■ ■

The team decided to do an interview with Joe to gather information on what conditions he believed contributed to his behavior. Joe's mother, the staff at his group home, and his roommates were interviewed along with relevant day-program staff. Direct A-B-C observational data were collected to help Joe's team determine the environmental contexts in which Joe exhibited the behavior and the consequences he typically received. Because multiple people would be collecting the data, they decided that the A-B-C cards would be best, as they allowed consistent information to be collected from everyone.

After collecting information for 2 weeks, a pattern began to emerge. Joe's noncompliant behavior happened most often during repetitive tasks, and after Joe exhibited the behaviors, work often got removed.

DEVELOPING A HYPOTHESIS

After the team collects information from the functional behavior assessment, the data are analyzed to determine patterns of antecedents that predict occasions of behaviors and consequences following behavior incidents that lead to a hunch about the behavior's purpose or payoff. This process results in a hypothesis, or written statement that describes the relation between the individual's behaviors and events in the environment. The hypothesis allows the formation of a multicomponent support plan that will include environmental modifications to the antecedents to prevent problem behavior, teaching of a replacement behavior that has a functional equivalence of the original behavior, and changing responses so that the problem behavior is no longer reinforced.

A hypothesis statement can follow several formats. The statement should include a description of the antecedents (setting events, if applicable, and immediate events), the behavior, and the purpose or function of the behavior. An example of a hypothesis statement is "When Joe oversleeps (setting event), and he is asked to do a nonpreferred task (antecedent), he will shake his head back and forth, say 'no' loudly, or cross his arms and bow his head down (behavior) to avoid doing the task (function)."

Behavior functions can be divided into two categories: 1) those intended to escape/avoid something, or 2) those intended to obtain something (O'Neill et al., 1997). People with Down syndrome may exhibit behaviors for the purpose of escaping or obtaining specific activities, objects, people, or environmental settings. In some cases, problem behaviors are the result of trying to alleviate symptoms of a medical condition. For example, refusing to comply with a request, along with lying down on the couch, may be an attempt to escape or ease the pain of a stomachache brought on by constipation. An important consideration for adults with Down syndrome is to evaluate whether any medical problems exist and are contributing to the problem behavior.

Systematic methods to analyze functional behavior assessment data have been developed, such as the Functional Analysis Observation tool (O'Neill et al., 1997). Figure 7.6 shows a sample pattern analysis form, whereas Figure 7.7 shows a completed form that assists in the examination of functional behavior assessment data collected from A-B-C cards. This pattern analysis tool provides a simple but structured way to analyze the A-B-C cards collected. It can be easily used by both families and professionals.

Using this method involves sorting the A-B-C cards collected by specific behaviors. For example, if Joe's team decided to collect data on two behaviors, noncompliance and oppositional behavior, the A-B-C cards would be sorted with all of the ones completed for noncompliance placed in one set and all of the ones completed for oppositional behavior in another set. The cards within each behavior are then reviewed to examine whether there are patterns in antecedent occurrence and consequences administered. After all of the cards have been reviewed and the information tallied, totals can be summed for each set of tallies. A hypothesis statement can be developed based on the antecedents and consequences receiving the highest sums.

■■■   Joe's team reviewed the interview information and the A-B-C cards collected by everyone. Joe's noncompliant events most often occurred when he was asked to do something that he either thought was boring or that he had been doing for a long period of time. More often than not, Joe's behavior got him out of the task or, at times, delayed or interrupted the time he spent doing the undesired activity. Along with removal of materials, Joe would usually get a fair amount of verbal redirects (e.g., "Hey, Joe Buddy. Calm down!") from the program staff and others. For example, when Joe visited his mother at home during the weekends, Joe would not comply with his mother's requests to clean up after he ate or to make his bed. His mother usually gave in to Joe's noncompliance because it took too much effort for her to continue to coax and plead with him to do the activities.   ■■■

Joe's team hypothesized that he mainly did the behavior to escape from the task, but he also gained some attention at the same time. Therefore, the hypothesis formulated by the team was: "When presented with a work-related or nonpreferred demand, particularly when the demand is a task that Joe has been doing for a long period of time (e.g., more than 30 minutes, more than 1 day), he will shake his head back and forth, say 'no' loudly, or fold his arms and bow his head down to escape from or interrupt his working on the task and to get attention from others (staff and family)."

DESIGNING A SUPPORT PLAN

A hypothesis sets the foundation for building a comprehensive support plan, which should address three things at a minimum. First, the plan

Individual: _____

Behavior: _____

Directions: Sort all of the antecedent-behavior-consequence cards by class of challenging behavior. Complete an analysis for each behavior class by tallying and recording the totals for each antecedent, consequence, and function.

Antecedent analysis	Number	Consequence analysis	Number	Perceived function	Number	Setting events	Number
Demand/request	___	Verbal redirect/coaxing	___	Escape/avoid	___	Medical/physical condition	___
Alone (no attention)	___	Physical redirect	___	Obtain	___	Hunger/thirst	___
Alone (no apparent assignment)	___	Ignored	___			Fatigue	___
Attention given to others	___	Activity/materials/task taken away	___			Sleep deprivation	___
Transition	___	Calming/soothing	___			Weather conditions	___
Specific person	___	Verbal	___			Family fight/conflict	___
Nonpreferred object/activity	___	Physical	___			Parties/social gatherings	___
Difficult task/activity	___	Both	___			Medication	___
Told "no"	___						

Figure 7.6. Pattern analysis form.

Repetitive or long activity   ___

Help/assistance given   ___

Change in schedule or routine   ___

Other:___

Other adults join in to coax   ___

Eating routines/diet   ___

___

Other:___

Sensory events   ___

___

Went home for week-end   ___

Other:___

Other comments: ___

Hypothesis/es: ___

Individual: _Joe_   **Behavior:** _Noncompliance—shaking head back and forth, saying "no," crossing arms and bowing head._

Directions: Sort all of the A-B-C cards by class of challenging behavior. Complete an analysis for each behavior class by tallying and recording the totals for each antecedent, consequence, and function.

Antecedent analysis	Number	Consequence analysis	Number	Perceived function	Number	Setting events	Number
Demand/request	10	Verbal redirect/coaxing	10	Escape/avoid	10	Medical/physical condition	
Alone (no attention)		Physical redirect		Obtain	5	Hunger/thirst	
Alone (no apparent assignment)		Ignored	1			Fatigue	
Attention given to others		Activity/materials/task taken away	3			Sleep deprivation	2
Transition	2	Calming/soothing				Weather conditions	
Specific person		Verbal				Family fight/conflict	
Nonpreferred object/activity		Physical				Parties/social gatherings	
Difficult task/activity	10	Both				Medication	
Told "no"							

Figure 7.7. Completed pattern analysis form for Joe.

Repetitive or long activity	8	Help/assistance given	___
Other: ___		Other adults join in to coax	7
___		Other: ___	

Change in schedule or routine	___
Eating routines/diet	___
Sensory events	___
Went home for weekend	3
Other: ___	

Other comments: _____

Hypothesis/es: _____ *When presented with a work-related or nonpreferred demand, particularly when the demand is a task that Joe has been doing for a long period of time (e.g., more than 30 minutes, more than 1 day), he will shake his head back and forth, say "no" loudly, or fold his arms and bow his head down to escape from or interrupt his working on the task and to get attention from others (staff and family).*

should include interventions that will prevent the problem behavior from occurring (i.e., prevention interventions). This includes modifying or changing the antecedent events identified in the functional behavior assessment as typically happening before the problem behavior. For example, if demands were identified as an antecedent, the team would develop an intervention that modifies the demand so that it is no longer aversive to the person with Down syndrome. Providing the person with a choice related to the demand or changing the content or presentation of the activity related to the demand may be effective prevention interventions. Redesigning the antecedents makes the problem behavior irrelevant; that is, the person no longer has a need to exhibit the behavior (Carr et al., 2002; O'Neill et al., 1997). Second, the plan should include proactive skill building to replace the problem behavior with a new, socially valid behavior (i.e., replacement behavior) that will make the old behavior inefficient. Third, the plan should include a description of how others will respond to the person's new behavior (i.e., responding strategies) so that the new behavior will be repeated and the old behavior will become ineffective.

Prevention Interventions

Prevention interventions, which modify the antecedents or context, can contribute greatly toward enhancing the life of a person with Down syndrome exhibiting behavior problems. In addition, they may have the greatest impact on promoting systemic change. Prevention interventions for adults with problem behaviors are extremely important in the positive behavior support process because it is easier to work on skill building and shaping appropriate behavior when problem behavior is not occurring (Carr et al., 2002). Therefore, prevention interventions must be applied before the problem behavior is exhibited. Examples include providing choices; providing short, frequent breaks between work-task steps; providing a photographic visual schedule for predictability and comprehension; and embedding preferences into living arrangements, working options, and recreational activities (Dunlap et al., 1994; Holburn & Vietze, 2002; Newman, Summerhill, Mosley, & Tooth, 2003; Stevens & Martin, 1999).

■ ■ ■   Functional behavior assessment data suggested that Joe's noncompliant behaviors most often presented with demands, particularly when the demands were involving work tasks or activities that were either repetitive, perceived as boring, or ones on which he had been working for a lengthened period of time. The team decided to provide Joe with some choices related to his tasks so that he would be more likely to want to engage in them. Each day, they displayed the jobs that were available from which Joe could choose. Next, he could choose the order in which he did the jobs (if there was not a tight deadline). Finally, he could choose how long he would work or an amount of time he would need to finish a job before he could take a break or switch to another task.   ■ ■ ■

Joe's team also recognized that many of the tasks Joe was performing were boring for him. They agreed that they would start a preference assessment and schedule visits to other possible jobs so that Joe could explore and determine his next job placement. During this exploration time, some adjustments were made in the tasks given to Joe. Higher-level tasks that would be of interest to him were provided. For times when Joe had to work on less meaningful tasks, the team decided that the tasks could be broken up into shorter segments so that Joe could get brief breaks from the nonpreferred tasks.

Joe's mother would also use similar interventions when he visited. She identified that the most problematic times were when she presented demands for Joe to do things he didn't like to do, especially if the demands took him away from preferred activities of eating and watching television. She would build in a choice opportunity when she asked Joe to do something. For example, she would give Joe the choice of when he would make his bed (e.g., before breakfast, after breakfast).

She identified some higher-level activities that embedded Joe's interests and were more meaningful to him. One of the activities she thought she would try was to give him choices of desserts he could make over the weekend. Because the desserts would be ones he liked, he could then make a shopping list of what he needed to buy at the supermarket. Joe could also choose from two or three different times of the day to schedule a trip to the supermarket.

Replacement Behaviors

Replacement behaviors are alternative, socially acceptable behaviors that a person can perform to get the same payoff as he or she did when the problem behavior was performed. By providing a socially valid communicative replacement for the problem behavior, which is honored with the same or better payoff than the problem behavior, the problem behavior will become *inefficient*. For example, Joe can be taught to request a short break from a boring activity rather than screaming at staff to escape. He can also be taught to request help from a specific staff person to get attention rather than shaking his head or saying "no." Requesting the short break or help from a specific staff member is the replacement behavior.

In addition to replacement behaviors, careful thought should be given to teaching the person with Down syndrome critical skills that can be used in several settings. For example, teaching the person to self-manage his or her activity compliance or completion can be used in home settings, work settings, and community settings. Another example of a critical skill is teaching the person to tolerate a delay in getting access to reinforcing events. This skill can be used across many of the environments that a person with Down syndrome encounters daily.

■ ■ ■   Because Joe's behavior appeared to be primarily for the purpose of escaping or interrupting work tasks, the team decided to teach Joe to ask for a break instead of not complying. Time was set aside to teach Joe how to use his new behavior. In the past, Joe would work an average of 5 minutes before shaking his head, saying "no," or crossing his arms and bowing his head. Right before he started any of his noncompliant behaviors, he would often stop working and look around the room. It was decided that Joe would be prompted to ask for a break using a break card after he had been working on a work activity for 3 minutes. If staff members noticed him stopping and looking around, they would prompt him at that time to take a break, even if it was before the 3 minutes were up. When Joe would request a break, his work tasks would be removed, and he could sit at his work area for 2 minutes. After 2 minutes, he would be urged to get back to work. If he requested a break again, the procedure would be repeated.   ■ ■ ■

The team agreed that Joe was capable of doing higher-level jobs. They also wanted to teach him the critical skill of self-managing the number of tasks he complied with and the number of tasks he completed. Joe talked with his boss and his family about how he would keep track of how many times he worked without stopping and how many activities he stayed with until they were finished. A simple self-management system was set up with Joe (see Figure 7.8 for an example). Joe would decide what skill (complying with a request or completing work) he would concentrate on each day. He would then make a checkmark each time he performed the behavior. At the end of the time, he would add up all of the checkmarks and put the total in the appropriate spot on his form. He would also put down the number of checkmarks he had earned the last time he worked on the same skill. Joe would then evaluate whether he did better, stayed the same, or did worse.

The team also planned how they would fade Joe's requests for breaks. Each week, a goal for how many breaks Joe could take per day was set between Joe and the program staff. Initially, Joe was request-

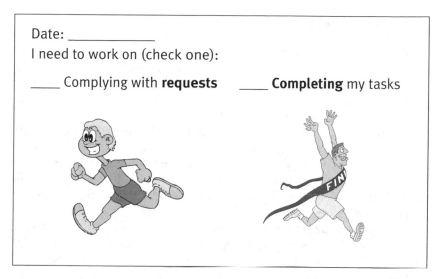

Date: _____

I need to work on (check one):

____ Complying with **requests**   ____ **Completing** my tasks

Figure 7.8.   Example of self-management form for Joe.

ing a break 10 times a day on average; therefore, the first week, the program staff members set a daily goal of 10 breaks. Joe was given 10 break cards and had to use a break card each time a break was requested. Once his quota of break cards was exhausted, he would not be able to request any additional unplanned breaks.

Joe was taught to look at his work schedule first thing in the morning and plan when he might need the breaks. These breaks were built into the schedule to remind him. He was taught to reserve one or two break cards not built into his schedule for those times that he did not foresee the need. If Joe had any break cards left at the end of the day, he would record those on a form. Each unused break card would earn him either 5 free minutes for a break to the lounge area, where he could purchase items from the vending machine (a very preferred activity) or 5 minutes to talk with a program staff member.

Each week, the number of break cards provided would be reduced until Joe reached five. At that time, the team would evaluate next steps. Use of this strategy allowed Joe to plan his days accordingly and also allowed the fading of the short breaks from tasks.

The team worked with Joe's mom to help plan similar strategies she could use during Joe's visits. She liked the break card system and decided that she would provide Joe with break cards at home. She started with five per day because she did not make as many demands on Joe as staff members did at the day program. She also had Joe use the same self-management system at home.

Responding Strategies

Problem behaviors are maintained by the reactions of others and the payoffs achieved. Often, other people (e.g., family members, day program staff, employers, peers, friends) inadvertently reinforce problem behavior by the interventions or responses they apply. The information collected in the functional behavior assessment will let the team know the typical responding strategies used after the person with Down syndrome exhibits problem behavior.

To change the responding strategies, the team members must first decide how they will respond when the person with Down syndrome 1) uses the replacement behavior taught; 2) does an appropriate behavior; and 3) does the problem behavior. When the person with Down syndrome uses the replacement behavior, everyone should respond to the behavior immediately. If the person is asking for a break, the break should be provided, even if the person asked for a break just a few minutes before the current request was made. It is important that the person sees that the new behavior is the one that is *more effective* than the old behavior at getting the same outcome.

Once the person begins using the replacement behavior on a consistent basis, tolerance for waiting a small time before getting the reinforcement can be taught. This can be done by responding to the replacement behavior request with a *delay signal* (e.g., "Do one more thing," "Wait one more second") and then releasing the person with a *safety signal* (e.g., "Okay, you did one more. It's time for the break.") Gradually, the time of the delay can be lengthened.

Careful consideration should be given to the reinforcement and responses that will be delivered when the person does prosocial or appropriate behaviors. The person-centered plan may be of assistance in this step. The team and the person with Down syndrome can look at what goals they want to achieve in the future and make a list of behaviors that would help to achieve the goal. For example, if a better-paying job is one of the dreams, behaviors such as following directions, complying with requests, and finishing tasks would be prosocial behaviors that would be employer-pleasing behaviors.

Upon selection of a behavior to be targeted, the team can determine how they will respond and how often they will reinforce when the person does the behavior. For example, at first, a positive verbal statement or gesture may be made after each occurrence of a specific behavior if the person with Down syndrome enjoys it (e.g., "Way to go!" thumbs up, high five, pat on the back). Gradually, the reinforcing responses are more intermittent but never completely removed so that the person with Down syndrome continues to perform appropriately.

Some individuals with Down syndrome may need other responses in addition to verbal praise or positive gestures. If this is the case, the team can determine how the person will "earn" a specific activity, object, or time with a preferred person by performing desired behaviors. Reinforcement delivery can be contingent on how many times the person performs the behavior. For example, if the person completes five tasks in the morning, he or she gets to watch an extra 15 minutes of television.

Finally, there should be a plan of how to react if the person exhibits the problem behavior. The response should be one that no longer gives the person the same outcome (escaping, avoiding, or obtaining something or someone). This is an important point because, if the person gets an outcome more often and more quickly with the problem behavior than the replacement behavior, there will be no reason to use the replacement.

The support plan should carefully consider which adults will need to take part in the interventions and should clearly describe the appropriate responses to both the new and the old behaviors. The new behaviors being taught should be reinforced, and at the beginning, the reinforcement should occur at a high rate (i.e., after each time the behavior is used). The old behaviors should be greeted with responses that will no longer provide the person with the same outcomes.

■ ■ ■　Joe's noncompliant behavior got an immediate reaction and attention from several adults in the day program and from his mother at home. They would usually call out Joe's name, ask him to do the task again, and try to coax him with cajoling and humor to continue to work on the task. If the noncompliance persisted, one or two additional people would go to Joe and join in the cajoling and pleading. The responses typically got Joe to delay getting back to work and provided him with many people to engage in a conversation and get attention. At home, Joe usually succeeded in getting his way because his mother would quit making the request and let Joe do whatever activity he preferred.　■ ■ ■

Functional behavior assessment information supported the hypothesis that Joe exhibited the problem behaviors to escape or interrupt the task and to get attention from others. The plan to address Joe's behavior problems described how others should respond to the problem behavior so that it no longer achieved the desired outcome. When Joe engaged in noncompliant behavior, other adults would not respond until Joe stopped shaking his head, stopped saying no, or put his head back up (even if only for 1 second). As soon as any of these behaviors happened, he would be prompted to use his replacement behavior to get a break.

Because Joe really enjoyed attention from others and talking with the staff at the day program, a plan was developed to give him attention for appropriate behavior rather than inappropriate behavior. If Joe completed a specific number of tasks, he could have a choice of which person he would want to talk with for 5–10 minutes. With consistent implementation of the strategy and the responses, the new behavior became more efficient and effective than the noncompliance did to get Joe attention. The self-management strategy also allowed Joe to have more positive interactions with others.

Joe's mom incorporated the same responding strategies at home with slight modifications. On the self-management plan, Joe could earn time for doing whatever he wanted to do if he complied with making his bed and with going shopping at the time he chose to do so with his mother.

IMPLEMENTING, EVALUATING, AND MONITORING THE PLAN

Once a support plan has been developed, an action plan that details the steps for implementation should be written. The action plan can be written by anyone who has a vested interest in the person with Down syndrome. This can be the family, agency, friends, employers, or even the person with Down syndrome, depending on the person's skills and involvement in the process. At the least, the person with Down syndrome should be actively included so that he or she can set goals and decide on appropriate steps to take to meet the goals. The person with Down syndrome can, at this point, identify other people who should be on the team to assist.

The action plan should include realistic goals and steps that can be accomplished in the timeline decided on by the person with Down syndrome and the team. The plan should identify who will be involved and responsible for each step, the timeline for intervention, the environments in which the plan will be implemented, how the plan will be generalized, and the methods of determining effectiveness. A critical feature of positive behavior support is the broadened perspective of plan effectiveness. Though it is always desirable to decrease the problem behavior and increase prosocial behaviors, positive behavior support also looks at quality-of-life changes, not only for the person with Down syndrome, but also for the people who support the individual, such as family members.

The action plan should be shared with everyone who will be doing the behavioral interventions. Meeting dates should be scheduled on a consistent basis for reviewing the plan so that the team can determine whether the interventions are effective and if progress is being made toward the goals. Scheduled meetings should occur at least once a month, if not more often.

Lifestyle changes do not come in a restricted timeframe; therefore, positive behavior support examines how supports can be applied and skills increased throughout a person's life span (Carr et al., 2002). Meaningful change, particularly for adults, takes many years to achieve (Turnbull, 1988; Vandercook et al., 1989). Plans may need to be constantly reviewed and altered, especially as people and settings change.

A conservative estimate of change is that it takes 2–3 months after the functional behavior assessment is completed before the staff members and/or family members believe they have a firm handle on the behavior, and it takes 1 year before lasting and substantive change occurs (Edmonson & Turnbull, 2002). The person-centered planning process is an approach that can be used to monitor behavior change and to maintain the momentum to continue to refine the positive behavior support strategies and to contribute toward having the person achieve a more enviable life (Kincaid, 1996).

■ ■ ■   Joe's team decided to record the occurrences of his problem behavior, the frequency of use of his replacement behavior, and his success of achieving his self-management goals. They decided that they would meet monthly to make decisions based on the data collected. The person centered plan action steps would also be reviewed during the monthly meetings to ensure that momentum would be maintained.   ■ ■ ■

After implementing the support plan for 1 month, data indicated that the interventions developed appeared to be successful. Prior to the plan's implementation, Joe's noncompliant behavior occurred on the average of 10 times a day. After 1 month of the implementation, Joe's noncompliant behavior had decreased to two episodes for the entire month. In addition, the first week showed that Joe started requesting a break at a high rate (i.e., mean of 10 times a day).

The self-management strategy for monitoring Joes's compliance and task completion was implemented during week two. Joe quickly caught on to the intervention and enjoyed charting how many times he did the specific behavior chosen each day. He especially enjoyed when he was able to circle that he did better than the previous time. By the end of the third week, Joe was complying about 70% of the time and was completing 75% of his tasks.

At the same time, the team decided to start fading out Joe's requests for breaks by giving him 10 break cards that he could use throughout the day. By the end of the first week, Joe had 2–3 break cards leftover daily. At the meeting held 1 month after the initiation of the support plan, Joe's break card allotment at the day program was set at 7.

The team wanted to help Joe achieve his vision of having a job that paid more money. The team completed a preference assessment of what types of jobs Joe would like to do and made a list of potential job sites for him to explore. Because Joe's behavior had become more appropriate, the team decided to start scheduling one trip a week to a job site during the next month. It was decided that at the end of 2 months, Joe could decide which jobs he liked best, and interviews could be scheduled.

Joe's mom attended the meetings when it was possible. If she couldn't attend, she gave information over the phone. She reported that things had improved to a point where she thought she might be able to have Joe come home for longer periods of time and eventually move back if he preferred.

Finally, program staff members, Joe's mother, and Joe were asked about their perceptions of the plan and their satisfaction with life after the plan. Both program staff members and Joe's mother rated the interventions high and stated that fewer disruptions were occurring. This improvement gave them more time to teach new skills to Joe and others. They also felt that Joe appeared to be more content. He spent more time engaged in activities and often smiled. In an interview with Joe, he said he liked working more than he did before, and he appeared excited about all the changes, including being able to have his coffee each morning and getting a new job. The team decided to continue the interventions and activity steps.

SUMMARY

Positive behavior support has made significant contributions toward meaningful changes in the lives of people with disabilities who have challenging behavior. This approach is a feasible and valuable one to use with adults with Down syndrome who have a history of problem behavior. The positive behavior support component of enhancing the quality of life is a crucial one to provide for this population. By using person-centered planning, positive behavior support enables the individual with Down syndrome to play an active role in the management and decrease of problem behaviors.

REFERENCES

Albin, R.W., Horner, R.H., & O'Neill, R.E. (1994). *Proactive behavioral support: Structuring and assessing environments.* Eugene: University of Oregon, Research and Training Center on Positive Behavioral Support, Specialized Training Program.

Bambara, L.M., Cole, C.L., & Koger, F. (1998). Translating self-determination concepts into support for adults with severe disabilities. *Journal of The Association for Persons with Severe Handicaps, 23,* 27–37.

Benson, B.A., & Havercamp, S.M. (1999). Behavioural approaches to treatment: Principles and practices. In N. Bouras (Ed.), *Psychiatric and behavioural disorders in developmental disabilities and mental retardation.* Cambridge, England: Cambridge University Press.

Carr, E.G., Dunlap, G., Horner, R.H., Koegel, R.L., Turnbull, A., Sailor, W., et al. (2002). Positive behavior support: Evolution of an applied science. *Journal of Positive Behavior Interventions, 4*(1), 4–16.

Carr, E.G., Levin, L., McConnachie, G., Carlson, J.I., Kemp, D.C., & Smith, C.E. (1994). *Communication-based intervention for problem behavior: A user's guide for producing positive change.* Baltimore: Paul H. Brookes Publishing Co.

Carr, J. (2002). Patterns of ageing in 30- to 35-year-olds with Down's syndrome. *Journal of Applied Research in Intellectual Disabilities, 16,* 29–40.

Clark, H.B., & Hieneman, M. (1999). Comparing the wraparound process to positive behavioral support: What we can learn. *Journal of Positive Behavior Interventions, 1,* 183–186.

Coe, D.A., Matson, J.L., Russell, D.W., Slifer, K.J., Capone, G.T., Baglio, C., et al. (1999). Behavior problems of children with Down syndrome and life events. *Journal of Autism and Developmental Disorders, 29,* 149–156.

Cohen, W.I., Nadel, L., & Madwick, M. (Eds.). (2002). *Down syndrome: Visions for the 21st century.* New York: John Wiley & Sons.

Desrochers, M.N., Hile, M.G., & Williams-Moseley, T.L. (1997). Survey of functional assessment procedures used with individuals who display mental retardation and severe problem behaviors. *American Journal on Mental Retardation, 101,* 535–546.

Dunlap, G., dePerczel, M., Clarke, S., Wilson, D., Wright, S., White, R., et al. (1994). Choice making and proactive behavioral support for students with emotional and behavioral challenges. *Journal of Applied Behavior Analysis, 27,* 505–518.

Dykens, E.M., Shah, B., Sagun, J., Beck, T., & King, B.H. (2002). Maladaptive behaviour in children and adolescents with Down's syndrome. *Journal of Intellectual Disability Research, 46,* 484–492.

Eber, L. (1996). Restructuring schools through wraparound planning: The LADSE experience. In R.J. Illback & C.M. Nelson (Eds.), *School-based services for students with emotional and behavioral disorders* (pp. 139–154). Binghamton, NY: Haworth Press.

Edmonson, H.E., & Turnbull, A. (2002). Positive behavioral supports: Creating supportive environments at home, in schools, and in the community. In

W.L. Cohen, L. Nadel, & M. Madwick (Eds.), *Down syndrome: Visions for the 21st century* (pp. 357–375). New York: Wiley-Liss.

Forest, M., & Lusthaus, E. (1987). The kaleidoscope: Challenge to the cascade. In M. Forest (Ed.), *More education/integration* (pp. 1–16). Downsview, Ontario, Canada: G. Allen Roeher Institute.

Hieneman, M., Nolan, M., Presley, J., DeTuro, L., Gayler, W., & Dunlap, G. (1999) *Facilitator's guide, positive behavioral support.* Tallahassee: Florida Department of Education, Bureau of Instructional Support and Community Services.

Holburn, S., & Vietze, P.M. (Eds.). (2002). A better life for Hal: Five years of person-centered planning and applied behavior analysis. In S. Holburn & P.M. Vietza (Eds.), *Person-centered planning: Research, practice, and future directions* (pp. 291–314). Baltimore: Paul H. Brookes Publishing Co.

Horner, R.H., Close, D.W., Fredericks, H.D.B., O'Neill, R.E., Albin, R.W., Sprague, J.R., et al. (1996). Supported living for people with profound disabilities and severe problem behaviors. In D.H. Lehr & F. Brown (Eds.), *People with disabilities who challenge the system* (pp. 209–240). Baltimore: Paul H. Brookes Publishing Co.

Horner, R.H., Sugai, G., Todd, A.W., & Lewis-Palmer, T. (2000). Elements of behavior support plans: A technical brief. *Exceptionality, 8*(3), 205–215.

Kincaid, D. (1996). Person-centered planning. In L.K. Koegel, R.L. Koegel, & G. Dunlap (Eds.), *Positive behavioral support: Including people with difficult behavior in the community* (pp. 439–465). Baltimore: Paul H. Brookes Publishing Co.

Koegel, L.K., Koegel, R.L., & Dunlap, G. (Eds.). (1996). *Positive behavioral support: Including people with difficult behavior in the community* (pp. 439–465). Baltimore: Paul H. Brookes Publishing Co.

Lohrmann-O'Roarke, S., & Gomez, O. (2001). Integrating preference assessment within the transition process to create meaningful school-to-life outcomes. *Exceptionality, 9*, 157–174.

Mount, B. (1987). *Personal futures planning: Finding directions for change.* Doctoral dissertation, University of Georgia.

Newman, D.W., Summerhill, L., Mosley, E., & Tooth, C. (2003). Working with an adult male with Down's syndrome, autism, and challenging behaviour: Evaluation of a programme of staff support and organizational change. *British Journal of Learning Disabilities, 31*, 85–90.

O'Brien, J. (1987). A guide to lifestyle planning: Using the activities catalog to integrate services and natural support systems. In B. Wilcox & G.T. Bellamy (Eds.), *A comprehensive guide to the activities catalog: An alternative curriculum for youth and adults with severe disabilities* (pp. 175–189). Baltimore: Paul H. Brookes Publishing Co.

O'Brien, J., Mount, B., & O'Brien, C. (1991). *Framework for accomplishment: Personal profile.* Decatur, GA: Responsive Systems Associates.

O'Neill, R.E., Horner, R.H., Albin, R.W., Sprague, J.R., Storey, K., & Newton, J.S. (1997). *Functional assessment and program development for problem behavior: A practical handbook* (2nd ed.). Pacific Grove, CA: Brooks/Cole.

Owen, D.M., Hastings, R.K.P., Noone, S.J., Chunn, J., Harman, K., Roberts, J.L., et al. (2004). Life events as correlates of problem behavior and mental health in a residential population of adults with developmental disabilities. *Research in Developmental Disabilities, 25,* 309–320.

Patterson, B. (2002). Behavior concerns in persons with Down syndrome. In W.L. Cohen, L. Nadel, & M. Madwick (Eds.), *Down syndrome: Visions for the 21st century* (pp. 215–219). New York: Wiley-Liss.

Pueschel, S.M., Bernier, J.C., & Pezzullo, J.C. (1991). Behavioural observations in children with Down's syndrome. *Journal of Mental Deficiency Research, 35,* 502–511.

Sailor, W. (1996). New structures and systems change for comprehensive positive behavioral support. In L.K. Koegel, R.L. Koegel, & G. Dunlap (Eds.), *Positive behavioral support: Including people with difficult behavior in the community* (pp. 163–206). Baltimore: Paul H. Brookes Publishing Co.

Smith, C., Hine, K., Freeman, R., Zarcone, J., Tieghi-Benet, M., & Kimbrough, P. (2004). *Person-centered planning quality indicators checklist.* Lawrence: University of Kansas, Lawrence.

Smull, M.W., & Harrison, S.B. (1992). *Supporting people with severe retardation in the community.* Alexandria, VA: National Association of State Mental Retardation Program Directors.

Stevens, P., & Martin, N. (1999). Supporting individuals with intellectual disability and challenging behaviour in integrated work settings: An overview and a model for service provision. *Journal of Intellectual Disability Research, 43,* 19–29.

Turnbull, A.P. (1988). The challenge of providing comprehensive support to families. *Education and Training in Mental Retardation, 23,* 261–272.

VanDenBerg, J.E., & Grealish, E.M. (1998). *The wraparound process training manual.* Pittsburgh: Community Partnerships Group.

Vandercook, T., York, J., & Forest, M. (1989). The McGill Action Planning Systems (MAPS): A strategy for building the vision. *Journal of The Association for Persons with Severe Handicaps, 14,* 205–215.

Wehmeyer, M., & Schwartz, M. (1997). Self-determination and positive adult outcomes: A follow-up study of youth with mental retardation or learning disabilities. *Exceptional Children, 63,* 245–255.

Wolfensberger, W. (1983). Social role valorization: A proposed new term for the principle of normalization. *Mental Retardation, 21,* 234–239.

8

Self Before Sex

Perspectives on Support, Self-Esteem, and Sexuality

Karin Melberg Schwier

*with invited contributions from Dave Hartzog,
Nannie Sanchez, Stefanie Ward, Karen Taylor, and Jim Schwier*

Let's say something right off the bat so that we can all relax and get through this chapter with everyone breathing normally. There are plenty of wonderful resources to help you as you support someone with Down syndrome explore issues like masturbation, sexual relationships, disease and abuse prevention, and birth control. Some will be listed in Table 8.1, and I encourage you to get comfortable with the resources that are available. Let's be clear. *Sexuality* is not merely *sexual intercourse*. There's still a lot to talk about before you start thinking about your son or daughter doing, you know, *that!* So take a breath. There, are you okay now? Then, let's begin.

"Down syndrome makes you different. People think you will be different in everything. They don't think you know about boyfriends and girlfriends and sex and families and babies." —Stefanie Ward

"People always freak out if anybody with a disability is in a sexual relationship, because they still see us as children and we do not have sexual drives like anyone else. People need to understand that we may be mentally challenged, but we still are interested in sex and have the same sex drives that everyone has." —Nannie Sanchez

The first step toward sex must be self. This fundamental principle guides many parents and professionals when they think about the sexuality and self-worth of adults with Down syndrome. *We connect better with others when we connect well with ourselves.* This tenet applies not only to adults with disabilities but also to those without.

105

In *Sexuality: Your Sons and Daughters with Intellectual Disabilities*, Melberg Schwier and Hingsburger (2000) offered this advice: Every infant, child, teenager, and adult who has an intellectual disability, like anyone else, is a sexual being. For all of us, sexuality is the integration of feelings, needs, and desires into a unique personality that expresses maleness or femaleness (Ludwig & Hingsburger, 1993). Sex can simply mean gender, but it can also mean the physical act of sexual intercourse. Sexuality, however, really refers to the whole person—thoughts, feelings, attitudes, and behavior toward oneself and others (Maksym, 1990a, 1990b). Learning how, when, where, and with whom to interact and express one's sexuality as a male or female is very important to one's well-being and to how well one will be welcomed and accepted by the community.

To go even further, the Sex Information and Education Council of the United States says that

> Human sexuality encompasses the sexual knowledge, beliefs, attitudes, values, and behaviors of individuals. It deals with the anatomy, physiology, and biochemistry of the sexual response system; with roles, identity, and personality; with individual thoughts, feelings, behaviors, and relationships. It addresses ethical, spiritual, and moral concerns, and group and cultural variations. (Haffner, 1990, p. 28)

CALLING IN THE EXPERTS

I am the stepmom of a young man with Down syndrome. This chapter started out as purely a parent's perspective on sexuality and relationships from my vantage point, but early on, it took a much-needed detour. Throughout this chapter are some thoughts—if not words of wisdom—that my husband and I have tossed around as we have grown up with our son, Jim, who is now 31 years old. We're certainly not experts in sexual development or sexuality education, but we have picked up ideas from other parents and good materials and resources along the way.

My son's father, other family members, and I developed a "plan." The plan is not much more than putting into practice our thoughts and beliefs about how to best help Jim grow into a confident, self-assured, interested, and interesting man, but the plan is always changing. It is sometimes messy because life is not nicely ordered and tidy. It involves many people who know and care about Jim. The plan takes constant attention, but it is a lot of fun. Because supporting Jim has often taken more deliberate and sustained action than did parenting his younger sister and brother, we have learned a lot about being open to new ideas and perspectives.

Some of our best insights have come from people with Down syndrome and other disabilities. Many of these people have shared some very intimate and personal feelings and profound thoughts on how they view themselves and the people they care about. I asked several of them who have Down syndrome to help with this chapter. They are Dave Hartzog of Charleston, South Carolina; Nannie Sanchez of Albuquerque, New Mexico; Stefanie Ward of Virginia Beach, Virginia; and Karen Taylor and Jim Schwier, both of Saskatoon, Saskatchewan, Canada. These people agreed to offer their perspectives on questions such as

- What is this thing called "sexuality"?

- Is sexuality something you grow into, or are you born with it?

- How do you feel about sexuality?

- What do you really like about yourself?

- What has helped you understand what it means to be a boy or a girl, a man or a woman?

- Why do people get so freaked out about the idea that someone with Down syndrome is a sexual person?

- What are the relationships you have in your lives, and how do you keep them healthy?

As parents or professionals, we want to support loved ones with Down syndrome to become confident, happy, giving, loving human beings who have a good sense of their own values and boundaries. Having a healthy understanding of one's own sexuality can mean that adults with Down syndrome are comfortable in their own skin with a secure and positive view of themselves as their bodies and attitudes mature. Growing into that view can happen slowly and steadily; building self-confidence and moving toward more intimate relationships isn't a race. The point is to develop an awareness and appreciation for that aspect of being human.

"Sexuality means to me when a man and a woman fall in love and have a healthy relationship that turns into two people getting married so they can engage in a sexual relationship. I feel you should really get to know that person before you get serious with him and then comes love and marriage. I believe that if you have a sexual relationship with anyone to fit in, [it] will get you in trouble and is not healthy." —Nannie Sanchez

Winifred Kempton of Haverford, Pennsylvania, has written some of the most widely used books and training materials on social and sexual health and feelings. The trouble for parents whose child has an intellectual or other disability, she says, is that they've sometimes been sidetracked from a positive attitude about their child's social and sexual identity. Sometimes those early and profoundly gloomy pronouncements have a way of hanging around long after the child becomes an adult. No matter what the age of the son or daughter, it's never too late to lay a good foundation of social sexual education and sexual self-image. Setting aside those limiting early predictions and learning to get a grip on the anxiety that a combination of disability and sexuality may evoke are necessary.

"We must insist that parents understand clearly that their children—with or without disabilities—all receive the same training that will deem them socially acceptable by an open-minded public."
—*W. Kempton (personal communication, 1996)*

How do we help individuals with Down syndrome feel good about themselves? It's easy—and sometimes unavoidable—to get caught up in and be exhausted by the mechanics of supporting someone with a disability. There always seems to be a barrage of external forces that many parents must battle with in order to get their son or daughter—and the family—the things they need to have a good life, from financial needs to emotional needs, to developing a sense of community and engaging in community connections.

Regardless of the level and type of stress experienced, it's critical for families and those closest to the person with Down syndrome to stop, take a breath, and reflect on who the person really is: a son, a daughter, a brother, a sister. This is someone with interests and desires who is on a journey, just like the rest of us. We want to be comfortable within ourselves as we discover and experience connections with others. Sometimes we've all got to slow down and remind ourselves and each other of this.

There's another thought that my husband and I find comforting as we continue to stumble forward on this journey as parents. There is such a wide range of intellectual abilities, behaviors, cultures, traditions, religious beliefs, languages and communication skills, family expectations, and interests among people with Down syndrome and their families that it is impossible—and probably dangerous—to look for a single recipe for healthy sexuality that suits everyone. Still, generally speaking, all people with Down syndrome have changing, evolving needs and perspectives as they make their way through life.

ACKNOWLEDGING FEELINGS

"I'm good with people and fun to be with. I'm hard-working, nice, and smart."
—Dave Hartzog

People with Down syndrome and others with disabilities sometimes find themselves living with and trying to respond to a dichotomy related to their sexuality. One view that someone with a disability is asexual leads parents and caregivers to ignore this aspect of humanness as a possibility. It doesn't exist. The other contradictory view is that there must be an inordinate amount of attention paid to the aspect of sexuality and every move is scrutinized, assessed, and supported somehow. As Freud once pointed out, sometimes a cigar is just a cigar. Widely differing views on a person's sexuality and emotional development as a man or a woman can be tempered with some good old common sense and a reasoned response. Expressions of sexuality should be treated with respect. While disability has an impact, the lens through which someone is viewed should be that of man or woman first, disability second.

"I am a person with a lot of energy and passion and committed to helping other people and to learn skills in becoming a self-advocate. I also think I am a pretty good political activist."   —Nannie Sanchez

Acknowledging the array of feelings experienced by an individual with Down syndrome as legitimate is the foundation of that respect. Is an expression of a dawning sense of sexual identity treated as "a behavior problem" at home or school? Is a "crush" dismissed as "inappropriate"? A sibling of a young man with Down syndrome remembers his older brother talking about Alice from *Alice's Adventures in Wonderland* (Carroll, 1865/2000), how much he liked her and his very serious declaration that she was his wife. The older brother with Down syndrome was in his teens at the time, and the younger brother recalled that his family members worried that such a fantasy was babyish; they pooh-poohed the older brother's expressions of loyalty and love or at least disregarded the thoughts as "cute."

But what if the older brother wasn't really talking about Alice but instead was trying to express that he found that *kind* of girl attractive? What if he was talking about liking someone who had adventures and looked pretty and who found her way out of trouble and was a hot blonde on top of everything else? If that's what he was really trying to say, how must it have felt to be told that his thoughts were just silly and unattainable?

Jim Schwier (left) relaxes on the back deck after a day of work at the YMCA. Stefanie Ward (right) gets ready to head out on the National Down Syndrome Society Buddy Walk on the Old Dominion University campus in Norfolk, Virginia.

How much of the sexual expression of someone with a disability is forced into "appropriate" or "inappropriate" boxes by families and professionals, even if it's all with good intentions? Somehow it's all right to knowingly tolerate "crushes" on unattainable and unrealistic movie stars and music icons, but if the fan in question has a disability, are we a little too quick to make sure our loved ones realize this is "unrealistic"? Do we kill dreams and fantasies in a rush to teach and reinforce appropriate behavior? After all, dreams and fantasies are all normal and healthy aspects of an evolving sense of sexuality. As parents and professionals, when do we become comfortable with and respect the decisions adults with Down syndrome make about having real, significant relationships? Even more complex, how do we know when to recognize that our notion of sexuality may be different from that of a person with Down syndrome?

Perhaps the notion of the conservative, traditional progression of having a relationship, marrying, and finally engaging in a sexual relationship might provide comfort to parents, but is it possibly limiting or stifling—maybe even unattainable? What about sexual experimentation? What about a desire for sexual relationships before marriage? What about gay and lesbian issues? The answers aren't easy and certainly aren't the same for everyone, but we should be open to thinking beyond our comfort zones.

"I have some friends that are boys, but they are not my boyfriend. I wish I had a boyfriend. I call my friends, I go out with . . . friends, I talk to them when they have problems. I tell my mom when I need help. If my friends get mad, I make them stop arguing and help them get back together. Sometimes boyfriends and

girlfriends fight over silly stuff, and I try to help them stop being mad."
—Stefanie Ward

"I have had four boyfriends in life, three of them were friends that I went out for lunch or dinner and the movies. The fourth I came close to being engaged to him; it got pretty serious. I always tell the men I date that I will not be in a sexual relationship unless we fall in love, become great friends, and get married. As I mentioned, the fourth person came very close. Currently, I do not have a boyfriend. I have been so busy I don't have time to date. But now my schedule is becoming not as busy, so I am going to start looking." —Nannie Sanchez

PICKING UP ON CLUES

Our son Jim can list some important elements he feels make up his identity as a man. We are conscious of the lack, as far as we can tell, of particular interest in having a romantic relationship with anyone for the time being. But we're keeping an eye out, not only for potential friends, but also for changes in how Jim views himself as he ages.

We want to encourage Jim to be in more situations where there is a greater possibility of him meeting someone he might click with. Still, who and what he clicked with even 5 years ago may not be of interest now. Since he had a strong interest in *Star Trek* for many years, we once thought maybe a Trekkie club for adults would be fun and open up new friendships. He came home and announced that the club members were "weird." *Star Trek* is still okay, but it doesn't hold the allure it once did.

When we casually ask if he might be interested in having a girlfriend, he shrugs and says, "Naww, maybe later." Is that apparent lack of interest in a relationship because he's not had one? What constitutes an informed choice about these things? And how "informed"—based on our definition—does that choice have to be? Who knows all there is to know about a relationship before getting into one?

Jim enjoys his time out with other people, but he's not a night owl like his musician brother. And while he's very sociable and friendly and enjoys being with others, he's not as gregarious as his sister. Sometimes, Jim's idea of a really good time is making a salad for supper, having a glass of wine as we barbeque a steak on the deck with some good tunes on the stereo, and maybe watching a movie later while having some popcorn. Jim is happy to enjoy an evening at home. Part of this, we suspect, is that Jim may just have a homebody personality. Also, being with other people is a lot of work.

Jim wears two hearing aids, and ambient noise in crowds is problematic. Communication, too, requires a great deal of effort because of difficult speech. Our role isn't to force him out into new experiences but to present legitimate opportunities for more social interaction and the risk of new experiences with other people while he has the security and sanctuary of a peaceful and loving home environment. We must gently help him risk.

"I'm glad to be a man."　　—*Dave Hartzog*

"I am glad I am a girl. I am glad I am pretty and smart. I am very nice, too."
—*Stefanie Ward*

LAUNCHING INTO ADULTHOOD

There is a time, just before puberty, when kids start to demand greater space from their parents. Parental closeness, emotional and physical, becomes embarrassing, and parents really feel an emotional wrench as the child pulls away, often with great force, from the parent–child bond. Given that this is the child's job, if the child doesn't do it, the parent isn't likely to force the child away. That means that parents of kids with intellectual disabilities need to begin to move away from their children.

Since the experience of adolescent launching can be substantially skewed by the presence of disability, parents need to help their sons or daughters "launch" themselves into the teenage and adult world by supporting more independent experiences and choices (Melberg Schwier & Hingsburger, 2000). The trick for parents is to discover and practice ways to help their sons and daughters become more confident adults. How do we balance the need for security and safety with a desire to risk, meet new people, and enjoy a taste of responsibility and independence from time to time? Think back and remember what it felt like to be "grown up."

"[Sexuality] it's whether you're a man or a woman. You grow into it."
—*Dave Hartzog*

"I think you are born with it, and it comes out when you get older."
—*Stefanie Ward*

"Everyone is born with sexual drives, but as we become adults our sexual drives become more real as our hormones start kicking in. I think people need to understand that we may be mentally delayed, but we have the same sexual drives as anyone else."　　—*Nannie Sanchez*

Our family constantly nurtures a network of friends for our son, drawing in new people from time to time, reconnecting with the veterans and getting everyone together now and then for a backyard barbeque. We make sure Jim is able to spend time away from us with people in his network. As parents, we continue the search for relationship possibilities and remain alert to Jim's expression of interest because when Jim thinks "maybe later," that time may be now. Listening to Jim's siblings is a critical element, and other family members have different perspectives that can help round out a rich and interesting life. It's up to us and those close to Jim to pay attention to how he responds to other people in a variety of situations.

In the meantime, however, being a man has some specific characteristics for our son that involve responsibility, caring for others, particular possessions, and his place in the family. Our role is to build on those interests and desires and make sure he has opportunities to feel good about himself and others. When we ask him what he likes about being a man, he says,

"I am a man. I shave. I have bankcard. My job cleaning, mopping. Towels and stuff at YMCA. I do cool man stuff. I babysit Simon. He is little boy. He needs help. I help him. Sam and Chris [Simon's parents] me, we take care of him. I gel for my hair. I have my room. I get DVD player, my birthday for 30 years old. I am the oldest brother." —Jim Schwier

As individuals with Down syndrome grow up, they experience a number of powerful drives. Some of these are a part of normal and healthy sexual development: learning how it feels physically and emotionally to be male or female and what it means socially to be a man or woman. Some of those drives involve the need to be social and develop friendships and relationships. It is all a process of discovery.

RECOGNIZING SEXUALITY

"Sexuality is how boys and girls like each other. Sexuality is how you feel when you get older and you want to have a boyfriend or girlfriend. It is how you feel about yourself." —Stefanie Ward

What are individuals with Down syndrome being taught when they learn about sexuality and what sexuality means?

- Learning about sexuality means being held, cuddled, and stroked by parents and caregivers.

- Learning about sexuality means finding out what it means to be a boy or a girl.

- Learning about sexuality is being curious about your body.

- Leaning about sexuality is running, playing, and wrestling with friends in the neighborhood.

- Learning about sexuality is coming to terms with the physical changes of puberty and wondering, "Am I normal?" (Maksym, 1990a, 1990b).

"My mom helped me learn things about being a girl. My friends in school talked about stuff, too. Sometimes at pajama parties we talk about boys. My friends' sisters do, too. Sometimes on TV I learned about what girls do."
—Stefanie Ward

"What has made me realize that I am different than a man is that I have breasts and a vagina, and I also have a monthly menstrual period, whereas a man has a penis, testicles, and tiny breasts."   *—Nannie Sanchez*

An individual's intensity of disability, and how much concentration and energy goes into daily life because of it, can influence the type and variety of relationships he or she experiences. How families and others respond to the sexual identity (and even orientation) of a person with Down syndrome will depend on a willingness to actively acknowledge sexuality as a positive and valuable part of every human being. Socializing someone to think he or she is not a sexual being, that he or she is not ready for sex, or never will be because he or she is "really only a child in an adult body" may suppress things for a while, but human needs have a way of making themselves known.

"I think [sexuality] can make you feel good about yourself. I like to dress up in nice clothes, and people tell me I look good. I like to dance with boys, and they like to dance with me. I like to flirt with the cute boys. I feel so good when boys want to spend time with me."—Stefanie Ward

"I like to look at magazines like Avon. I enjoy looking at all that. Oh, and I like to look at designing magazines, too, so I think about how to decorate my bedroom, but I haven't done it yet. It's just interesting."—Karen Taylor

Dick Sobsey is a professor at the University of Alberta in Edmonton, Canada, and is a parent of a son with disabilities. Much of his most well-known research has been in the area of violence, sexual

Dave Hartzog (left) with a bevy of friends, (left to right) Jennifer, McKenzie, and Kelley. Karen Taylor (right) works in a library.

abuse, and victimization of people with disabilities. He cautions parents who feel they can ignore the issue of their children's developing sexuality or those who feel they can simply "put their foot down" and cut it off at the metaphoric knees.

"They find out their daughter was kissing the neighbor's son in the basement and it's, 'Okay, that's it. You're grounded for life and you'll never see him again.' A part of the motivation for this young woman may be sexual, but a big part of it is social," says Sobsey (personal communication, 2004). Simply isolating the person merely frustrates very natural drives and emotions. "If you don't give them any opportunity to move forward and develop some relationships, you may run into problems."

"People want to have sex. You have to be careful. It is better to wait until you are married to have sex. If you have sex, you should use a birth control. You don't want a baby if you not ready to take care of one. Sex disease can kill you. You have to watch out who you are with and be careful. You don't want to get a disease. I don't want babies because they are hard work. They need lots of care. You have to take care of them for a long time."—Stefanie Ward

Preventing Sexual Abuse

One of the most frightening and uncomfortable "problems" or truths that Sobsey, both as a researcher and a parent, and so many others are concerned about is that people with disabilities are sexually abused in huge numbers. There are many reasons for this, but we know families and responsible caregivers must prepare people with disabilities for the real world. Self-protection skills must be taught, learned, and reinforced. This teaching should ideally start in childhood, but adults with disabilities—even adults who have been taught to be compliant and "nice"—can learn strategies to reduce risk. What parents and professionals should not do is create a sterile environment where people with Down syndrome are denied any access to the world because there is risk.

It's a scary but true cliché: there are some bad people out there. Even more disturbing is that the bad people "out there" may not be so far away. Abuse at the hands of people known to the victim is a significant possibility and, for some, a reality.

Part of the best defense against abuse and exploitation is to teach an individual with Down syndrome to be a confident and assertive person. This will take practice, and the best practice is real life. It's virtually impossible to teach children about abuse and exploitation in a vacuum. It must be taught in the wider context of sexuality, sex, relationships, and values. Self-protection requires an assertive child, yet many children with disabilities are taught to comply. They know that the quickest way to approval and favor is to just do what they are told. A very frightening study showed that people with disabilities would do what they were told even if they knew it was wrong and even if they knew it was dangerous (Flynn, Reeves, Whelan, & Speak, 1985). This comes from a lifetime of being told what to do and being expected to just do it. People who "just do it" have lost the discrimination skills about how and when to comply or not comply (Melberg Schwier & Hingsburger, 2000).

The issue of sexual abuse prevention deserves far more than a mention in this chapter. Luckily for families and people with disabilities, a great many good resources have been developed. Some are listed in Table 8.1. Get them. Go to your local advocacy association and check into their lending library. Call some organizations to see how you might find these resources, and pick something that works for your loved one with Down syndrome.

This is not an issue to put on a to-do list for future consideration. What we do have to think about seriously is that the traditional approach of *us* protecting *them* (people with disabilities) hasn't worked so well. The startling rates of abuse and victimization attest to that. We are beginning to realize that people with disabilities can and must learn, at the very least, to be their own first line of defense.

Encouraging Self-Assertion

Developing a strategy around giving a loved one with Down syndrome more freedom, good information, and decision-making skills can guide

Table 8.1. Recommended resources about sexuality

Internet resources

http://www.aamr.org—The American Association on Mental Retardation has a Special Interest Group on Sexual/Social Concerns. Go to this web site and click on groups.

http://www.nichcy.org—This web site, for the National Information Center for Children and Youth with Disabilities, includes information on defining sexuality and how it develops, social skills, teaching children about sexuality, effects of disability on sexuality, and relationship issues for young adults. It also includes information on sexual orientation, reproduction, birth control, protection against sexually transmitted diseases, sexual exploitation, and sexual abuse.

http://www.qualitymall.org—This web site is a place where you can find lots of free information about person-centered supports for people with developmental disabilities. Each of the mall stores has departments you can look through to learn about positive practices that help people with developmental disabilities live, work, and participate in our communities and improve the quality of their supports. You can do a search for key words such as *sexuality* and *sexual abuse prevention.*

http://www.siecus.org—This web site is for the Sexuality Information and Education Council of the United States (SIECUS). Also visit www.siecus.org/pubs/biblio/index.html and see *sexuality and health, and sexuality and disability.* Though not specific to disability issues, there is also a link to an annotated bibliography on religion, spirituality, and sexuality at http://www.siecus.org/religion/index.html.

Print resources

Brown, R.I., Lawrence Patricia, L., Mills, J., & Estay, I. (1995). *Adults with Down syndrome: Together we can do it!* North York, Ontario, Canada: Captus Press.

Canadian Down Syndrome Society. (1999). *Sexuality, relationships and me: Sexuality booklets for young adults.* Calgary, Alberta, Canada: Author.

Hingsburger, D. (1995). *Just say know!: Understanding and reducing the risk of sexual victimization of people with developmental disabilities.* Eastman, Quebec, Canada: Diverse City Press.

Ludwig, S., & Hingsburger, D. (1993). *Being sexual: An illustrated series on sexuality and relationships.* Toronto: Sex Information and Education Council of Canada.

Macon Resources. (2003). *We can stop abuse peer training manual.* Decatur, IL: Author.

McKee, L., Kempton, W., & Stiggall-Muccigrosso, L. (1997). *An easy guide to loving carefully for women and men.* Los Gatos, CA: Lynne Stiggall-Muccigrosso Associates.

Kempton, W., Stiggall-Muccigrosso, L., & Davies, T. (1998). *Socialization and sexuality, A comprehensive training guide for professionals helping people with disabilities that hinder learning* (Rev. ed.). Syracuse, NY: Program Development Associations.

Melberg Schwier, K., & Hingsburger, D. (2000). *Sexuality: Your sons and daughters with intellectual disabilities.* Baltimore: Paul H. Brookes Publishing Co.

Regional Residential Services Society & the Nova Scotia Department of Health Community Health Promotion Fund. (1998). *Relationships and sexuality: A guide to policy for individuals with intellectual disabilities and their regional residential service providers.* Dartmouth, Nova Scotia, Canada: Authors.

Vredeveld, R.C. (2001). *Caring relationships: Helping people with mental impairments understand God's gift of sexuality.* Grand Rapids, MI: CRC Publications.

Multimedia resources

Hingsburger, D. (1995). *Hand made love: A guide for teaching about male masturbation through understanding and video* [Videotape]. Eastman, Quebec, Canada: Diverse City Press.

Hingsburger, D. (1998). *Tall tales: Self-concept and people with developmental disabilities* [Audiotape]. Angus, ON: Diverse City Press.

Hingsburger, D., & Haar, S. (2000). *Fingertips: Teaching women with disabilities about masturbation through understanding and video* [Videotape]. Eastman, Quebec, Canada: Diverse City Press.

(continued)

Table 8.1. (continued)

Hingsburger, D., & Harber, M. (1998). *The ethics of touch: Establishing and maintaining appropriate boundaries in service to people with developmental disabilities* [Videotape]. Eastman, Quebec, Canada: Diverse City Press.

Macon Resources. (2004). *We can stop abuse: A sexual abuse prevention curriculum for persons with developmental disabilities* [Videotape]. Decatur, IL: Author.

PACER Center (1996). *I am a beautiful person—Sexuality and me: A video for parents of teens with disabilities* [Videotape]. Minneapolis, MN: PACER Center.

Walker-Hirsch, L.W., & Champagne, M.P. (1986). *Circles II: Stop abuse* [Videotape]. Santa Barbara, CA: James Stanfield.

Walker-Hirsch, L.W., & Champagne, M.P. (1988). *Circles III: Safer ways* [Videotape]. Santa Barbara, CA: James Stanfield.

Walker-Hirsch, L.W., & Champagne, M.P. (1993). *Circles I: Intimacy and relationships* (Rev. ed.) [Videotape]. Santa Barbara, CA: James Stanfield.

growth in a progressive way. Parents and professionals can create an atmosphere where there is good communication; they should never create a situation in which an individual with disabilities feels there are things he or she cannot tell them. If such a situation exists, most certainly exploitation and abuse will fall into that category.

Of course, there are people with such profound disabilities that the kinds of support for growth and risk-taking they require will be different from someone with Down syndrome who has only a mild disability, for example. Still, sexuality is the essence of every person. Parents and professionals must guard against the fear of abuse and the temptation to think of sexuality and sex education as something for next year's to-do list. If it's difficult for you to see a loved one with Down syndrome as a full human being, or even as an adult, find some resources to help discuss the person's sexuality and what it means to be an adult.

Part of healthy sexuality is a generous helping of self-assertion. People with disabilities can be—and have been—taught to be compliant. They are constantly expected to do what others tell them to do. They are often used to other people controlling many, if not most, aspects of their lives. Parents and professionals can help individuals with Down syndrome seize the opportunity to be more assertive and confident. If they try to take that away and don't support some self-reliance and decision-making skills development, they are increasing the chance their loved one will be victimized (D. Sobsey, personal communication, 2004).

DIFFERENTIATING PUBLIC AND PRIVATE

Most often when someone with Down syndrome makes a social-sexual mistake, it involves a lack of understanding about what is public and what is private. Dave Hingsburger is a sexuality consultant who has worked with many people with disabilities, families, and educators on this issue. He says part of the difficulty is rooted in two competing myths about the sexuality of people with disabilities. Both lead to ineffective ways to support someone's sexual identity.

One myth is that people with disabilities are sexually innocent, and another myth is that they are sexually deviant. Interestingly, when a social-sexual mistake is made, people almost always jump to the second myth (Melberg Schwier & Hingsburger, 2000). Luckily, the opportunities for teaching and reteaching these concepts present themselves daily in many different ways. In fact, the mother of one of the young adults who offered her opinions for this chapter said just the activity of sitting down to help her daughter with some of the questions made her realize that she may need to do some refresher-type discussions more frequently. She also indicated that it was an opportunity to reflect on the fact that as parents "we do the balancing act lifelong to respect our children's rights to explore and experience with our desire to keep them as safe as possible."

"[I learned about sexuality] from classes in high school. My teacher showed slides about puberty."   —Dave Hartzog

The balancing act happens in nitty-gritty, day-to-day ways, too. In a harried household, it may be easier to dress a child in the kitchen while making breakfast, but the message being taught is that public nudity and a lack of privacy is okay and tolerated in any room of the house with anyone around. Sometimes parents and professionals forget that their actions are lessons in themselves to people with disabilities and those around them. If the fundamental concepts of public and private are not thoroughly taught, understood, and refreshed, then a healthy and normal sexual outlet like masturbation (or even activity that will be mistaken for it) suddenly becomes "sexually perverted behavior" if it's conducted in the wrong place at the wrong time.

There must be a very clear distinction between public and private. It's okay in private in your room. It's not okay in the living room as everyone watches *As Good As It Gets* with Uncle Nels and Aunt Gwen, who are visiting from Oregon.

"Parents can teach you what is okay to do in public and what is for private. Lots of people don't even know what PDA means. Public display of affection makes other people feel embarrassed for you."   —Stefanie Ward

"I think sex can be a beautiful thing, but as people with disabilities, we are always told that we should never have sex nor do we have the right to get married. I feel sex between two people who have made a lifetime commitment to you is a great thing."   —Nannie Sanchez

When discussing this chapter with Jim's younger brother, Ben, a sibling's perspective on self and sexuality was gently offered as a reminder that respect for privacy should be practiced and not just preached: writing about Jim's sexuality might be an invasion in itself.

"If it was me and you were writing about my sexual feelings and identity, really personal stuff, I might be a little creeped out."   —Ben Schwier

Point taken, and some issues initially discussed in a draft of this chapter have been discarded. Giving someone privacy reinforces the concept of public and private behaviors and underscores the fact that privacy should be respected on a variety of levels. Parents and professionals shouldn't walk into the bedroom of an individual with disabilities without first knocking on the door (and getting an invitation). They shouldn't barge into the bathroom or flip back the shower curtain to ask when the person is going to be finished. If an individual with Down syndrome wants to spend time in his or her room doing whatever he or she feels like (and that includes masturbation!), parents and professionals should leave him or her alone. I'm not saying that everyone is always good at these things; we all make mistakes. I'm just saying we should remember to be better!

If parents and professionals need any more motivation than just common courtesy to reinforce the concepts of public and private, consider this: These concepts are relevant to the topics of abuse and exploitation and the safety of the individual with disabilities because too many people with disabilities learn that their bodies are very public. All sorts of people touch them, usually while providing some kind of support service. Begin at the beginning, and ensure that your loved one with Down syndrome knows that there are parts of his or her body that no one sees or touches without permission. Don't worry about upsetting some service provider in the future. If the provider hasn't learned to ask permission, let it be your son or daughter who teaches him or her through protests that permission is necessary (Melberg Schwier & Hingsburger, 2000).

MODELING

You can teach the distinction between public and private most effectively through modeling, explanation, and persistence. When you teach the skills of personal grooming, for example, do so in a private place. You teach much more than public and private by modeling desired behaviors. You also teach important lessons about relationships and how to treat others.

My husband and I had a layover at an airport recently and killed some time over coffee. At a nearby food court table sat three Mom-looking types and four young women with Down syndrome. They were having a supper of various selections from food court vendors, and there were frequent trips in twos and threes to the washroom. The thing I particularly noticed was that the young women, possibly in their late teens or early twenties, looked absolutely *cool*. Three of the four had those precarious high platform shoes, two had on Capri pants and belly shirts. I didn't see any bellybutton or nose rings, but I wouldn't have been surprised. Everything about their style was current fashion. One carried a well-stuffed Gap shopping bag. I had to use the washroom, too (honest, I did, I wasn't just eavesdropping), and the conversations among the twos and threes who visited the facilities included movies, hair, advice on each other's makeup, school, exams, jobs, outfits, the cute guy on the plane, younger siblings (sigh), who's no longer speaking to whom, and who is now so-and-so's best friend ever.

All four of these young women were expressing very loudly and clearly their own unique expression of their female sexuality. I liked these girls! What's more, I found myself, without ever meeting them, really liking the three Mom-types, who could have been parents, other relatives, professionals, or just friends. They were entirely comfortable with just letting the young women *be themselves*. While I surreptitiously spied, I didn't see any hovering, correcting, admonishing, babying, or stepping in to do for unless it was absolutely necessary (there was some minor difference of opinion over departure times). By simply modeling confident and relaxed behavior, they were teaching those young women about shared decision making and a balance of power. They were helping the four young women grow up with a healthy sense of what being an adult woman was like.

So even if your loved one is no longer a child, as a parent or professional you can still shift your perspective and begin to treat the person more like the grownup he or she has become. Whatever your child's chronological age, stand back, bite your tongue, or sit on your hands; do what you must to allow your loved one to mature (Melberg Schwier & Hingsburger, 2000). Has your teenager been given the opportunity to go shopping at the mall with a friend or relative without you? Has he or she ever traveled to visit a relative on a plane without you? Teenagers and young adults with intellectual disabilities need a variety of experiences not only to broaden their own view of the world and its possibilities but also to give them a more mature message content in their communication and to be perceived as more mature people (Horstmeier, 1990).

"My mother and I always discuss sex and the choices I have to make when I have a man in my life and how you keep your relationship healthy. I have always been taught that my body is mine and I own it. If I choose to share my body there might be some consequences or a great relationship."
—Nannie Sanchez

"[You have] to have lots of exercise to keep your body healthy and very happy, and to keep your fitness, and… to enjoy yourselves…and to make your body healthy, too. I do my exercises every day, and I feel better." —Karen Taylor

CREATING A NETWORK OF CONNECTIONS

Social isolation is probably one of the most debilitating barriers for people with disabilities, particularly for those who rely on others— professionals, family members, volunteers, or friends—to keep them connected to the community. Research indicates that a relatively high percentage of people with intellectual disabilities don't visit family or friends outside their home, participate in social activities, or even speak on the telephone very often, if at all (The Roeher Institute 1995). Many more cope with periodic isolation. Data from the 1991 Health and Activity Limitation Survey (HALS) shows the total number of people 15 and older with disabilities was 3,533,000. Of those, 315,000 adults with disabilities never attend social activities or visit with family or friends (9%); 147,000 of these people never attend or take part in community activities such as religious and related activities, volunteer work, sporting events, concerts, plays, movies, museums, libraries, art galleries, parks, or seminars (4%); 40,000 of these people never talk with others by telephone (1.1%); and 20,000 of these people (0.6%) consider themselves housebound (i.e., restricted to their personal home) (C. Crawford, personal communication, 2004). Data from the older 1986 HALS tell much the same story (Melberg Schwier & Schwier Stewart, 2005).

Thinking of a future for loved ones with Down syndrome without friends or social connections is certainly a nightmare that keeps many parents and professionals awake at night. A critical aspect to developing a good sense of self-identity is to experience friendships and relationships with other people. One of the most important tasks that you can do is to create a network of people around your son or daughter. Make sure the people truly like your loved one and want to spend time and stay connected. Your primary role is not just to pull in your own friends but to seek out people who will be connected to your son or daughter first and you second. Find people your loved one's age. Find people with similar interests or who do things your son or daughter may find intriguing. Look outside just the immediate group of people you know. It's very

Nannie Sanchez enjoys being a self-advocate and political activist.

important that your son or daughter learns about relationships by having them.

Part of the responsibility that a person learns to take on when he or she is in a friendship or a more intimate relationship is taking care of the other person. Considering the other person's feelings and needs in a friendship can teach some valuable lessons that come into play when, for example, a sexual partnership develops in adulthood. Taking care of someone else means making sure the other person doesn't get sick; early lessons can be adapted to personal hygiene and protection from sexually transmitted diseases. Taking care of someone means preventing unwanted pregnancy, so part of the responsibility of being a grownup engaging in a sexual relationship is to learn how to use birth control methods. These complex concepts are more easily understood and practiced if they are based on lessons learned first in friendships and other social connections.

"I have family relationships. I have friends. I don't have a girlfriend. I'm still looking and waiting for the right one to come around."   —Dave Hartzog

"[For a good marriage] you have to like each other. You have to be partners. You have to listen and be nice to each other. That is good communication. You have to agree and not fight. You have to like the same things and share. You have to be like a friend to each other."   —Stefanie Ward

There are some families we know who have "arranged" relationships and even set up marriages between their sons and daughters with disabilities. It's a bit unusual in North American culture, so it may serve to set the couple apart as odd, and it may be assumed the choice to be together was not theirs. But arranging social experiences so that people can make connections and perhaps discover some mutual attraction seems not only helpful but also necessary for people who often lack opportunities to meet new people.

RAILING AGAINST STEREOTYPES

Some lessons need to be reinforced and retaught during the lifetime of an individual with Down syndrome. These are not necessarily lessons you must teach only to your loved one again and again, but to all those people who will come into contact with him or her. This begins when a child is born and lasts throughout his or her lifetime.

Right from the start, you need to talk about your family member as an individual with a future and with potential. When people offer sympathy or pity on the birth of a child, cut them off. Do not allow this outpouring of pity to occur. Do not allow people around your loved one to begin to talk about him or her as "hopeless" or "futureless." Let them know that *you* see your son or daughter as a child who will grow into a competent adult. Let them know that *you* intend for your son or daughter to be treated like a legitimate member of the family. Let them know that *you* intend for your loved one to go to school and work, get married, and live independently (Melberg Schwier & Hingsburger, 2000).

"My mother call[s] me a beautiful princess."   —Karen Taylor

SUMMARY

One important thing to remember—and probably forcefully remind ourselves of from time to time—is that individuals with disabilities grow and change and demand different expressions of the parent–child relationship. The kind of person you hope a child with disabilities will become is not determined by his or her disability but by his or her family, friends, teachers, medical professionals, and him- or herself. The child needs to learn that he or she is loved, valued, witty, gorgeous, strong, and an irreplaceable part of the family.

Our son Jim is 31 and sees himself very clearly as a man, an adult. Though we mess up from time to time, support for him in his daily life is always offered with that in mind. That doesn't mean everything is serious; adults play, too! But the lens through which we view our son guides us and reminds us to respect him as an adult. And when we do slip up, he gently—usually gently—corrects us. After a recent trip to the grocery store, Jim hopped out of the car and fished his house keys out of his pocket to let us in. When I said, "Atta boy, Jim," he turned to us and raised an eyebrow. With a grin he said, "Man. 'Member?"

We do.

REFERENCES

Carroll, L. (2000, December). *Alice's adventures in Wonderland* (Reissue ed.). New York: Signet Classics. (Original work published in 1865)

Flynn, M.C., Reeves, D., Whelan, E., & Speak, B. (1985). The development of a measure for determining the mentally handicapped adult's tolerance of rules and recognition of rights. *Journal of Practical Approaches to Developmental Handicaps, 9,* 18–24.

Haffner, D.W. (1990, March). *Sex education 2000: A call to action.* New York: Sex Information and Education Council of the United States.

Horstmeier, D. (1990). Communication. In S.M. Pueschel, *A parent's guide to Down syndrome: Toward a brighter future* (pp. 233–257). Baltimore: Paul H. Brookes Publishing Co.

Ludgwig, S., & Hingsburger, D. (1993). *Being sexual: An illustrated series on sexuality and relationships—teaching manual* (Number 17). North York, Ontario, Canada: The Roeher Institute.

Maksym, D. (1990a). *Shared feelings: A parent guide to sexuality education for children, adolescents and adults who have a mental handicap.* North York, Ontario, Canada: The Roeher Institute.

Maksym, D. (1990b). *Shared feelings: A parent guide to sexuality education for children, adolescents and adults who have a mental handicap: Discussion guide.* North York, Ontario, Canada: The Roeher Institute.

Melberg Schwier, K., & Hingsburger, D. (2000). *Sexuality: Your sons and daughters with intellectual disabilities.* Baltimore: Paul H. Brookes Publishing Co.

Melberg Schwier, K., & Schwier Stewart, E. (2005). *Breaking bread, nourishing connections: People with and without disabilities together at mealtime.* Baltimore: Paul H. Brookes Publishing Co.

Roeher Institute, The. (1995). *Harm's way: The many faces of violence and abuse against persons with disabilities.* North York, Ontario, Canada: Author.

9

■■■

Having a Life

JEFFERY D. MATTSON

■■■

I have the best life! Last year, I received my first romantic kiss. A young lady came into my life at the National Down Syndrome Congress Youth and Adult Conference in Philadelphia, Pennsylvania, in 2003. When I first saw her, I thought, "I like her face." After the conference, we e-mailed and called one another a couple times a week.

I invited her to California and showed her the sights. We went out to eat at some of my favorite restaurants. I used my credit card to take her out. I always pay my credit card off, but it makes eating out easy. I introduced her to some of my friends at work, and we double dated with my brother and his girlfriend.

I took her to Disneyland. At the Happiest Place on Earth, I got my first kiss. It was very romantic. We spoke every other night on the phone, and then I flew across country to see her a few months later. She showed me the sights where she lives.

Since then, we have decided against a long-distance relationship, and we are just friends. Sometimes, I see her picture or a gift she has given me or hear a song we liked. I think about how much I really loved her.

My life is full because of good friends. I have friends from work, from church, from where I volunteer, and from school and my community. Even though I have been out of college for almost 2 years, I still see some of my school friends. My community college is a place where I learned skills for being a good student and future employee.

Some of my favorite classes there were swimming and music because I like to stay fit and I like to play guitar and write songs.

Having friends is very important to me. I think I am a good friend. Friends put others first. I feel so honored to have been asked to be in two of my friends' weddings. This year, my brother will be married, and I will have been in three weddings. I have been an usher and a candle lighter, and I will be the best man.

My life is full because I have a job I love. I work Monday through Thursday. I get up early, get ready, and I always put on a necktie from my necktie collection before I walk to the bus stop. I am a courtesy clerk for Pavilions in Laguna Beach. I have been with Pavilions for 2 years. The people I work with are good guys. They are my good friends. I have made friends with the people that work next door at Gina's Italian restaurant, where I like to sometimes eat after my job.

My life is full because I can give back to my community by volunteering. My High Roller friends are my best friends. High Rollers Club is a part of Young Life. Young Life is an organization for teens that has been around for over 60 years. My dad was a volunteer Young Life leader when he was at Stanford, my mother is a volunteer Young Life leader, and my brother was a volunteer Young Life leader at the University of Michigan. Even my grandparents were volunteer Young Life leaders in the 1960s.

In 1999, the local Young Life staff guy asked me to be a volunteer leader for High Rollers, a club for kids with special needs. I am fully included in the Young Life Leadership, and I have been a volunteer for 5 years now. I like giving back to the community, and I like being part of the team.

Last January, I was asked to speak to over 3,400 people at the Young Life All Staff Conference in Orlando, Florida. I have spoken on disability awareness in schools and at church. I have spoken for local parent groups and other disability organizations. I have spoken at the National Down Syndrome Congress and the National Down Syndrome Society, but I had never spoken before 3,400 people before. I loved it!

In my PowerPoint presentation, I show photos. I say, "I am just a guy. I am more like you than unlike you." Then I say, "I like girls," and I show a photo of me and the babe I took to prom. Then, I say, "I really like girls," and show a picture of me with two of my best friends, who are really cute blonds. Then, I say, "Did I mention I like girls?" and show a picture of me and the entire cheerleading squad from Dana Point.

After I spoke, a couple of Young Life staff guys asked me to be in one of the skits the next morning. The skit started out with me surrounded by lots of girls, and it got a big laugh. The president of Young Life sent me a great letter and a DVD of the weekend. I like watching it.

I live life to the fullest because I went to school, I work, I volunteer, I have hobbies, and I have many important relationships. I stay healthy, too. This year, I lowered my cholesterol and lost 14 pounds. I have a supportive family. This year, I am getting a new sister to be a part of our family. My brother's fiancée is my forever friend, and that is what I always call her. My family helps me be the best I can be in everything I try.

The most important thing in my life is my faith. People with Down syndrome want to live life to the fullest. For me, a full life has to include God. People with disabilities have the right to make their own decisions about their faith. God is in my life. He loves me so much. I want to tell others how much He loves them, too. My favorite verse I know by heart. It is Jeremiah 29:11, "For I know the plans I have for you...plans to give you hope and a future."

I have the best life. How do I live life? To the fullest!

... 10 ...

Person-Centered and Collaborative Supports for College Success

Cate Weir

■■■ Many people believed that Lynn's label of Down syndrome defined her as a person and would shape her future. Lynn, however, was determined to attend college and create an ordinary, challenging environment in which she could learn and grow along with students without disabilities. Through the creative, collaborative teamwork of her school district, Vocational Rehabilitation services, good friends, and community-based supports, Lynn overcame the barriers of limited academic preparation, low placement test scores, and low expectations. Today, as a result of creativity, perseverance, and teamwork, Lynn is pursuing an associate's degree at a community college close to her home. ■■■

This chapter is sprinkled with stories like Lynn's about the personal journeys of adults with Down syndrome and other significant disabilities who are pursuing their dreams of a postsecondary education through the creative use of person-centered and collaborative supports. The participation of individuals with significant disabilities in postsecondary education illustrates the impact that new ways of thinking about resources, support, and control can have on the lives of individuals with Down syndrome. These stories, and others like them, would not have happened without some key ingredients:

- Preplanning that emphasizes the goals and dreams of the student

- Creative use of existing community resources

- Interagency collaboration

- Willingness to challenge assumptions about the capacity of individuals with disabilities to learn and succeed

Individual supports for college are designed around a student's desires and unique needs. Using this individualized approach, students are not part of a specially designed program for individuals with disabilities but instead make use of existing supports available through the college, local school district, Vocational Rehabilitation services, and other relevant support agencies in a collaborative and empowering way. Person-centered planning and creative collaboration are key features of this approach to postsecondary education. Family, friends, Vocational Rehabilitation services, local school districts, and the college or university all have a role in planning and support (O'Brien & Lovett, 1992; Weir, Tashie, & Rossetti, 2001). *Any* student who is interested in college may use this approach to attend regular college classes and participate in typical activities.

PROVEN CYCLE OF SUCCESS

The following eight steps are proven to be effective when providing individualized, person- and community-centered supports for students with disabilities who are planning to go to college. The first step is for students with Down syndrome to pursue academic coursework in high school that will prepare them for college, as opposed to simply taking community-based and life skills instruction courses. Joan, whose story is presented next, did not take advantage of classes during high school that would prepare her for postsecondary education. Although she was still able to attend college, she missed the obvious positive impact that the expectation for and support of academic goals during high school can have on the success of students in college.

■ ■ ■   Joan's identified goal through person-centered planning was to work with children in a child care center. She, however, needed six college credits to make this dream a reality. Because Joan had been in life skills classes for her entire high school career, she was concerned about whether she could handle college courses. A supportive and creative Vocational Rehabilitation counselor designed an employment plan with her that allowed for financial and tutorial support so that she could meet state licensing requirements by completing two college courses in child development.   ■ ■ ■

Vocational Rehabilitation paid for professional tutoring for Joan in order to supplement the peer tutoring available at the college. Joan and her tutor developed grids for the child observations that were required in her class and were a historically difficult area for *all* students. The grids were so successful that all of Joan's classmates adopted the approach.

The second step toward individualized supports is for a student with Down syndrome to establish a group of family, friends, and/or professionals from both secondary and postsecondary education who can work together to support his or her educational needs. Jenny, whose story is presented next, received essential support from her family.

■ ■ ■ Although Jenny had intellectual disabilities, she and her family believed in her ability to get a college education and a rewarding career. Together with her college advisor, Jenny was able to design a major that highlighted her strengths and interests. For those classes that were particularly difficult, Jenny audited the class first and then took the course for credit, allowing her more time to learn the essential material. Jenny took advantage of various supports, such as 1) college-provided peer tutors, 2) regular work with the instructors at the college learning center, 3) meetings with her academic advisor, and 4) her mother's help with homework. ■ ■ ■

Now, Jenny is a college student. Like many of her classmates, she works diligently and sometimes fails classes along the way. One of the things she is fond of saying sums up the way Jenny feels: "When I was born, my parents were told that I would be in an institution, and now I am, but it's another kind of institution—a college!"

The third step toward individualized supports is for team members to meet with a student with disabilities and identify goals through the use of a person-centered planning approach, such as Planning Alternative Tomorrows with Hope (PATH; Pearpoint, O'Brien, & Forest, 1991; see also Chapter 7), that helps the student articulate his or her dreams for the future and how college fits into those dreams. The student and a team of people, representing both personal and professional relationships, meet to identify dreams, objectives, and supports needed to attain that goal.

The essence of individual supports is that they are person centered (Falvey, Forest, Pearpoint, & Rosenberg, 1994). Supports are student driven and may be coordinated by the student or a person chosen by the student (e.g., friend, high school teacher, Vocational Rehabilitation counselor, family member, staff person from an adult support agency). Because of the collaborative and responsive nature of individualized support, ongoing communication between the student and those people involved in his or her support is required.

The fourth step is for the team to determine the student's college of choice. This can be done through talking with the high school guidance counselor and other students, attending college open houses, visiting campuses through tours provided by college admissions offices, and attending college fairs. College catalogs will describe courses of study available and will outline the supports provided through the disability support offices and the learning centers at the college.

The fifth step is for the team to develop knowledge of the college culture and the supports available on the college campus, including those that are specifically designed for students with disabilities and those that are provided to all students. This process is known as *resource mapping.* The team should understand the protections afforded by the Americans with Disabilities Act of 1990 (PL 101-336) and Section 504 of the Rehabilitation Act of 1973 (PL 93-112) and Rehabilitation Act Amendments of 1992 (PL 102-569). Because these protections differ from those provided under the Individuals with Disabilities Education Act (IDEA) of 1990 (PL 101-476) and its amendments, students and their advocates will be much better able to locate and advocate for supports with the college when they understand these distinctions.

The sixth step toward individualized supports is for the team to continue resource mapping by identifying partners and potential resources. These resources include the community agencies that are available to support postsecondary education, such as Vocational Rehabilitation and adult developmental services agencies. For those students who are 18–21 and still eligible, services and supports may be available through the high school. Potential resources also include college-based supports, college financial aid services, and family and friends.

State Assistive Technology Programs provide information and advocacy services to individuals with disabilities regarding assistive technology issues. Each program's goal is to make sure that the state's residents with disabilities get access to assistive technology. The programs are funded by a grant from the National Institute on Disability and Rehabilitation Research. Each state has a technology center where individuals are able to explore technology, borrow things to try out, and purchase and donate used assistive technology devices. (A list of each state's Assistive Technology Program can be found at http:// www.ataporg.org/stateatprojects.asp.)

■ ■ ■   Gil, Sara, and Joe all attend college courses at universities of their choice. They each use a variety of assistive technology solutions in class, at home, and in the library in order to complete assignments. They use audiotape recorders for recording lectures, textbooks on CD, reading software for the computer such as Kurzweil (Kurzweil Educational Systems) or Read:Outloud (Don Johnston), magnifiers and other low vision aids, and speech-recognition software such as Dragon NaturallySpeaking (Nuance Communications). Utilizing Vocational Rehabilitation support, low-interest technology loan programs, and the services of the state's federally funded Assistive Technology Program, Gil, Sara, and Joe are all able to be evaluated for and effectively use technology in the attainment of their goals.   ■ ■ ■

The seventh step is for the team to work with faculty and staff at the college. Once a college (or colleges) have been chosen and support providers have been identified, the team members should schedule a meeting with disability support services personnel at the chosen college(s). Team members should

- Be prepared with questions about the types of supports and the resources available at the college.

- Be sure to discuss strengths and support needs of the student.

- Look for commitment on the part of the college to provide ongoing support to the person with disabilities who has chosen to study there.

- Discuss how additional supports will be provided by the partners who have been identified.

- Consider whether the student will apply for admission to the college and a particular program, or take courses through the Division of Continuing Education as a nonmatriculated student.

For students, like Tom (presented next), who do not meet all the requirements for matriculation into a college or course of study, such as a standard high school diploma, applying to the Division of Continuing Education is a very useful option to exercise.

■ ■ ■   Tom and his family believed that his lack of a high school diploma and standardized test scores would prohibit him from taking willing classes at his local university. His Vocational Rehabilitation counselor, however, encouraged him to try courses through the university's Division of Continuing Education. Through this division, Tom's lack of a typical high school diploma was not a hindrance.

He now attends the university with support from his family, an adult support agency, and Vocational Rehabilitation in addition to the supports provided to him as a student with disabilities through the Access Office on his campus. Tom's family provides him with help with schoolwork he needs to complete at home, and the adult support agency provides transportation to school and staff support while Tom is attending classes. Vocational Rehabilitation assists by providing tuition assistance and by helping Tom to determine the best courses to take to meet his vocational goals.   ■ ■ ■

Many students do not perform well on standardized tests, and they may be prevented from participating in college classes because their scores on placement tests in math and English make them ineligible for admission. The poor scores may indicate that the students will have a difficult time in college-level classes, and students may be advised to forgo the dream of a higher education and move on. There are, however, continuing education classes that do not require placement scores. Students can meet with professors to design effective evaluation methods for their learning styles, use the supports available to all college students, and call upon staff from community support agencies to help with assignments.

While visiting the college(s), team members should consider if there are any *extracurricular activities* that the student may want to participate in, including special interest and discussion groups. Team members should also meet with the faculty members teaching the classes the student will attend. This allows the student to find out what is required in the class, and to determine the supports he or she will need to be successful. If a student chooses to audit a class, there is flexibility in the work requirements. If the course is taken for credit, the student will be expected to meet the established goals of the class. It is important to remember that when a student takes a college course for credit, there are no course modifications that are possible, although accommodations will be provided. Determine what accommodations are needed to make the coursework accessible and who will be providing them.

The eighth step is for the team to meet regularly with the student to solve problems when concerns or issues arise. Even if supports are well designed and thought out at the start, there are always issues that arise that were not anticipated. Having regular team meetings prevents those issues from getting out of control. The team can address the issues and look together for creative solutions. For example, if a student is having trouble walking across campus from the parking lot, the team may address this by helping the student learn to use the university bus service.

In addition to these eight steps, there are also important underlying *beliefs and values* that are present in teams successfully supporting individuals in college. These values and beliefs can be characterized in the following ways:

- People with disabilities have the right to pursue their dreams, including dreams that involve postsecondary education.

- A creative and positive approach to potential barriers and ability to collaborate with others to overcome these barriers is essential.

- Attitudinal barriers that exist for individuals with disabilities must be confronted.

- One can never fully know the capacity of any person, and opportunities to reach beyond perceived limitations should be afforded to every human being.

WHY CONSIDER INDIVIDUAL SUPPORTS OVER SPECIAL PROGRAMS?

Many adults with Down syndrome participate in support programs run by human services agencies or local school districts and housed on a college campus (Neubert, Moon, Grigal, & Redd, 2001). This option is not optimal because programs that are established specifically for students with Down syndrome and other disabilities do not offer the fully inclusive college experience that students may wish for (see Table 10.1). These programs may be in segregated rooms on a college campus, offering training in daily living skills and other skills to enhance independence for young adults. They typically do not involve attending regular college classes of the student's choosing and do not result in the obtainment of any type of college certification or degree.

One university describes its "life skills" program as being designed for young adults with intellectual disabilities to provide instruction in functional literacy skills, technology, career exploration/employment, and living skills. Life skills classes follow the college's academic calendar schedule but are taught exclusively for the program's students. Classes meet each day from 9 A.M. to 3 P.M. Although the program is university based, students are not admitted to the college itself. Students receive a certificate upon completion of the program.

Table 10.1. General disability support programs versus individualized supports

General disability support programs	Individualized supports for students with disabilities
Students are directed to colleges and programs that they "should" or "must" choose.	Students can choose colleges and programs based on interests and personal preferences.
Students register for a preestablished curriculum.	Students register for classes based on interests and personal preferences.
Students are on campus at preestablished times (e.g., 8 A.M. until 2 P.M., which are the hours during which such programs are typically in session).	Students are on campus when their classes are scheduled, based on the curriculum they have designed.
Students establish paid supports for college attendance.	Students establish natural supports for college attendance.

Another possible drawback of special college programs for students with Down syndrome and other disabilities is the lack of personal choice that may be allowed.

■ ■ ■   As a young man with Down syndrome who had completed 4 years of high school, Mark could have accepted 3 years of "transition" support at his local high school, but he instead expressed his dream to attend college. He wanted to learn more about computers so that he could work in the field. His school district organized and provided supports that allowed him to attend his local community college. Availing himself of supports from a community-based support agency, his family, and the community college, Mark is currently enrolled in a college class. In the introduction to computers course, he is increasing his computer skills. He also uses the Learning Center at the college to improve his writing skills and often chooses to have lunch at the college's cafeteria. When he is not at class or working on schoolwork at the college, Mark occupies himself with a part-time job at an office supply store.   ■ ■ ■

A key distinction between program-based services and the individual-support model lies in the *person-specific* nature of the supports offered to students (Hart, Zafft, & Zimbrich, 2001). In contrast to special programs that are developed on campus with the goal of addressing the needs of a *group* of students, and where students are compartmentalized by needs and directed into that program, individual support systems start out with the unique needs and desires of the student him- or herself (Weir, Tashie, & Rossetti, 2001). Mark was not given a set of standard options offered to students with Down syndrome. Instead, his specific postsecondary goals were the first criteria considered, and then the accommodations required to make those goals possible were taken into account.

A second important distinction is in the role the student plays on the college campus. The individual with Down syndrome is viewed as an independent student, not a program participant or "special" student. This integration reinforces the notion that students with and without disabilities are, at the heart of the matter, all students in the same college environment.

Finally, a support program located at a college campus may be provided only for the "transition" years—those years between the ages of 18 and 21 when many students continue to receive special education services through their local school district—and students only have the option of attending college while affiliated with the transition program. In contrast to a program-based model, the use of individually designed supports and collaborative teamwork empowers students to continue their college education on their own timetable and in their own unique way. School-district employees, parents, and students themselves can use their own experiences and expertise to collaborate with adult supports on behalf of an individual student and widen the base of support for each student in this way.

SUMMARY

Sixteen years after the passage of IDEA and with at least a decade of a policy of inclusive education, inclusive and "typical" college experiences must be available as an option for students with Down syndrome and other disabilities. Through person-centered planning that emphasizes the goals and dreams of the student, creative use of existing resources, and a willingness to challenge assumptions about the capacity of individuals with significant disabilities, students with disabilities are attending college in increasing numbers. The percentage of college freshmen reporting disabilities has increased from just under 3% in 1978 to more than 9% in 1998 (U.S. Department of Education, 2003).

The stories in this chapter represent just some of the ways that students with Down syndrome and other disabilities are finding success in reaching their own college goals. The stories illustrate the many strategies that have been tried and also may lead the reader to imagine other solutions to what may seem to be insurmountable barriers. Each story offers both information and inspiration to others who will come next.

Although colleges and universities have recently experienced an increase in the numbers of students with Down syndrome and other disabilities that they support (Blackorby & Wagner, 1996), and more students with significant disabilities are considering or attending college, their participation in postsecondary education is still very limited. In 1999–2000, 11% of all undergraduate students in degree-granting institutions reported having a disability (U.S. Department of Education, 2003). When students with significant disabilities attend college as typical, fully participating students, they challenge long-held assumptions about disability, the nature of intelligence, and the role of postsecondary education. These challenges call for a significant paradigm shift for many people, and barriers still remain to full participation. Each student profiled in this chapter was successful because of a creative and flexible support system that was willing to figure out ways around existing systemic barriers to collaboration and financial support.

Postsecondary education for students with intellectual disabilities should be a choice that is available to students and their families. Supporting this choice requires flexible service systems. At this point, there are few situations that systemically support the choice of post-secondary education for students with significant disabilities.

The alignment of support and services on the local, state, and federal level is a place to begin to discern where the supports and services currently exist to support students with significant disabilities in colleges. Recent studies of innovative supports and services in postsecondary education reveal more effective and cooperative mechanisms with which to provide supports to individuals with disabilities (Stodden, Jones, & Chang, 2002; Whelley, Hart, & Zafft, 2002). Colleges and universities can design supports that permit individual choice while avoiding the establishment of isolating parallel "service systems." Providing individual supports to students with significant disabilities will establish new and creative alliances driven by the wishes and dreams of the students.

REFERENCES

Americans with Disabilities Act of 1990, PL 101-336, 42 U.S.C. §§ 12101 *et seq.*

Blackorby, J., & Wagner, W. (1996). Longitudinal post-school outcomes of youth with disabilities: Findings from the national longitudinal transition survey. *Exceptional Children, 62,* 399–413.

Falvey, M., Forest, M., Pearpoint, J., & Rosenberg, R. (1994). *All my life's a circle: Using the tools: Circles, MAPS, and PATH.* Toronto: Inclusion Press.

Hart, D., Zafft, C., & Zimbrich, K. (2001). Creating access to college for all students. *Journal for Vocational Special Needs Education, 23*(2), 19–31.

Individuals with Disabilities Education Act of 1990, PL 101-476, 20 U.S.C. §§ 1400 *et seq.*

Neubert, D.A., Moon, M.S., Grigal, M., & Redd, V. (2001). Post-secondary educational practices for individuals with mental retardation and other significant disabilities: A review of the literature. *Journal of Vocational Rehabilitation, 16,* 155–168.

O'Brien, J., & Lovett, H. (1992). *Finding a way toward everyday lives: The contribution of person centered planning.* Harrisburg: Pennsylvania Office of Mental Retardation.

Pearpoint, J., O'Brien, J., & Forest, M. (1991). *PATH: Planning possible positive futures.* Toronto: Inclusion Press.

Rehabilitation Act Amendments of 1992, PL 102-569, 29 U.S.C. §§ 701 *et seq.*

Rehabilitation Act of 1973, PL 93-112, 29 U.S.C. §§ 701 *et seq.*

Stodden, R., Jones, M., & Chang, K. (2002). *Services, supports, and accommodations for individuals with disabilities: An analysis across secondary education, postsecondary education and employment.* Retrieved October 24, 2003, from http://rrtc.hawaii.edu/products/phases/phase3.asp

U.S. Department of Education, National Center for Education Statistics. (2003). *The condition of education 2003* (NCES 2003-067). Washington, DC: U.S. Government Printing Office.

Weir, C., Tashie, C., & Rossetti, Z. (2001, September). Inclusion goes to college: A call to action. *TASH Connections, 27*(9).

Whelley, T., Hart, D., & Zafft, C. (2002). *Coordination and management of services and supports for individuals with disabilities from secondary to postsecondary education and employment.* Retrieved October 24, 2004, from http://rrtc.hawaii.edu/products/phases/phase3.asp

11

...

College Years and Future Job

ANDREW LEE JONES

...

My name is Andrew Lee Jones, and I live in my own apartment in Kansas City, Missouri. My typical day starts out with a good workout. My workout includes lifting weights, working on abdominals and obliques, walking on the treadmill, and riding a bicycle. I walk on the treadmill 3 days a week. I usually do the treadmill on Mondays, Tuesdays, and Fridays. I do the bicycle on Wednesdays and Thursdays. At the end of the workout, I walk around the track three or four times to cool down.

After the workout, I come home and have lunch. After lunch, I read my Bible, and sometimes I check e-mail or pay bills. Once I get my bills paid, then I watch television until 2:30. When 2:30 comes around, I start getting ready for work. I put on my uniform and get all the stuff that I need for work. Then, I watch television until 3:15 P.M. When 3:15 comes around, I leave for work at the YMCA.

Before I had a job, I had to set goals that would help me to guide my job search. These goals were to use my degree that I got in college and to live independently in my own apartment. In my apartment, I would be able to set my own rules and to do whatever I wanted to. Secondly, I wanted to live in a small town where I could drive. Third, I wanted to work with people with disabilities. I did accomplish those goals.

In college, I had job interviews for potential jobs. I found my job with suggestions made by family friends. I found the right place in

Arkadelphia, Arkansas. I worked for an agency serving individuals with developmental disabilities. But the downside was that I knew no one in the town. The town was the right size for me to drive in, and the job did involve working with people with disabilities. The independence was great, but it was a little lonely at first until I got involved in some activities.

On the first day I drove myself to work, I really felt grown up and independent. After 2 years at the job, I reviewed all my goals. They came out really good. The one goal that I did accomplish is that I was working with people with disabilities, and I had a job with benefits.

When I was working for the agency, they wanted me to create a recreational program for the clients. While that was going on, I was working as a staff aide in the day program. I liked teaching the clients life skills, but after 2 years I became angry when they did not start the recreational program.

In December 2002, I decided to quit the agency. That was a hard step to do because I liked the staff and the clients. I was really bored with the job, and I wasn't using my degree. It was really hard to give up a job with benefits. I learned my lesson that it is not good to work in a job that you don't like.

All of the YMCAs of Greater Kansas City got together to have an awards banquet. I was nominated for the "Rookie of the Year." After they announced all the nominees, they announced the winner of the award. They announced my name for the award. I was excited that I got the award. Everybody got up and applauded for me. This was a great accomplishment.

In the year 2001, I went to the NDSS (National Down Syndrome Society) Conference. I really enjoyed the conference. I participated in the workshops at the conference. They were really interesting and helpful. At the NDSS Banquet, I received the NDSS Community Award. It was given to me by the National Down Syndrome Society for graduating from college and for work promoting activities in the community for people with disabilities. I was really excited that I got the award.

... 12 ...

Work and Vocational Training for Individuals with Down Syndrome

Paul Wehman, Pam Targett, and Jacob A. Neufeld

The advent of vocational services such as supported employment has offered new opportunities for social and economic integration for adults with disabilities, including individuals with Down syndrome (Wehman, Revell, & Kregel, 1998). Yet despite the use of supported employment, improved transition to work services, and laws like the Americans with Disabilities Act (ADA) of 1990 (PL 101-336), the unemployment rate for people with disabilities remains high at around 60%–70% (Kiernan, Gilmore, & Butterworth, 1997; National Organization on Disability, 2004; U.S. Census Bureau, 2004). When compared with working-age individuals with disabilities, working-age adults with intellectual disabilities have much lower rates of competitive employment (Olney & Kennedy, 2001). In addition, the majority of vocational services continue to be provided in segregated work settings such as sheltered workshops (Kregel & Dean, 2002; Wehman, 2001). A national sample revealed that approximately 50% of adults with intellectual disabilities who received vocational services were placed in segregated employment settings.

In recent years, some additional strides have been made to improve competitive employment. For example, the expansion of eligibility for supported employment under Medicaid waiver (West et al., 2002) and the 1998 Amendments to the Rehabilitation Act (part of the Workforce Investment Act of 1998 [PL 105-220]) that emphasize vocational services for individuals with the most severe disabilities have helped with payments for job coaches, personal care assistants, and assistive technology in the workplace (Olney & Kennedy, 2001); how-

---

Preparation of this chapter was partially supported by Grants No. H133B040011 and E9420117-03.

ever, the bias toward segregated placement remains and cannot be changed by legislation alone. Change must also occur on other levels if individuals with more significant disabilities are going to become productive citizens (Kiernan & Schalock, 1997; Wehman et al., 1998).

Unfortunately, service providers may have limited knowledge on how to serve someone with more significant support needs (Unger, Parent, Gibson, & Kane-Johnson, 1998; Wehman, Barcus, & Wilson, 2002). For example, they may not know how to successfully negotiate work opportunities with employers, use systematic instruction, or facilitate workplace supports. Yet the successful application of employment support for individuals with Down syndrome requires the ability to implement these and other best practices.

One powerful way to educate direct-service personnel is to provide positive examples of how individuals with disabilities have succeeded at work. This chapter highlights some best practices and presents a case study to further illustrate how a package of supports can be assembled to help facilitate community employment for an individual with Down syndrome.

BEST PRACTICES

There are a number of practices that can help promote community employment for individuals with Down syndrome. This includes, but is not limited to, the following: vocational education, vocational transition planning, supported employment, family support, employment negotiations, and workplace supports. Each is touched on in the following sections.

Vocational Education

The professional literature contains few examples of students with intellectual disabilities who participate in academic programs in either community colleges or 4-year institutions; however, some students are choosing to attend 2- or 4-year colleges or community colleges with learning disability programs. Others are opting for noncredit transitional programs on college campuses. Such programs usually have strong independent living and recreational components in addition to academic and vocational training. Still other individuals with Down syndrome are opting to bypass the aforementioned to immediately pursue employment, where they will receive on-the-job vocational skills training, sometimes with the assistance of a job coach.

Two reasons why employment may be a more desirable option for some individuals follow. First, often there is variability in how a particular occupation is performed depending of the environment. For instance, a storeroom clerk may have a very different work scope in a food service versus a retail setting. In addition, the workplace environments and management expectations would differ. Thus, teaching vocational skills in a classroom, simulated setting, or even in a real work setting where one will not eventually be employed may not equate to the future place of employment.

Second, each person with Down syndrome possesses unique talents and will have varying support needs. This means that some individuals may require individualized vocational support services even after successfully completing a postsecondary education program. For instance, an individual may require assistance with locating suitable work opportunities, describing his or her strengths and support needs to employers, learning how to do the job to meet a specific employer's standards, and/or obtaining other supports to enhance his or her success at work. This is why some individuals may find going straight to work a more desirable option. Under such circumstances, vocational skills training takes place on the job once an individual is employed. What makes it possible for students to leave high school and work in the community for good pay and benefits is a life skills curriculum that is community based and practices authentic instruction. This chapter focuses on this particular approach to employment.

Trying to decide whether postsecondary education or employment is the best option for a student with Down syndrome will need to be determined with help from the individualized education program (IEP) team and revisited throughout the student's education. It may be useful to consider the following:

- What is the person's ultimate goal?
- What is the best way to achieve it?
- What are the person's academic strengths and weaknesses?
- What are the person's future life goals?
- What are the person's career goals?
- How does the person best learn new skills?
- How much support is anticipated to be needed in a postsecondary setting?
- How much support is anticipated to be needed at work?
- What supports are available to the person?

Answers to these and other questions should assist those involved with making a decision about which path to pursue. When a student decides to pursue the postsecondary education option, close collaboration between the transition team at the secondary school and college is essential.

Students with Down syndrome should have access to a vocational education component starting in their elementary years. This type of program can help prepare students with the most significant disabilities for community-based employment by delivering vocational education and training to students in typical community work settings rather than in conventional school environments (Moon & Inge, 2000; Rizzolo, Hemp, Braddock, & Pomeranz-Essley, 2004; Wehman, 2001; Wehman et al., 1998; Wehman & Kregel, 2004). Four major themes that should guide program development are 1) individualized and person-centered services, 2) functional and practical curriculum, 3) community-based activities, and 4) workplace and community supports.

It is recommended that students, particularly those with the most significant disabilities who are age 14 years or older, gain opportunities to engage in nonpaid vocational exploration, assessment, and training experiences to identify their career interests, assess their employment skills and training needs, and develop the skills and attitudes associated with paid employment. Then, prior to leaving school, students should engage in paid employment, through either cooperative vocational education experiences or competitive employment with any necessary supports, including job coach/supported employment services.

Typically there are four distinct components to the community-based vocational education approach: vocational exploration, vocational assessment, vocational training, and paid employment. Students may progress sequentially through all four components; however, some students, depending on their instructional needs, may participate in only one or two components before moving to paid employment. A brief description of each component is provided in Table 12.1.

Community-based vocational education gives students an opportunity to learn more about the world of work, build skills, and become employed prior to leaving school. This approach may also increase parents' confidence by demonstrating the vocational capacity of a student and allowing parents to see firsthand how their child can work in the community when provided with the right type and intensity of on- and off-the-job supports. For example, it may help parents form a career vision as part of their child's future and alleviate fears associated with independence. Educating students in business settings also exposes business personnel to students with disabilities. This, in turn, may help employers better understand the abilities of individuals with disabilities and change any negative reactions they may have to the perceived differences of people with Down syndrome. For some students, part-time and/or full-time college will be a possibility. Work can be an important supplement to college for those students as they balance real-life work experiences with on-campus college activities.

Table 12.1. Overview of components of a community-based vocational education program

Vocational exploration

The *vocational exploration* component briefly exposes students to a variety of work settings. The exploration process investigates likes and dislikes across various work environments. During vocational exploration, students might talk to employers, watch work being performed, or actually try out some tasks under direct supervision of school personnel. Exploration can help students make choices regarding career or occupational areas they wish to pursue and develop future individualized education programs (IEPs). *According to Fair Labor Standards Act (FLSA) of 1938 (PL 75-718), this activity should not exceed 5 hours per job experienced.*

Vocational assessment

The *vocational assessment* component helps determine a student's individual training objectives The student rotates through various work settings, and assessment data are systematically collected about the student's interests, learning styles, work habits, social skills, physical stamina, support needs, and so forth. As a result, future training objectives are developed and become a part of the student's IEP. *According to FLSA, this activity should not exceed 90 hours per job experienced.*

Vocational training

The *vocational training* component places the student in various employment settings for work experiences. Training is closely supervised by a representative of the school or a designated employee/supervisor. After the training objectives in a particular employment setting are met, the student moves to other employment environments where additional or related learning or reinforcement of current competencies and behavior can occur. *According to FLSA, training should not exceed 120 hours per job experienced.*

Paid employment

Paid employment may come in the form of *cooperative vocational education*. This is an arrangement between the school and an employer in which each contributes to the student's education and employability in designated ways. The working student may receive payment from the employer; from the school's cooperative vocational program; from another employment program operating in the community, such as those supported by the Workforce Investment Act of 1998 (PL 105-220); or a combination of these. Students may engage in several placements as part of their educational experience.

In other instances, the student may obtain supported employment to assist him or her in gaining and maintaining work in the community. As needed, supports are provided or facilitated by an employment specialist or job coach. Both approaches require the student to be paid the same wage as employees without disabilities.

From Cobb, B., Halloran, W., Simon, M., Norman, M., and Bourexis, P. (1999, Nov.). *Meeting the needs of youth with disabilites: Handbook for implementing community-based vocational education programs according to the Fair Labor Standards Act* (2nd ed., p. 6). Minneapolis: University of Minnesota, National Transition Network; adapted by permission.

Vocational Transition Planning

Helping students with Down syndrome make the transition from school to work requires movement through school instruction to employment in the community. Special education and vocational rehabilitation programs are required by legislation to cooperatively plan for the transition of students with disabilities into the workplace. Vocational transition planning consists of the student, parents, teachers, and rehabilitation personnel meeting and crafting a plan for movement from school to adulthood in the community. Vocational transition planning does not have to be complicated or labor intensive; however, it does require willingness, cooperation, creativity, and determination among those involved (Wehman, 2001). Although the school's role is extremely important, others, such as family members and vocational rehabilitation providers, must get involved.

For too long, vocational rehabilitation and schools have struggled over who bears the legal and financial responsibility for providing services to assist students with disabilities with employment. Each state's agreement between these agencies should clearly delineate roles and responsibilities. School administration and staff, vocational rehabilitation personnel, and family members should fully understand rights, roles, and responsibilities. Without this pertinent information, employment services may be poorly coordinated, nonexistent, or inconsistent. Communication and commitment across participating agencies is essential.

Supported Employment

Supported employment was initiated through the Rehabilitation Act Amendments of 1986 (PL 99-506) to specifically assist individuals with the most severe disabilities with employment. It is one of the few specialized programs that has grown in size to the point where it has the potential to make a real national impact on the hundreds of thousands of unemployed people with disabilities (Wehman et al., 1998). It is also a program that has documented positive employment outcomes (Wehman, 2001).

The major premise of a supported employment program is to give necessary support to the people with the most significant disabilities (those deemed unemployable) so that they can work. With the assistance of a job coach, impediments to work are reduced through the provision or facilitation of an array of individualized supports both at and away from work (Wehman et al., 1998). Despite PL 99-506 and the Rehabilitation Services Administration's emphasis and priority of supported employment, a pattern of noncompetitive, segregated, or group-model employment for individuals with intellectual disabilities persists (Wehman, Inge, Revell, & Brooke, 2007).

Efforts need to be made to track those individuals who are not working competitively and offer them services. Those with the most significant disabilities (for whom the service was intended) need to take a stand either alongside of and/or instead of those individuals with less significant disabilities and fight for their right to this service option.

Supported employment is a highly individualized service option. To be successful, personnel need to use proven strategies, be creative problem solvers, and provide different types and levels of support within the workplace to meet the individual's unique needs.

Family Support

As adults with Down syndrome age, so do their parents. Many of those parents have carried the full responsibility for day support. Work experience can be challenging, given the transportation requirements and different expectations that employers have in the business community. Families increasingly need to turn to community providers and other families for help, guidance, and support to oversee these challenges. At the same time, increased independence by the individual with Down syndrome will make things easier.

Employment Negotiations

Sometimes a person with Down syndrome will be able to perform in a position with an accommodation or change to the original job design. In the business community, this is often referred to as *job restructuring* and is an example of a reasonable accommodation under ADA. Although simply reassigning or reallocating a marginal job duty may be effective for qualified individuals with disabilities, it may not lead to employment for people with more significant support needs. This occurs because some individuals with disabilities may not be qualified or able to perform all of the essential job functions of a position, even with reasonable accommodation.

If an individual with Down syndrome is unable to perform the essential job functions of an existing position, it may be useful to negotiate the design of a new job. This innovative job development strategy, which is often a common practice in supported employment, can lead to a customized work opportunity for the job seeker who has a disability. Under these circumstances, a job is restructured when some of the duties or tasks typically performed by one or more workers are changed to develop a customized job for the person with disabilities. Hagner and DiLeo (1996) described three typical methods for carving jobs: *cut and paste, fission,* and *fusion.* When used, such efforts must always ensure that the new worker is making a genuine contribution to the workplace and that the person with the disability is not being relegated to performing undesirable tasks.

Cut and paste involves trading duties between an open position and a current employee. For example, a warehouse person works in shipping and receiving at a large retail store. In addition to unloading trucks and removing merchandise from boxes, his or her job entails collecting customer shopping carts from the parking lot. The worker is not able to learn how to perform collecting shopping carts, so he or she trades duties with a floor stocker, who among other things, is required to keep the front end cashiers stocked with bags. The warehouse person keeps the cashier's station stocked with bags, and the stocker brings in the customer shopping carts.

The cut-and-paste method may also be used in a professional setting. For example, in a legal library in a large law firm a person may hold a clerk's position. The clerk is responsible for photocopying briefs, checking out books, updating a database, and delivering copied briefs to attorneys. The worker is not able to enter the information into the database in a timely manner, so he or she trades a shelving duty with the librarian's assistant.

A second method, *fission,* involves dividing a single position into two or more jobs. For example, a position in a greenhouse might be restructured to take advantage of the capabilities and accommodation needs of an employee who can repot and water plants. The position of greenhouse worker becomes two positions—one that specializes in customer service activities and plant maintenance (e.g., treatment for insects, fertilizing, cleaning), and another that focuses on repotting and watering the plants. The maintenance worker makes a meaningful contribution to the workplace while leaving some more complex tasks to another employee.

Fission can also take place in a professional setting. For example, a marketing firm plans to hire a research specialist who is required to contact the public, complete a survey by telephone or mail, and enter the data into a database for analysis. This job is divided into two part-time opportunities in which one employee focuses on the telephone surveys while the other handles those by mail. Both employees are required to enter data into the database.

A third carving method, *fusion,* is the reassignment of similar functions from several employees to a newly created position. For example, in a sandwich shop all employees are required to perform a variety of different functions (e.g., food prep, making sandwiches, cashiering, cleaning dining area, washing dishes). A position might be created by taking some of the duties that all staff members used to perform and combining these to form a new job (i.e., making pasta salad, filling condiments, cleaning front entrance and windows, bussing tables, and refilling customer drinks in dining area). This allows existing staff members to spend more time on the other functions (i.e., taking orders, making sandwiches, and cashiering) and creates a job for someone else.

In all instances, the end result is a customized employment opportunity that maximizes a job seeker's strengths and abilities, minimizes disability, and meets a business need. This strategy has proven to be particularly effective for individuals with disabilities whose specific vocational strengths might not otherwise be recognized or given credence under an existing work structure or position description. Vocational rehabilitation professionals need to be well versed on how to negotiate work opportunities that not only add value to business but also capitalize on a particular job seeker's strengths and abilities.

Workplace Supports

Vocational service providers are professionals who provide individualized support to assist people with disabilities with locating and retaining work in their communities. Assistance may entail providing on-the-job instruction and arranging for or providing workplace supports. For example, some individuals will require very specific and intensive systematic instruction, self-management procedures, and other workplace supports.

Effective instruction involves many decisions and an ability to adapt basic strategies to meet the unique characteristics of the worker and demands of the workplace. Vocational rehabilitation specialists need to know how to develop effective vocational instructional programs. This includes determining the best way to teach a task and may entail developing creative ways to perform it and establishing suitable learning objectives. Also, instead of using a trial-and-error approach to teaching, systematic instruction may be needed. When teaching is systematic, it is a defined replicable process that reflects current best practices (e.g., task analytic instruction, prompting error correction procedures, reinforcement) and uses performance data to direct modifications. This systematic plan moves the worker from initial acquisition to complete mastery of the skill (Moon & Inge, 2000).

The use of self-management procedures is also important because these procedures involve an individual in the learning process or behavior change. The nature of self-management procedures, which include self-observation and self-reinforcement, requires the person him- or herself to be quite involved in knowing what he or she is doing and how to control the activity. Unfortunately, many people with severe disabilities have never achieved the ability to monitor their performance because teachers, parents, and others usually do this for them. What often results is prompt dependence on others that reduces independence at work. Oftentimes, an employee with a disability will need to learn how to monitor his or her own work performance in order to become as independent as possible. Thus, those providing or facilitating support need to be familiar with an array of strategies to promote self-management, such as self-monitoring, self-instruction, and self-reinforcement.

In addition, vocational service providers (e.g., community program agencies) should learn to facilitate existing workplace and co-worker support and remember that they are there to complement what employers do, not supplant existing practices. For example, a new hire should participate in his or her employer's new employee orientation and initial training if at all possible. Afterward, more intense systematic instruction is provided by a job coach.

Employment often offers many benefits beyond receiving a paycheck and benefits. For instance, meaningful work and social inclusion can lead to new or renewed feelings of self-worth and self-esteem. Knowledge about the workplace culture can provide a basis for understanding social inclusion. It can also assist direct services staff to develop strategies to maximize inclusion. For example, if part of the culture involves taking turns cleaning the employee breakroom or walking down to the local market for coffee in the morning, the new hire should be told of these "office customs" and invited to participate. This helps indoctrinate the person into the workplace culture and promotes inclusion.

Strategies to enhance and facilitate the inclusion of the adult with Down syndrome may also be used to maximize success at work. For example, to work independently, a worker may require spontaneous prompting to remain on or return to a task. Because the goal is for the vocational specialist to eventually fade from the job site, if instructional programs fail to produce continuous on-task behavior, support from a couple of co-workers and a verbal or physical prompt may be needed to get the worker back on task.

ROBERT'S STORY

Robert is an 18-year-old man with Down syndrome. Over the years, he has participated in a number of vocational explorations, assessments, and training activities through his school's community-based vocational education program. His vocational skills training took place at a department store, hotel, and health club. He worked in each setting performing a variety of tasks throughout the week during a 7-month time period. Training sessions were scheduled between the regular school hours of 7:30 A.M. and 3:00 P.M. Some of the information gained during his community-based vocational training experiences is highlighted in Table 12.2. After the training experiences, a team meeting was held to discuss Robert's next steps and transition from school to work.

Supported Employment

The transition team included Robert, his mother, his special education teacher, his regular education teacher, the school's vocational education coordinator, a state vocational rehabilitation counselor, and an employment specialist/job coach from a local supported-employment provider. Supported-employment services were recommended because it appeared that Robert would need one-to-one on-the-job skills training and an array of workplace support to assist him with gaining and maintaining employment in his community.

Table 12.2. Summary of Robert's community-based vocational training experiences

	Site 1: Retail store	Site 2: Hotel	Site 3: Health club
Activities	Fronted shelves Brought in carts Hung merchandise Processed shoes	Prepared veggies for salad bar Baked cookies Folded linens	Swept floors Cleaned equipment
Time	Noon to 2:45 P.M., Monday through Friday	7:30 A.M. to 11:30 A.M., Monday, Tuesday, and Wednesday	7:30 A.M. to 11:30 A.M., Thursday and Friday
Information learned	Learned to say, "See service desk." Increased standing tolerance to 3 hours before a break (initially required a break every hour) Mastered the task of recognizing damaged items and setting aside opened packages Learned to match to a sample Learned to lift stock weighing up to 15 lb Learned to maneuver a loaded stock cart	Went from 2 hours to prepare lettuce, cucumber, and tomato to 1 hour (the production standard was 30 minutes) Was slow on the food preparation task Learned self-management strategy using a picture cue implemented with some success Liked folding some linens Responded well to systematic instruction	Began to recognize clean equipment without prompting Used a modified cleaning spray bottle Was slow but increased productivity when a self-management check card was initiated Worked well with different specialists and co-workers Expressed the desire to "work out" Discovered that his loud voice was usually not noticeable due to background stimuli (e.g., talking, music)

Career Direction

During the meeting, the team used information obtained from previously held person-centered planning meetings and community-based vocational education activities to further develop Robert's vocational portfolio. The portfolio included pictures of Robert performing various community-based activities and a functional resume that listed Robert's interests, strengths, abilities, and potential support needs.

In addition, the team spent some time generating ideas on places where Robert might want to explore employment and determining the roles of the various members. After the meeting, the employment specialist had a better sense of who Robert was and what he liked and did not like to do; however, she needed additional knowledge to further her understanding of his abilities and potential support needs. Consequently, the employment specialist visited Robert and his family in their home, which gave her an opportunity to observe Robert in his natural environment. She also interviewed him and his family about his work preferences, abilities, and support needs.

Afterward, she arranged to spend some additional time with Robert in the community. They went on an outing to the local mall so that the specialist could observe Robert's ability to orient to the environment, respond to various conditions, interact with others, and order a simple meal from the food court, among other things.

Based on the information gained from the vocational training experiences and other activities, the employment specialist recognized that while Robert had a number of abilities, it was highly likely that an employment situation would need to be specifically negotiated for him (see Table 12.3 for a list of Robert's strengths and challenges). She would need to find an employer who would consider developing a work opportunity that would highlight and maximize Robert's abilities, while providing a valuable service to the business. In the vocational rehabilitation field, this is often referred to as *job carving* or *creation*.

Job Search and Employment Negotiations

Over the next few weeks, the employment specialist approached a number of businesses, including hotels, manufacturers, retail stores, fast food, and full-service restaurants, to inquire about business needs and hiring practices. Many employers were not hiring at the time and/or not interested in pursuing a job creation. Some employers expressed fears about hiring someone with a disability. The specialist knew that such fears were not uncommon and left educational information with these employers with a promise to follow up with them at a future date.

Table 12.3.   Robert's vocational strengths and challenges

Vocational strengths	Vocational challenges
Has outgoing and pleasant personality	Is easily distracted
Is friendly, polite, and cooperative	Is overly talkative
Often volunteers to help	Raises voice
Wants to please	Dislikes pressure on fingertips
Follows simple instructions	Has difficulty processing multiple instructions
Follows a routine	Has limited transportation options
Prints personal information	Has slow rate of performing manual tasks
Prepares simple meals	Dislikes washing and drying dishes
Recognizes mistakes	May act age inappropriate to gain attention
Enjoys wrapping items	Loses control of temper (rare)
Likes to pour things	May complain to get attention
Likes to fold towels	Cannot express when sick
Likes to go bowling	Needs forewarning of changes to routine
Responds well to systematic instruction and follows very specific verbal cues	Becomes frustrated when unable to complete a task

A couple of weeks later, the employment specialist met with a manager of a restaurant who agreed to explore the idea of hiring someone with a disability who might not be able to perform all of the duties required within an existing job description. The employment specialist spent some time at the employment site in order to learn more about the business's needs and its practices. During this time, she observed various jobs including that of food preparer. The employment specialist learned that this particular job entailed more than 25 different duties. For example, among other things, the food preparer was required to make 10 different pasta salads and 6 desserts, tray desserts, prepare and bake potatoes, assemble salads, and rotate items in the small and big walk-in refrigerators.

While learning about this job, the specialist noted a number of tasks that Robert might be able to learn how to do, such as preparing potatoes for baking, making different types of salads, preparing salad dressing to go, and portioning desserts. With this in mind, she asked the prep worker and manager certain questions to help stimulate their thoughts about job carving. She probed about possible ways of improving the prep worker's efficiency or reducing overtime expenditures by hiring someone to perform certain tasks.

The employment specialist also observed the employees interacting with one another. She noted that everyone seemed to be friendly and willing to help each other out. She also learned that senior workers trained new employees. The employment specialist was pleased to hear this and explained how she would be available to offer training tips to a co-worker on instructional strategies that were proven to be effective for a worker with a disability. She reiterated that if they hired someone, she could offer an on-the-job site skills training service at no cost to the business.

The employment specialist also inquired about the possibility of establishing a mentor for a new hire and gave some examples of how past relationships had worked. A co-worker mentor's role might include introducing the new worker to others, promoting workplace friendships by modeling a positive relationship, and teaching the person certain aspects of the job.

With this information in mind, the employment specialist considered how this particular job and place of employment might match Robert's interests, abilities, and the types of supports he might need to succeed there. She recalled that during his vocational training experience Robert had tried some food preparation tasks like preparing vegetables for the salad bar and wrapping baked cookies. In addition, Robert's mother had described how he liked to assist her in the kitchen at dinnertime. The employment specialist contacted Robert and his family and a few other key team members (i.e., transition specialist, special education teacher, and vocational rehabilitation counselor) to discuss this possibility, and all were in favor of the idea. During the conversation with Robert's mother, the employment specialist learned that the family frequented this particular restaurant a couple of times per month. This, along with other information, seemed to indicate that this may be a good match for Robert, so an interview was arranged.

During the interview, the employer asked Robert his name, where he went to school, and if he wanted to work, among other things. He also showed Robert the kitchen and introduced him to some workers. At the end of the interview, the employer offered Robert the job. Robert replied that he thought he could work, but he needed to ask his mom. The employment specialist, knowing his parents were agreeable, reminded Robert of this fact, and Robert then accepted the job. The employer scheduled Robert to begin work the following Monday from 8:00 A.M. until noon.

On-the-Job Training and Workplace Supports

The daytime food prep specialist, Antonio, agreed to provide initial skills training to Robert and serve as his co-worker mentor. He received some basic tips on systematic instruction from the employment specialist because this was a proven way to teach Robert new skills. In addition, Robert's mother provided some other points that others should keep in mind when teaching Robert a new task, such as Robert will say, "What?" even when he has heard what was said.

The food preparer, Antonio, provided 2 days of skills training. Afterward, management requested that the employment specialist provide the additional training. The employment specialist had participated in the employer's initial training alongside Robert and was ready to provide instruction. She used various prompts like verbal instruction, indirect verbal cues, modeling, and physical assistance on each step to determine which ones would solicit the right response (i.e., the next step of the task) from Robert. This strategy utilizes a response where the trainer progresses from the least amount of assistance (usually a verbal prompt paired with a physical prompt) to the most intrusive (usually a physical prompt), until one prompt results in the correct response (Moon & Inge, 2000; Wehman & Kregel, 2004). Table 12.4 gives a brief description of how Robert's least intrusive prompt program was designed.

By keeping track of the number and type of prompts required over time, the employment specialist was able to determine when she could start gradually moving away from Robert during training. Initially, she was located beside Robert when she provided direct instruction. When he performed 75% of the steps in the task analysis independently, she moved about 4 feet away from him. If a prompt was needed, she would move back toward Robert. Once the correct response was initiated, she moved to the designated distance. In this manner, the employment specialist gradually faded her physical proximity to Robert as he began to independently perform the majority of steps in the task analysis. Eventually, she removed her presence from the immediate work area and eventually off the job site.

One major challenge during job skills training related to Robert's becoming accustomed to touching various textures (i.e., lettuce, potatoes, grease) and putting pressure on his fingers. Robert was required to pick up a baking potato, grease it, and wrap it in aluminum foil prior to baking it. He found the grease texture adverse and would refuse to grease the potato. To alleviate this issue, Robert was taught to use a food prep sponge to apply the grease. This technique worked, and Robert was successful at applying the grease to potatoes.

Supportive staff have been important throughout Robert's employment. For example, after about 8 months of employment, Robert started leaving his work station early and would go sit in the breakroom. When prompted to return to work, he would refuse. The employment specialist was alerted to the problem during one of her

Table 12.4. Overview of Robert's least intrusive prompts program

Instructional program components	Robert's program components
Prompt hierarchy	Robert responds well to verbal instructions. Gesturing and modeling prompts have been effective. Robert is sensitive to touch and prefers to work independently; therefore, physical prompts should be avoided.
Reinforcer	Robert is not currently motivated by the natural reinforcer (paycheck). A reinforcement system will be used to teach him about pay. Robert's mother will instruct him to use a money card with a picture of an item to purchase and the amount it costs. At the end of the week, Robert will go to the bank, cash his paycheck, match his money to the card, and go purchase the specified item.
	Robert will also learn to use a vending machine during break. Arrangements will be made to make sure he has some change on a daily basis. The money card method described previously will be used.
	Robert responds well to verbal praise.
Schedule of reinforcement	Verbal praise will be given after successful completion of each step. When Robert performs 60% of the steps in the task analysis independently, reinforcement will only be delivered after nonprompted completion of the entire task. When Robert reaches 80% independence, reinforcement will only be delivered on every other nonprompted correct response and at the completion of the entire task.
Time period for worker's response	Robert will be given 5 seconds for self-initiation of the steps in the task analysis.
Error correction procedure	Errors will be interrupted using a system of least prompts (verbal, gesturing, modeling). Upon initiation of an incorrect response or no response within 5 seconds, the trainer will begin with the least intrusive prompt (verbal). If an incorrect response is initiated or there is no response within 5 seconds, a gesture will be simultaneously provided along with the verbal cue. If Robert does not respond correctly in 5 seconds, a modeling prompt paired with a verbal cue will be given.

ongoing monthly follow-up visits. Her investigations revealed that in the previous weeks Robert had been scolded on a number of occasions for arriving "late" to catch his ride home with the disability transportation provider.

The employment specialist also learned that a new driver was on duty and had not been coming up to the establishment's door to escort Robert to the vehicle. Instead, she waited for him in the parking lot. The specialist met with the transportation provider. The provider agreed that they could come to the back door to pick up Robert. This not only eliminated the need for him to walk through a busy parking lot, but he could remain in the breakroom and see his ride when it arrived. Over time, Robert learned that his ride would be out back waiting, and he stopped leaving his workstation early.

Outcome

Robert has been employed at the restaurant for more than 2 years. Management reports that he is doing very well and is a valued member of their team. Robert seems to enjoy going to work, and his family would like to see him increase his work hours. The employment specialist, Antonio, and management are trying to identify some additional job duties. Over the years, Antonio and Robert's relationship has grown both at and away from the workplace. Antonio continues to introduce Robert to new employees and provides tips on how to support him. Outside of work, during pro baseball season Antonio has invited Robert to attend several home games with his family.

SUMMARY

If a primary goal of education is to help all people become productive citizens, then the concepts presented in this chapter must not only be duly noted but also followed. As this chapter points out, young adults with significant disabilities need to participate in community-based vocational training and receive transition to employment services (using supported employment as needed) prior to the last year of school. Supported employment services can assist those with the most significant disabilities with gaining and maintaining work. Creative work structures that highlight the job seeker's abilities and that benefit the business can be negotiated. People with disabilities can work in their communities. Some individuals may need minimal supports to work while others may need an array of supports to assist them with reaching their career goal. Thus, supports should always be individualized and provided in a way that capitalizes on the person's strengths, abilities, and existing support system.

These practices are often recognized as "best" in the field by those charged with overseeing and providing transition and adult employment services; however, in actuality, they are not always followed. In addition, individuals with disabilities and family members may not even be familiar with these practices or may choose to accept less. To truly become "best practices," these practices must become customary; they must be the rule rather than the exception. When these practices are routine, community-based employment will be closer to becoming a reality for individuals with all disabilities, including Down syndrome.

REFERENCES

Americans with Disabilities Act of 1990, PL 101-336, 42 U.S.C. §§ 12101 *et seq.*

Cobb, B., Halloran, W., Simon, M., Norman, M., & Bourexis, P. (1999, Nov.). *Meeting the needs of youth with disabilites: Handbook for implementing community-based vocational education programs according to the Fair Labor Standards Act* (2nd ed., p. 6). Minneapolis: University of Minnesota, National Transition Network.

Fair Labor Standards Act of 1938, PL 75-718, 29 U.S.C. §§ 201 *et seq.*

Hagner, D., & DiLeo, D. (1996). Negotiating job designs and salaries. In D. Hagner & D. Dileo (Eds.), *Working together: Workplace culture, supported employment and people with disabilities.* Cambridge, MA: Brookline Press.

Kiernan, W.E., Gilmore, D., & Butterworth, J. (1997). Integrated employment: Evolution of national practices. In W.E. Kiernan & R.L. Schalock (Eds.), *Integrated employment: Current status and future trends* (pp. 17–29). Washington, DC: American Association on Mental Retardation.

Kiernan, W.E., & Schalock, R.L. (1997). *Integrated employment: Current status and future trends.* Washington, DC: American Association on Mental Retardation.

Kregel, J., & Dean, D.H. (2002, May). Sheltered versus supported employment: A direct comparison of long-term earning outcomes for individuals with cognitive disabilities. In J. Kregel, D.H. Dean, & P. Wehman (Eds.), *Achievements and challenges in employment services for people with disabilities: The longitudinal impact of workplace supports* [Monograph]. Richmond: Virginia Commonwealth University, Rehabilitation Research and Training Center on Workplace Supports.

Moon, M.S., & Inge, K. (2000). Vocational preparation and transition. In M.E. Snell (Ed.), *Instruction of students with severe disabilities* (pp. 591–628). Upper Saddle River, NJ: Merrill.

National Organization on Disability. (2004). *N.O.D./Harris survey of Americans with disabilities: Landmark survey finds pervasive disadvantages.* Washington, DC: Author.

Olney, M.F., & Kennedy, J. (2001). National estimates of vocational service utilization and job placement rates for adults with mental retardation. *Mental Retardation, 39*(1), 32–39.

Rehabilitation Act Amendments of 1986, PL 99-506, 29 U.S.C. §§ 701 *et seq.*

Rizzolo, M.C., Hemp, R., Braddock, D., & Pomeranz-Essley, A. (2004). *The state of the states in developmental disabilities.* Washington, DC: American Association on Mental Retardation. Available at http://www.cu.edu/ColemanInstitute/stateofthestates/

Unger, D.D., Parent, W.S., Gibson, K.E., & Kane-Johnson, K. (1998). Maximizing community and workplace supports: Defining the role of the employment specialist. In P. Wehman & J. Kregel (Eds.), *More than a job: Securing satisfying careers for people with disabilities* (pp. 183–223). Baltimore: Paul H. Brookes Publishing Co.

U.S. Census Bureau. (2004). *American community survey.* Retrieved July, 2005, from http://www.census.gov/hhes/www/disability/data_title.html#2003

Wehman, P. (2001). *Supported employment in business: expanding the capacity of workers with disabilities.* St. Augustine, FL: TRIN Publishing.

Wehman, P., Barcus, M., & Wilson, K. (2002). A survey of training and technical assistance needs of community based rehabilitation providers. *Journal of Vocational Rehabilitation, 17,* 39–46.

Wehman, P., Inge, K.J., Revell, W.G., Jr., & Brooke, V.A. (2007). *Real work for real pay: Inclusive employment for people with disabilities.* Baltimore: Paul H. Brookes Publishing Co.

Wehman, P., & Kregel, J. (2004). *Functional curriculum for elementary, middle, and secondary age students with special needs* (2nd ed.). Austin, TX: PRO-ED.

Wehman, P., Revell, W.G., Jr., & Kregel, J. (1998, Spring). Supported employment: A decade of rapid growth and impact. [On-line]. *American Rehabilitation, 24*(1), 31–43. Available at http://soe.eastnet.ecu.edu/sped/articles-html%20form/42-supporEMPDecade.html

West, M., Hill, J., Revell, W.G., Jr., Smith, G., Kregel, J., & Campbell, L. (2002). Medicaid HCB Waivers and supported employment: Pre- and post-Balanced Budget Act of 1997. *Mental Retardation, 40*(2), 142–147.

Workforce Investment Act of 1998, PL 105-220, 112 Stat. 939.

13

■■■

The Future Is Ours

CHRIS BURKE

■■■

Many, many years ago, when I was still at school, someone asked me what I was going to be when I grew up. I thought about it and then said, "I want to be an actor, and I want to help the handicapped." Those two things really interested me, along with writing for the school newspaper. So, in reality, I had three ambitions.

While I was still attending Don Guanella School, I enjoyed working with the counselors and helped in the evenings with the younger boys, reading to them, encouraging them to talk, and helping them to get ready for bed. Thanks to that experience, I was able to get a job as a volunteer in a school for the multihandicapped in New York City when I graduated from Don Guanella. The children at Public School 138 were wonderful and needed so much help. It made me feel good to be there for them. I loved them, and they loved me. It was a great experience and led to a full-time job with the New York City Board of Education. It was a great job, and I would still be there if Hollywood hadn't beckoned.

But Hollywood did beckon, and I had an unbelievable opportunity to star in the series *Life Goes On* for 4 years. Show business is my true love. That's why I was always first in line when school shows were being cast. It didn't matter what the show or play was about; all I knew is that I wanted to be a part of it. The experience of being on a television series was beyond my wildest dreams. Sure, it was hard work: early morning calls, long hours, working in all weather situations, learning my lines, and hitting my mark. But I put my heart into it and was lucky that the cast and crew became my friends, encouraged me, and included me in everything. After *Life Goes On* ended, I was fortunate to get several other roles in various TV series, so I continued to work in the industry for a number of years.

Immediately upon returning to New York City, the National Down Syndrome Society (NDSS) asked me to come work for them. I was thrilled, especially since they had decided to launch a publication to be written for and by people with Down syndrome. I became the editor, and it has been very challenging but also quite a learning experience. It was so amazing that I had been a reporter for my school newspaper—it helped to make me feel comfortable in my new role. I have been trained and encouraged by some wonderful people. We worked hard at NDSS on a new format and new name for the magazine so that we could continue to bring the latest and best to all my cohorts with Down syndrome. I also act as the Goodwill Ambassador for the society. I am very proud to be a spokesperson for this outstanding organization. Everyone at NDSS works so hard trying to improve life for all people with Down syndrome. They are the best!

In addition, my friends and former day camp music counselors and I have formed a group, and we travel the country, entertaining and making people aware of the ABILITY of so-called "dis"abled people. My friends have always worked with challenges, and it means so much to them to see the hope that they give to children and parents alike.

My days are full with all these endeavors, and I want to continue to be involved. To me, it's like when you are watching television and have a remote control in your hand; you have a choice of two buttons, rewind and fast forward. Well I have just rewound by reminiscing about my school years, my many experiences, and my jobs. Now, I think I'll push fast forward and try to visualize what I want to do in the future. It's almost like a Christmas wish box: I want to continue to work for the National Down Syndrome Society and get more involved with self-advocacy. I truly believe that we should learn to speak up for ourselves so people know how we really feel about all matters concerning our lives.

I want to continue working and traveling with my friends, spreading the word *ABILITY*, not *disability*, to everyone.

Show business is still of great interest to me. I would like to become a project consultant, write and perform and create my own ideas . . .

and

I want to be independent, living and doing things on my own.
I believe in myself, I like to work hard, and I will never give up
when I want to accomplish something.

We all must keep in mind: The Future is Ours!!

14

■■■

Aiming High

MIA PETERSON

■■■

GROWING UP

I grew up in a small town called Webster City, Iowa. When I was growing up, I did most of the same things other kids did. I went to school in my neighborhood with my two sisters, Missy and Jana. I also went to the library for "storytime" with them. I learned how to check out books. I took swimming lessons and was even on the swim team. I was in 4-H, and I played softball. I also took piano lessons and performed in recitals in front of a lot of people. I graduated from high school with my friends in 1993. In Webster City, I learned how to get around town by walking everywhere I needed to go. Now that I am an adult living in Cincinnati, Ohio, I *still* walk almost everywhere I need to go!

SUPPORTS AND DREAMS

The kind of supports that I need are ones that teach me how to be more independent and safe in my neighborhood, like living on a budget and learning to cook and shop for food. I am good at making friends in my community, working out at my YMCA, serving as a lector at my church, and getting around in my neighborhood. The way I learned these things is by making friends who taught me how to do these things.

Because I was new to Cincinnati and I never lived on my own, I began my new move to Cincinnati by living with a family. For 6 months, I lived with a family in Hyde Park who had two children. I helped take care of the children for my room and board. The oldest child, age 2, has Down syndrome. I was excited to use my child care skills and help her learn new things.

After 6 months, I was ready for more independence. At Capabilities Unlimited, we have a "visitors apartment." Our office is in a two-family house. So if I needed help, there was always someone close by. Most of the time, I do things by myself. I moved there so I could learn more of what it is like to be independent. I had a bedroom, kitchen, and bathroom. I learned how to cook, how not to be scared living by myself, how to take care of cleaning my home, and how to start living on a budget.

In 1999, I met one of my biggest dreams, and that was living on my own in my own apartment! Another big dream was being able to take college classes. I have taken two so far and look forward to taking more.

One of my biggest dreams was to have a boyfriend. I met my boyfriend 2 years ago at a self-advocacy conference in California, where I was a keynote speaker. He lives in California, and I live in Ohio. We talk on the telephone every day, e-mail each other, and visit each other as often as we can. We have a very good relationship with each other, and our families like one another. We have gone on vacation together. We have gone to Hawaii and to Las Vegas so far. We are planning another trip to Las Vegas right now.

The last dream I want to talk about is the one of starting my own business. In 2001, I started my own business called Aiming High. What I do is give presentations on different topics related to self-determination and self-advocacy. I also recorded a song on a CD called "I Am Here." It is based on a poem I wrote. A young girl was sitting on a corner, feeling all alone. A friend took her hand, wiped her tears away, and said, "I am here." I want other people to know I am here for them.

I am also a certified co-facilitator for "Using the 7 Habits of Highly Effective People." This is an adapted version of Stephen Covey's *The Seven Habits of Highly Effective People* for people with developmental disabilities.

ACCOMPLISHMENTS

I trained to run the 5-mile leg of the Cincinnati Flying Pig Marathon. I have done that for 3 years now, and I met my goal. Because I like to run, my running has brought me a very big honor, and it was so exciting! The United States Olympic Committee asked me to carry the torch for the 2002 Winter Olympic games! I ran with the torch as it went through the streets of Cincinnati on its way to Salt Lake City, Utah. Isn't that cool?!

I also gave testimony in front of the United States Senate Hearing in celebration of the 10 years of the Americans with Disabilities Act. I was the only person with Down syndrome presenting at that hearing.

I was a researcher for two research studies. One project was on how people with Down syndrome learn language with a linguist from California, and the other was on "Healthy Lifestyles for Adults with Down Syndrome: What Do We Know" with a registered dietician from Oregon. For both research studies, we wrote surveys that self-advocates answered. What we learned about language was that when we talked to strangers it was harder for us to speak, but if we talked to our family and friends, we learned how to speak faster. That was very important to find out.

The second research program on healthy lifestyles taught me one very important thing. Many people with Down syndrome have a problem gaining weight . . . even me! When I talk about this project I like to tell a story. "If you had a cookie and ate it, you would burn the calories a lot faster than me. Now, if I had a cookie and ate it, I would not burn the calories as fast as you do. The reason is my metabolism rate is slower than people who do not have Down syndrome."

For a long time people have made decisions about people with disabilities by discussing what they think and do. Now, we are finding out what people with Down syndrome really think and do by asking them. That is why I think this research is so important. I am asking about what WE know, not what our parents know. This could really be important in understanding people with Down syndrome better.

For my future, I would like to continue my personal business, buy a house or condo, continue my relationship with my boyfriend, keep being independent, finish my book *Take the Challenge, Take the Risk,* do an exercise video, start another CD, and learn how to drive. Mostly, I want the opportunity to keep being a self-advocate and advocate for others as well because I know it is one way I can make a difference.

Please remember to reach out towards the stars because we are the stars. Keep learning, living, and giving. Keep aiming high! Trust me—if I can do it, you can do it, too!

REFERENCES

Americans with Disabilities Act of 1990, PL 101-336, 42 U.S.C. 12101 *et seq.*
Covey, S.R. (1990). *The seven habits of highly effective people: Restoring the character ethic.* New York: Fireside.

... 15 ...

Supporting Adults to Live in the Community

Beyond the Continuum

Steven J. Taylor

Recent years have seen the emergence of new approaches for supporting people with Down syndrome and other developmental disabilities to live in the community. Referred to as *supported living, housing and supports,* or *self-determination* (individualized funding), these approaches represent a radical departure from the traditional continuum of residential services. This chapter provides critiques of the principle of least restrictive environment and the traditional residential services continuum and also describes the characteristics of a supported-living approach that is more desirable because it gives people with Down syndrome and other developmental disabilities clearer control over where and how they live.

RESIDENTIAL CONTINUUM

Since its earliest conceptualization, residential considerations for people with Down syndrome and other developmental disabilities have been defined in terms of a continuum, an ordered sequence of placements that vary according to the degree of restrictiveness (see Figure 15.1). A

The preparation of this chapter was supported through a subcontract with the Research and Training Center on Community Living, University of Minnesota, supported by the U.S. Department of Education, Office of Special Education and Rehabilitative Services, National Institute on Disability and Rehabilitation Research (NIDRR), through Contract No. H133B031116. Members of the Center are encouraged to express their opinions; however, these do not necessarily represent the official position of NIDRR, and no endorsement should be inferred. This chapter is a revised version of a chapter originally published in Nadel, L., & Rosenthal, D. (1995). (Eds.), *Down syndrome: Living and learning in the community.* New York: Wiley-Liss; reprinted with permission from John Wiley & Sons, Inc. For further information on issues raised in this chapter, please visit http://thechp.syr.edu.

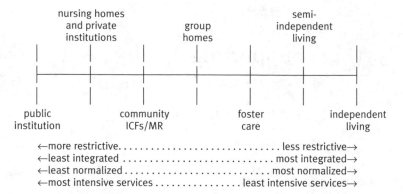

Figure 15.1. The traditional residential continuum. (From Taylor, S.J. [1988]. Caught in the continuum: A critical analysis of the principle of the least restrictive environment. *Journal of The Association for Persons with Severe Handicaps, 13*[1], 45–53; adapted by permission.) (*Key:* ICFs/MR, intermediate care facilities for people with mental retardation.)

common way of representing the least restrictive environment continuum is a straight line running from the most to the least restrictive alternative or, alternatively, a hierarchical cascade of placement options (Hitzing, 1980; Reynolds, 1962; Schalock, 1983). The most restrictive placements are also the most segregated and offer the most intensive services; the least restrictive placements are the most inclusive and independent and offer the least intensive services. The assumption is that every person with a developmental disability can be located somewhere along this continuum based on individual needs.

The residential continuum runs from institutions (the most restrictive environment) to independent living (the least restrictive environment). Between these extremes are nursing homes and private institutions, community intermediate care facilities for people with mental retardation, community residences or group homes, foster care, and semi-independent living or transitional apartments. A common justification of institutions is that they prepare people with developmental disabilities, especially those with severe disabilities, to live in less restrictive environments (see Crissey & Rosen, 1986; Walsh & McCallion, 1987). The residential continuum assumes that people with Down syndrome and other developmental disabilities will move progressively to less and less restrictive environments, until they are able to live independently.

LEAST RESTRICTIVE ENVIRONMENT PRINCIPLE

Outside of discussions of its legal and constitutional dimensions (Burgdorf, 1980; Turnbull, 1981), the least restrictive environment principle, as a policy direction, has received relatively little critical analysis in the field of developmental disabilities. The soundness of the principle generally has been assumed by practitioners and scholars. Although books, articles, and policies have been written on living and learning in the least restrictive environment (Bruininks & Lakin, 1985), the meaning and implications of the principle as a foundation on which to build services have not been thoroughly and critically explored.

Arriving at a precise definition of *least restrictive environment* is difficult because the term is used so variously by people in the field; however, out of the many usages a common meaning can be identified. The principle of least restrictive environment for residential, educational, vocational, and other services may be defined as follows: Services for a person with developmental disabilities should be designed according to a range of program options varying in terms of restriction, normalization, independence, and inclusion, with a presumption in favor of environments that are as independent and inclusive as can be accommodated by the severity of the person's disability. Nevertheless, while it has its advantages, the least restrictive environment principle and the associated residential continuum model are characterized by several serious conceptual and philosophical flaws (Taylor, 1988, 2001).

1. *The least restrictive environment principle legitimates restrictive environments.* Implicit in the principle is the assumption that there are circumstances under which the most restrictive environment would be appropriate. In other words, to conceptualize services in terms of restriction is to legitimate more restrictive settings. As long as services are conceptualized in this manner, some people will end up in restrictive environments. In most cases, they will be people with severe disabilities.

2. *The least restrictive environment principle confuses segregation and inclusion, on the one hand, with intensity of services, on the other.* As represented by the continuum, least restrictive environment equates segregation with the most intensive services and inclusion with the least intensive services. The principle assumes that the least restrictive, most inclusive settings are incapable of providing the intensive services needed by people with severe disabilities. When viewed from this perspective, it follows that people with severe disabilities will require the most restrictive and segregated settings; however, segregation and inclusion, on the one hand, and intensity of services, on the other, are separate dimensions. In fact, some of the most segregated settings have provided the least effective services (Blatt & Kaplan, 1966; Blatt, Ozolins, & McNally, 1979; Center on Human Policy, 1979; Kim, Larson, & Lakin, 2001; Stancliffe & Lakin, 2004).

3. *The least restrictive environment principle is based on a "readiness model."* Also implicit in the least restrictive environment principle is the assumption that people with developmental disabilities must "earn the right" to move to the least restrictive environment. In other words, the person must "get ready" or "be prepared" to live, work, or go to school in inclusive settings, with many residential and vocational programs designed to be "transitional." The irony is that the most restrictive placements do not prepare people for the least restrictive placements. Institutions do not prepare people for community living, segregated day programs do not prepare people for competitive work, and segregated schooling does not prepare students for inclusive schooling.

4. *The least restrictive environment principle supports the dominance of professionals' decisions over the decisions of individuals receiving services.* Inclusion is ultimately a moral and philosophical issue, not a professional one, yet least restrictive environment invariably is framed in terms of professional judgments regarding "individual needs." The phrase *least restrictive environment* is almost always qualified with words such as *appropriate, necessary, feasible,* and *possible* (and never with *desired* or *wanted*), and professionals ultimately determine what is appropriate, possible, feasible, or necessary for individuals receiving services.

5. *The least restrictive environment principle tends to allow infringements on people's rights.* Least restrictive environment is a seductive concept; government should act in a manner that least restricts the rights and liberties of individuals. When applied categorically to people with developmental disabilities, however, the least restrictive environment principle sanctions infringements on basic rights to freedom and community participation beyond those imposed on people without disabilities. The question implied by least restrictive environment is not whether people with developmental disabilities should be restricted but to what extent (Turnbull, 1981).

6. *The least restrictive environment principle implies that people must move as they develop and change.* As the least restrictive environment principle is commonly conceptualized, people with Down syndrome and other developmental disabilities are expected to move toward increasingly less restrictive environments. Schalock wrote, "The existence of a functioning system of community services would provide a range of living and training environments that facilitate client movement along a series of continua" (1983, p. 22). Even if

people moved smoothly through a continuum, their lives would be a series of stops between transitional placements. People with developmental disabilities sometimes move to "less restrictive environments" only because new programs open up or space is needed to accommodate people with more severe disabilities. This can destroy any sense of home and may disrupt relationships with roommates, neighbors, and friends.

7. *The least restrictive environment principle directs attention to physical settings rather than to the services and supports people need to be included in the community.* As Gunnar Dybwad (personal communication, February, 1985) has stated, "Every time we identify a need in this field, we build a building." By its nature, the principle of the least restrictive environment emphasizes facilities and environments designed specifically for people with developmental disabilities. The field of developmental disabilities has defined its mission in terms of creating "facilities" (first large ones and now smaller ones) and "programs," rather than providing the services and supports to enable people with developmental disabilities to participate in the same settings used by other people.

NEW COMMUNITY-BASED CONTINUUM

Critical examination of the principle of the least restrictive environment has led to the creation of a new "community-based" continuum. Critics of the traditional continuum rightfully reject the most restrictive and segregated environments and the assumption that segregated settings prepare people with Down syndrome and other developmental disabilities to function in inclusive settings (Bronston, 1980; Galloway, 1980; Haring & Hansen, 1981; Hitzing, 1980, 1987). Yet these critics stop short of rejecting the least restrictive environment principle itself, which underlies the residential continuum.

The community-based continuum has become a guiding principle for the design of services for people with developmental disabilities and their families. Like the traditional residential continuum, this new continuum envisions a series of options varying in degrees of restriction, inclusion, and normalization, with a preference—but not a mandate—for the least restrictive and most inclusive and normalized settings. It is also generally assumed that people with the most severe disabilities will be found in the more restrictive and less inclusive environments. In contrast to the traditional continuum, the community-based continuum eliminates totally segregated environments located at the most restrictive end of the scale. The range of acceptable options is confined to settings "in the community" that provide for at least some degree of interaction with people without disabilities.

The community-based residential continuum includes settings that range from group living arrangements on the most restrictive end to independent living on the least restrictive end. Specific residential programs found in the community-based continuum include small community-based intermediate care facilities, community residences or group homes, three- to four-person "mini-group homes," apartment clusters, supervised apartments, and "semi-independent living situations" (Halpern, Close, & Nelson, 1986). As in the case of the traditional continuum, it is assumed that people with severe disabilities will be served in the more restrictive congregate settings, albeit small by institutional standards according to the number of people served, and people with mild disabilities will live in less restrictive, smaller apartments.

HOMES, NOT FACILITIES

In contrast to the least restrictive environment continuum model, a supported-living approach focuses on the person, not the facility or the program. As developed by an increasing number of agencies (Taylor, Bogdan, & Lutfiyya, 1995; Taylor, Bogdan, & Racino, 1991; also see O'Brien, 1994), this approach has the following characteristics.

1. *Separation of housing and support services*—In traditional residential programs, a single agency both owns or rents the facility and provides the staff services and supports needed by the people living there. In a supported-living approach, people with disabilities or their families own or rent their homes; agencies coordinate or provide the services people need to live successfully in the community (Taylor et al., 1995). Since people are not guests in someone else's residence, they have maximum control over their personal living space. They do not have to fit into an existing program.

2. *Choice in living arrangements*—Such matters as the location of people's homes and the selection of roommates are based on personal preferences and choices, rather than being predetermined by agency policies. Although some people may choose to live alone, supported living should not be equated with one person per home.

3. *Flexible services*—Under the residential continuum approach, people were expected to leave their residence as their service needs changed. If they required less intensive services, they moved to a less restrictive setting; if they required more intensive services, they moved to a more restrictive setting. Because a supported-

living approach separates housing and supports, people can receive more or less intensive services while remaining in their homes. The services can range from live-in support to various forms of part-time or drop-in assistance. This support or assistance can be provided by paid roommates, neighbors, and personal-assistance aides as well as regular agency staff.

4. *Increased control over services*—Traditionally, people with developmental disabilities have had little or no say over who provided support for them. Many supported-living agencies are attempting to involve people with disabilities and their families in the selection and supervision of support staff or personal-assistance aides. For example, some agencies help many of the people they support to find and hire personal-assistance aides.

5. *Emphasis on personal relationships*—Supported living should not be viewed as a "model" or "program," but a different philosophy of helping people with developmental disabilities to enjoy meaningful lives in the community. Central to this philosophy is an emphasis on personal relationships between people with developmental disabilities and friends, family members, and community members without disabilities. Some supported-living agencies employ "community builders" or include this role in the job descriptions of all staff. Friendships and unpaid relationships are not intended to replace paid staff but to assist people in becoming part of the community (Bogdan & Taylor, 1987).

NEW APPROACHES

A more recent approach for supporting people with Down syndrome and other developmental disabilities is referred to as *self-determination* (Kennedy & Lewin, 1997; Moseley & Nerney, 2000; Sands & Wehmeyer, 1996; Wehmeyer, 1998) or *individualized* or *direct* funding (Moseley, Gettings, & Cooper, 2004; Moseley, Lakin, & Hewitt, 2004; O'Brien, 1999, 2001). Under this approach, individuals or their families receive funding directly, which they can use to purchase or arrange for their own services and supports. The services or supports may be offered by an existing agency or be provided by friends, acquaintances, neighbors, community members, or others recruited by individuals or their families.

According to Nerney and others (Center on Self-Determination, n.d.; Nerney & Shumway, 1996), self-determination is based on the following principles:

1. *Freedom*—ability for an individual, together with freely chosen family and friends, to plan a life with necessary support rather than purchase a program

2. *Authority*—ability for a person with disabilities (with a social support network or circle if needed) to control a certain sum of dollars in order to purchase services

3. *Autonomy*—arranging of resources and personnel, both formal and informal, that will assist an individual with disabilities to live a life in the community rich in community affiliations

4. *Responsibility*—acceptance of a valued role in a person's community through competitive employment, organizational affiliations, spiritual development, and general caring of others in the community, as well as accountability for spending public dollars in ways that are life-enhancing for people with disabilities

SUMMARY

The principle of the least restrictive environment was extremely forward-looking for its time. It emerged in an era in which people with developmental disabilities and their families were offered segregation or nothing at all. As a legal concept and policy direction, least restrictive environment helped to create options and alternatives.

It is now time to find new ideas, concepts, and principles to guide us. The least restrictive environment principle defined the challenge in terms of creating less restrictive and more integrated and normalized environments and programs. Now, we must define the challenge in terms of helping people with developmental disabilities to live successfully in their own homes in the community and to have maximum control over the services they receive.

REFERENCES

Blatt, B., & Kaplan, F. (1966). *Christmas in purgatory: A photographic essay on mental retardation.* Boston: Allyn & Bacon.

Blatt, B., Ozolins, A., & McNally, J. (1979). *The family papers: A return to purgatory.* New York: Longman.

Bogdan, R., & Taylor, S.J. (1987). Conclusion: The next wave. In S.J. Taylor, D. Biklen, & J. Knoll (Eds.), *Community integration for people with severe disabilities* (pp. 209–213). New York: Teachers College Press.

Bronston, W. (1980). Matters of design. In T. Apolloni, J. Cappuccilli, & T.P. Cooke (Eds.), *Towards excellence: Achievements in residential services for persons with disabilities* (pp. 1–17). Baltimore: University Park Press.

Bruininks, R.H., & Lakin, K.C. (Eds.). (1985). *Living and learning in the least restrictive environment.* Baltimore: Paul H. Brookes Publishing Co.

Burgdorf, R.L., Jr. (Ed.). (1980). *The legal rights of handicapped persons: Cases, materials, and text.* Baltimore: Paul H. Brookes Publishing Co.

Center for Self-Determination. (n.d.). *Principles of self-determination.* Ann Arbor, MI: Author.

Center on Human Policy. (1979). *The community imperative: A refutation of all arguments in support of institutionalizing anybody because of mental retardation.* Syracuse, NY: Syracuse University, Center on Human Policy.

Crissey, M.S., & Rosen, M. (Eds.). (1986). *Institutions for the mentally retarded.* Austin, TX: PRO-ED.

Galloway, C. (1980). *The "continuum" and the need for caution.* Unpublished manuscript.

Halpern, A.S., Close, D.W., & Nelson, D.J. (1986). *On my own: The impact of semi-independent living programs for adults with mental retardation.* Baltimore: Paul H. Brookes Publishing Co.

Haring, N.O., & Hansen, C.L. (1981). Perspectives in communitization. In C.L. Hansen (Ed.), *Severely handicapped persons in the community* (pp. 1–27). Seattle: Program Development Assistance System.

Hitzing, W. (1980). ENCOR and beyond. In T. Apolloni., J. Cappuccilli, & T.P. Cooke (Eds.), *Towards excellence: Achievements in residential services for persons with disabilities* (pp. 71–93). Baltimore: University Park Press.

Hitzing, W. (1987). Community living alternatives for persons with autism and severe behavior problems. In D.J. Cohen & A. Donnellan (Eds.), *Handbook of autism and pervasive developmental disorders* (pp. 396–410). New York: John Wiley & Sons.

Kennedy, M., & Lewin, L. (1997). *Fact sheet: Summary of self-determination.* Syracuse, NY: Syracuse University, Center on Human Policy, National Resource Center on Supported Living and Choice.

Kim, S., Larson, S., & Lakin, K.C. (2001). Behavioral outcomes of deinstitutionalization of people with intellectual disabilities: A review of U.S. studies conducted between 1980 and 1999. *Journal of Intellectual and Developmental Disability, 26*(1), 35–50.

Moseley, C., Gettings, R., & Cooper, R. (2004). *Having it your way: Understanding state individual budgeting strategies.* Alexandria, VA: National Association of State Directors of Developmental Disabilities Services.

Moseley, C., Lakin, K.C., & Hewitt, A. (Eds.). (2004). Feature issue on consumer-controlled budgets and persons with disabilities. *IMPACT, 17*(1).

Moseley, C., & Nerney, T. (2000, November/December). Emerging best practices in self-determination. *AAMR News & Notes, 13*(6), 1, 4–5.

Nadel, L., & Rosenthal, D. (Eds.). (1995). *Down syndrome: Living and learning in the community.* New York: Wiley-Liss

Nerney, T., & Shumway, D. (1996, September). *Beyond managed care: Self-determination for people with disabilities.* Durham: University of New Hampshire, Institute on Disability.

O'Brien, J. (1994). Down stairs that are never your own: Supporting people with developmental disabilities in their own homes. *Mental Retardation, 32*(1), 1–6.

O'Brien, J. (1999). *Community engagement: A necessary condition for self-determination and individual funding.* Lithonia, GA: Responsive Systems Associates.

O'Brien, J. (2001). *Paying customers are not enough: The dynamics of individualized funding.* Lithonia, GA: Responsive Systems Associates.

Reynolds, M. (1962). A framework for considering some issues in special education. *Exceptional Children, 28,* 367–370.

Sands, D.J., & Wehmeyer, M.L. (Eds.). (1996). *Self-determination across the life span: Independence and choice for people with disabilities.* Baltimore: Paul H. Brookes Publishing Co.

Schalock, R.L. (1983). *Services for developmentally disabled adults.* Baltimore: University Park Press.

Stancliffe, R., & Lakin, K.C. (2004). *Costs and outcomes of community services for people with intellectual disabilities.* Baltimore: Paul H. Brookes Publishing Co.

Taylor, S.J. (1988). Caught in the continuum: A critical analysis of the principle of the least restrictive environment. *Journal of The Association for Persons with Severe Handicaps, 13*(1), 41–53.

Taylor, S.J. (2001). The continuum and current controversies in the USA. *Journal of Intellectual & Developmental Disability, 26*(1), 15–33.

Taylor, S.J., Bogdan, R., & Lutfiyya, Z.M. (Eds.). (1995). *The variety of community experience: Qualitative studies of family and community life.* Baltimore: Paul H. Brookes Publishing Co.

Taylor, S.J., Bogdan, R., & Racino, J.A. (Eds.). (1991). *The community participation series: Vol. 1. Life in the community: Case studies of organizations supporting people with disabilities.* Baltimore: Paul H. Brookes Publishing Co.

Turnbull, R., with Ellis, J.W., Boggs, E.M., Brookes, P.O., & Biklen, D.P. (Eds.). (1981). *Least restrictive alternatives: Principles and practices.* Washington, DC: American Association on Mental Deficiency.

Walsh, K.K., & McCallion, P. (1987). The role of the small institution in the community services continuum. In R.F. Antonak & J.A. Mulick (Eds.), *Transitions in mental retardation: The community imperative revisited* (Vol. 3, pp. 216–236). Norwood, NJ: Ablex.

Wehmeyer, M.L. (1998). Self-determination and individuals with significant disabilities: Examining meanings and misinterpretations. *Journal of The Association for Persons with Severe Handicaps, 23,* 5–16.

16

■■■

Independent

KATIE MALY

■■■

Let me introduce myself. My name is Katie Maly, and I'm 26 years old. How did I find out about this book? One of my doctors from way back called me to see if I would help him on a book called *Down Syndrome*. I told him I would like to help him.

I was born to Bob and Joyce Maly on May 24, 1978, and they found out that I had Down syndrome. I have one older brother and two sisters and one older sister-in-law. When I was little, my parents wanted me to do all the things that other children were doing, so I played with my neighborhood kids. My parents thought I couldn't do things, but they were wrong, so I joined Girl Scouts, took swim lessons, etc.

When I was little, I went to a lot of public schools, and I was a mainstream kid that went to regular classes. I had three special classes that I went to: math, reading, and therapy for extra help. I'm still not very good at math, but I'm good at reading. When I was still in public schools, I had a hard time of making friends; that's when we had to move to Richmond, VA, and then back here to Cincinnati, OH. When I was in a junior high school, I had a chance to get involved in school activities. After junior high school, I had a chance to go to a Catholic high school. I did more activities there like Queens Men Drama Club.

After I graduated from Purcell Marian in 1997, I was working at two jobs that kept me busy. They were interesting, and I enjoyed both of them. One job was at the YMCA; the other was at the Inclusion Network.

During my senior year of high school, I was asked to think about what kinds of jobs I might want to do. At that time, I went to the people at CUI, which stands for Capabilities Unlimited, Inc. CUI is an organization that trains people with disabilities to speak out for themselves. This is called *self-advocacy*. CUI helps individuals with specific job-related skills.

At CUI, they also asked me what things I might want to do. I have been a member at the YMCA since I was little girl, so I really liked the things the YMCA does. I really wanted to work at the YMCA because I could make new friends. During my junior year of high school, I volunteered there to see if I liked the job and if the staff thought I was a good worker. When it was decided that we both liked each other, we met with CUI to identify the work supports I needed.

I became an intern with CUI to learn the work skills, and the YMCA paid for my training. My job had a lot of responsibilities like taking care of the front desk, answering the telephones, and passing out towels and more. After only 8 months, I was a permanent part-time employee of the YMCA. A new assignment that I did work on was to start a newsletter for the YMCA because they value me as a part of their TEAM.

Another skill I wanted to learn was how to use computers better. CUI was working with the Inclusion Network to find an intern to do desktop publishing for their quarterly newsletter. Because I wanted to learn those skills, I was asked to volunteer for 8 weeks to see if I could learn the job and would like to work there. I became an Inclusion Network intern while I was with CUI. During my internship at the Inclusion Network, I was working on the *Inclusion 2000* project. My next step was to move to the Inclusion Network office that is located in downtown Cincinnati, OH.

I'm on the board at the Down Syndrome Association of Greater Cincinnati (DSAGC). That means I go to a lot of meetings and events that we have. DSAGC gave me an award as the 2001 Self-Advocate of the Year. I gave a speech about what being a self-advocate means to me. It means many things.

It means I have learned to speak for myself about things that are important to me like:

- What hobbies I have
- How I want to dress
- Who my friends are
- What I learned in school
- Plans for my future

Being a self-advocate means that I am not afraid to decide where I will work and live. I work at two jobs right now because I like them both. Each one helps me learn different job skills. It is important to me to keep on learning new things.

Being a self-advocate also means that I have responsibilities to do my part to make the community a better place in which to live and to work.

Finally, I think being a self-advocate means being open to trying new things that I am not always comfortable with, like:

- Meeting new people

- Taking a new bus route

- Learning new jobs

- Going to new places

I would like to say that all of us have abilities and disabilities. Some of us have disabilities that you can see like Down syndrome, and some of us don't. People with different disabilities are proud of themselves. I would like to ask you to let everyone speak and do things for themselves. This is why we are ALL here, to listen and to learn about what other people have to say and to share ideas.

What I do now is that I'm living on my own in Cincinnati, OH, in an apartment that is near Hyde Park square so that I can walk to places. I do my rent and utilities. I have two jobs that I like very much. One of my jobs is to work for Great American Insurance Co. What I do is sort and deliver the mail to different departments.

My other job is at the Inclusion Network (I'm there on Tuesday and Thursday in the afternoon from 1:00 till 5:30). I'm an office assistant. I answer phones, make copies, etc. The easiest way to explain the Inclusion Network is for me to ask a question, "How do you include people with disabilities in your community?" That makes people think and realize there are lots of ways.

Yes, I do sneak my workouts into my schedule before and after work. I have a personal trainer. Her name is Lea. She helps me throughout my workouts.

... 17 ...

Recreation Through Special Olympics

Sports, Fitness, and Well-Being

Siegfried M. Pueschel and Courtney Pastorfield

When the daily work is done and the day comes to a close, everyone needs moments of relaxation to engage in non–work-related activities. After a busy week, when the dust settles and the weekend nears, all people should be able to engage in fun activities, sports, and various other recreational pursuits. Individuals with Down syndrome are no exception. There are also other time periods such as during holidays and vacations when individuals with Down syndrome can find enjoyment engaging in numerous leisure activities.

A wide spectrum of delightful recreational events can contribute to the fulfilling life of a person with Down syndrome, from a simple get together with friends to a splendid cruise on an ocean liner. This multitude of leisure time experiences was just not available decades ago when people with intellectual disabilities were segregated from society and often warehoused in institutions. Fortunately, changes have taken place, and adults with Down syndrome are more often included in regular community life, thanks in large part to the introduction of the Americans with Disabilities Act of 1990 (PL 101-336).

This legislation indicates that all individuals with intellectual disabilities have the right to actively participate in their neighborhood recreation programs. The Americans with Disabilities Act also spells out that all public agencies must provide reasonable physical and programmatic accommodation to support the participation of people with disabilities. Moreover, the law favors inclusive community recreation as the optimal environment for the development of social interaction and friendships for people with Down syndrome and others who may or may not have intellectual disabilities (Schleien, Meyer, Heyne, & Brandt, 1995). Recreational opportunities in the community should provide possibilities for social growth and foster personal development. Although this legislation spells out in detail what recreational involvement should entail, some significant challenges still remain.

Schleien et al. (1995) pointed out that leisure education can play a critical role in the instruction and community life of individuals with Down syndrome. Adults with intellectual disabilities need to find out what recreational opportunities are available and how these activities can enrich their lives. There are a variety of physical activities, including weight lifting, martial arts, soccer, running, and baseball, that can improve motor performance, muscle strength, and cardiovascular fitness. Going to a dance, enjoying an extended walk, learning to draw or paint pictures, or playing an instrument can also build self-confidence and self-esteem. Moreover, joining a gym program, partaking in workouts at the YMCA, taking aerobics classes, engaging in hiking trips, participating in yoga exercises, going fishing, swimming, and canoeing or kayaking are other recreational opportunities that can bring about fitness and provide fun.

There are other recreational possibilities that encourage building social relationships, promoting physical fitness, nurturing creativity and self-expression, and increasing independent functioning.

■ ■ ■ Katherine is a very pleasant 29-year-old lady with Down syndrome who has always enjoyed good health, except for a thyroid disorder that is being treated successfully and a dry skin condition called *xerosis*. She has also been diagnosed to have mitral valve prolapse that, however, does not prevent her from participating in various sports activities. During her school years, Katherine was involved in general physical education activities, and later she joined a health club where she primarily performed aerobic exercises. She is currently working part time at a fast-food restaurant, has a paper route, and enjoys volunteering in a nursing home.

She shares a home with her mother and her younger sister. Katherine often helps with household chores. Her deceased father was a martial arts instructor and introduced Katherine to karate. Katherine is determined to get her black belt next year.

In the evening, Katherine likes to go for walks with her mother, and on weekends she often invites friends to go bowling. During the wintertime, she likes to ski. She has not done so well with skating, however, because she has some problems with balance.

While on vacation, Katherine was hiking in the mountains but had difficulties keeping up with her sister. She had gained some weight during the last year and decided to limit her caloric intake and avoid starchy and fatty foods. With her savings, Katherine has also bought a stationary bicycle and uses it almost daily.

Katherine loves to go to dances. Last year, she joined a group of friends and went on a cruise. There she met a nice young man with Down syndrome, and they have been dating since. Katherine visited him once, and he in turn stayed with

Katherine's family for a few days. They watched movies, went out for dinner, and took long walks.

Katherine's leisure activities and her physical involvement most likely have contributed to her overall good health and fitness. She has been fortunate to be supported by her family and her community and has gained confidence and self-esteem. She intends to continue to be actively involved in community life and to be a vigorous self-advocate. ■ ■ ■

Recreation improves the quality of life of many people with Down syndrome. Successful involvement in recreation will also provide people with Down syndrome with confidence, increase their self-esteem, teach them to take chances, and allow them to have a good time. Among the many recreational activities available to individuals with intellectual disabilities, one stands out in particular—the Special Olympics. Adults with Down syndrome with various abilities may participate without age limit, have fun, and enjoy their accomplishments during training and competition at the Special Olympics.

TRAINING AND COMPETITION

"In a world where poverty, war and oppression have often dimmed people's hopes, Special Olympics athletes rekindle that hope with their spiritual strength, their moral excellence, and their physical achievements. As we hope for the best in them, hope is reborn in us." —Eunice Kennedy Shriver (1995)

Since 1968, when Eunice Kennedy Shriver founded Special Olympics, the organization has been providing outstanding preparation for and competition in more than 26 sports categories for people with intellectual disabilities, including those with Down syndrome (Dinn, 1996). These athletes may participate in various training programs and compete at local, state, national, regional, and world Special Olympics Games. Athletes with Down syndrome who meet the established eligibility criteria can join Special Olympics by contacting their local Special Olympics group or may be referred to Special Olympics by parents, special education programs, The Arc of the United States, and other organizations.

At the outset, it is important to determine the athlete's skills, what sports activities will be of primary interest to the individual, and in what way the coach can be of assistance to the athlete. Also, specific objectives will need to be developed that will allow the athlete to experience success. Specially trained volunteer coaches, students, the athletes' family members, and others will work with the athletes and prepare them for the games.

Athletes usually train with a volunteer coach for at least 8 weeks before competing in the sports of their choice. Pertaining to team sports, initially basic skill training will be pursued, later leading to team practice sessions. The training program will often entail one or more practice sessions each week. In addition to individual and group training, athletes may also find extra practice time during the week or on weekends. Also, family home training programs can help the athletes to develop their sports skills.

In order to perform optimally, before each training session, competition, and other sports activities, athletes should engage in warm-up, stretching, and range-of-motion exercises, aerobics, and/or physical conditioning activities. During various activities, including warm-up sessions, training exercises, and competition, it is advisable to use a reward system and positive reinforcement with words of praise, pats on the back, and an approving smile that will encourage the athletes to perform at their best.

After having engaged in a successful 8-week or more training program, the athletes are now ready for competition. Athletes are placed in a division so that they can compete against others of similar age and ability. Thus, each athlete or team will have a chance of winning. Although winning is a goal for everyone, the real meaning of Special Olympics is well expressed in the Special Olympics Oath: "Let me win, but if I cannot win, let me be brave in the attempt." After the competition, each athlete receives a medal (gold, silver, or bronze) or a ribbon.

Because Special Olympics athletes have to abide by the rules of their sports just like athletes in any other sports program, trained officials for every event will be present during the competition. Nowadays, Special Olympics athletes are also participating as game officials. These individuals are certified officials through sports governing bodies and usually are joined by a mentor official to officiate sports at the games.

Moreover, Special Olympics athletes are vocal advocates for their own causes, and many are eloquent speakers who can ably convey their Special Olympics experiences. These advocates give presentations at meetings of civic groups, at governmental and policy hearings, and at other places where people are discussing various issues relating to Special Olympics and intellectual disability in general.

Special Olympics Unified Sports

In the mid-1980s, Special Olympics Unified Sports was introduced, where athletes with and without intellectual disabilities train and compete as a team. This program has been very successful because it offers a challenge to all participants. The Unified Sports activities not only encourage athletes with Down syndrome and other intellectual disabilities to improve their skills but also have a positive effect on athletes without disabilities. Unified Sports provides a feeling of equal status among the athletes and encourages new friendships. Special Olympics Unified Sports are carried out in basketball, softball, soccer, volleyball, bowling, golf, and skiing, among others. No other program has a better track record of bonding athletes with and without intellectual disabilities in a way that promotes understanding and acceptance in the realm of sports. To learn more about this program, please visit http://www.specialolympics.org/Special+Olympics+Public+Website/English/Compete/Unified_Sports/default.htm.

Motor Activities Training

Special Olympics has also developed a program for athletes with significant physical disabilities who ordinarily would not be able to participate in regular training and competition. These individuals may be enrolled in the Motor Activities Training Program that focuses on building basic motor skills. With enhanced training, some of these athletes will improve in their motor skills to a point where they may move on to regular competition events for athletes with lower ability levels. Other athletes may remain in the Motor Activities Training Program and continue to work on activities at their own ability level.

Special Olympics World Games

Although local, state, national, and regional Special Olympics Games enjoy great popularity, the Special Olympics World Games are a rising star. Every 2 years, athletes from all over the world gather to join the Special Olympics World Games, alternating between summer and winter. In an atmosphere of peace and brotherhood, athletes from numerous countries travel to compete in various sports activities, have fun, and make new friends. There are opportunities to learn about the customs of athletes coming from different parts of the world.

■■■ Paul is an outgoing, friendly 32-years-young man with Down syndrome with a cheerful personality. He started to become involved in Special Olympics sports at the age of 8 years and has not stopped since then. He is so proud of his accomplishments and likes to display his large collection of gold and silver medals. He has demonstrated so well that individuals with Down syndrome are capable of participating and succeeding in various sports activities.

After he came in first in the 100-meter dash during the last competition and heard the applause and cheers of so many onlookers, Paul's facial expression of pride said it all. Paul is not only a good runner, but he also excels in gymnastics and swimming. Actually, free-style swimming is his favorite, and he was invited twice to participate in the Special Olympics World Summer Games. Recently, Paul became involved in Special Olympics Unified Sports, where he competed with athletes without disabilities during a softball game.

Beyond Special Olympics, Paul loves to engage in other sports activities such as soccer, basketball, and tennis. He likes to keep himself fit and watches his diet. As Paul demonstrates so well, his involvement in Special Olympics has enhanced his well-being and his quality of life. He has gained self-confidence and self-worth. ■ ■ ■

HEALTH ISSUES

Most athletes with Down syndrome desire to succeed and to win. Success, however, can only come through hard work. Athletes will first have to learn about the sport they would like to become engaged in. Moreover, they should learn to pursue a healthy lifestyle, find out about eating a balanced diet in moderation, keep their bodies fit, and of course, practice hard for the sports of their choice. Training appropriately and pursuing a healthy and happy lifestyle will also improve other areas of the athletes' lives.

All Special Olympics athletes are required to have a physical examination prior to participating. If a person with Down syndrome continues to partake in sports, he or she should be reexamined every 3 years and will need to undergo a radiological examination of the cervical spine. If atlantoaxial instability (described in Chapter 3) is identified, then the person should not participate in certain sports activities, such as diving at the start of swimming, butterfly stroke, pentathlon, high jump, soccer, equestrian sports, alpine skiing, and other sports that potentially could lead to neck injuries with subsequent neurologic damage. There are, however, many other sports and recreational activities in which people with atlantoaxial instability can participate, such as bowling, running, golf, and skating.

In the course of conducting training and competition, Special Olympics has found that athletes often have undetected or unappreciated medical or physical conditions. Therefore, Special Olympics developed Healthy Athletes Health Promotion Programs that offer free screening and health education services at many of its games. The various components of the Healthy Athletes Health Promotion Programs include Special Smiles (dental), Opening Eyes (vision), Healthy Hearing (audiology), FUNfitness (physical therapy), Fit Feet (podiatry), and Health Promotion (health and wellness). The latter component, Health Promotion, provides athletes with information to establish healthy lifestyle choices relating to diet, exercise, and disease prevention. These efforts are now extending into local communities with year-round Health Promotion to maintain fitness and good lifestyles. The success of the Healthy Athletes Health Promotion Programs became particularly apparent during the 2003 Special Olympics World Games that were held in Dublin, Ireland.

RESEARCH

Pertaining to individuals with Down syndrome, it is of interest to analyze the Special Olympics Games that took place in 1991, 1993, and 1995. At that time, more than 13% of all participating athletes were individuals with Down syndrome. Those athletes reportedly had fewer medical concerns such as heart problems, seizure disorders, and hearing and vision impairments than athletes without Down syndrome did. Athletes with Down syndrome participated in all Special Olympics sports alongside individuals with other intellectual disabilities. In particular, athletes with Down syndrome had higher participation rates in gymnastics, aquatics, distance running, figure skating, golf, bowling, power lifting, and equestrian events compared with other athletes with intellectual disabilities. These data indicate that individuals with Down syndrome, if given the opportunity, will actively take part in Special Olympics events in large numbers (Songster, Smith, Evans, Munson, & Behen, 1997).

Dykens and Cohen (1996) carried out an important study. The results of this investigation indicate that the myth that people with Down syndrome have more health problems and accomplish less than individuals without Down syndrome is indeed incorrect. Previous assumptions that individuals with Down syndrome have lower skills than other Special Olympics athletes are likewise not true. These authors clearly showed that adults with Down syndrome, when provided with appropriate instructions, adequate training, and good coaching, will succeed and contribute significantly to the achievements of Special Olympics.

There has been ample documentation that, among other factors, Special Olympics is improving the quality of life of many athletes with Down syndrome. Successful involvement in Special Olympics sports will also provide athletes with confidence, increase their self-esteem, teach them to take chances, and allow them to have a good time. Pertinent research data as well as anecdotal reports mention the effect of Special Olympics on self-esteem. Dykens and Cohen (1996) found that Special Olympics athletes had higher social competence scores and more positive self-perception than individuals in the control group who had never participated in Special Olympics activities. The authors also noted that the length of time individuals had taken part in Special Olympics was a powerful predictor of social competence.

Beyond the personal triumph of the athletes and their accomplishments, Special Olympics is demonstrating to society what people with intellectual disabilities are capable of doing. Individuals who previously have been shunned, institutionalized, maltreated, and forgotten now are showing the world that they are brave, resilient, and competitive people. With their involvement in Special Olympics, they display their enormous strength of character, varied skills, discipline, and foremost their exuberant humanity. As free citizens in a democratic society, individuals with Down syndrome and other intellectual disabilities have the right to be fully integrated in every aspect of society (see also Chapter 19).

LOOKING TOWARD THE FUTURE

As we have witnessed the exponential rise of Special Olympics during the past decades, from the early beginning in Eunice Kennedy Shriver's backyard to the ever-expanding international programs culminating in exemplary Special Olympics World Games, we have to ask ourselves what the future will hold for athletes with Down syndrome. With the increase in life expectancy of people in general, and in individuals with Down syndrome in particular, and when taking into consideration medical, educational, and other advances, in the future, we will most likely see older people continuing to participate in the Special Olympics movement. Thus, the community will have to adjust to this trend and help in developing healthier lifestyles for this aging population, and specific programs like Special Olympics will have to expand both the availability and the types of sports programs that they provide to optimize the functional participation of this aging group of still-active people. Other Special Olympics programs, such as the Partners Club, a peer coaching program and sports partnership that integrates Special Olympics teams and school varsity teams, will most likely continue to grow and will hopefully be encountered more often in the future.

There is a continued need for community outreach to attract people to Special Olympics programs as coaches and volunteers. More importantly, we must strive to include the millions of people with intellectual disabilities who have never heard of Special Olympics, including those people who live in developing countries, so that they also may become part of the Special Olympics movement.

In the future, we hope that individuals from all walks of life will be inspired to celebrate the unlimited spirit by sharing the skills, courage, and joy expressed so vividly by the many people with Down syndrome who take part in recreation activities and the Special Olympics.

SUMMARY

Individuals with Down syndrome deserve to relax after a hard week through participation in recreational activities. There are numerous recreational possibilities that encourage building social relationships, promoting physical fitness, nurturing creativity and self-expression, and increasing independent functioning. Special Olympics is one example of a program that encourages individuals with Down syndrome to participate in sports and improve their self-esteem. Further discussion on general recreational involvements is provided in Chapter 19.

REFERENCES

Americans with Disabilities Act of 1990, PL 101-336, 42 U.S.C. §§ 201 *et seq.*

Dinn, S. (1996). *Hearts of gold. A celebration of Special Olympics and its heroes.* Coodbridge, CT: Blackbirch Press.

Dykens, E.M., & Cohen, D.J. (1996). Effects of Special Olympics International on social competence in persons with mental retardation. *Journal of the American Academy of Child and Adolescent Psychiatry, 35,* 223–229.

Schleien, S.J., Meyer, L.H., Heyne, L.A., & Brandt, B.B. (1995) *Lifelong leisure skills and lifestyles for persons with developmental disabilities.* Baltimore: Paul H. Brookes Publishing Co.

Shriver, E.K. (1995). *You have the right* [Opening ceremony speech]. Washington, DC: Special Olympics International.

Songster, T.B., Smith, G., Evans, M., Munson, D., & Behen, D. (1997). Special Olympics and athletes with Down syndrome. In S.M. Pueschel & M. Sustrova (Eds.), *Adolescents with Down syndrome. Toward a more fulfilling life* (pp. 341–357). Baltimore: Paul H. Brookes Publishing Co.

18

###

Imagine the Possibilities

KAREN ELIZABETH GAFFNEY

###

My friend, Dr. Pueschel, asked me to tell you, his readers, a little bit about myself and my experiences growing up with Down syndrome. I would like to start by telling you a little bit about who I am and what I am doing now. Then, I will tell you a little bit about how I got to where I am today.

I am Karen Gaffney, and I am 26 years old. I live in Portland, Oregon, with my parents and my brother, Brian. I graduated from St. Mary's Academy, here in Portland, Oregon, where I earned a regular high school diploma. I was on the swim team at St. Mary's, and I earned my letter for swimming in my sophomore, junior, and senior years. I joined the Science Club, too, mainly because it was a nice group of girls who invited me to join!

After I graduated from St. Mary's, I went on to Portland Community College, where I earned my associate of science degree and a teacher's aide certificate. I worked with a counselor there who helped me pick the right classes to take. He also talked to the professors ahead of time to make sure there were no surprises on the first day of class!

And there never were any surprises the first day of class.

I am currently working 3 days a week as a teacher's aide. I work with 3-year-olds in a Head Start program. I work part time because I have other responsibilities. I wanted to be able to share my experiences with others and give back to those who helped me.

About 6 years ago, a professor from Portland State University, Dr. Jean Edwards, helped me start a non-profit organization that is dedicated to championing the journey to full inclusion in families, schools, the workplace, and the community for people with Down syndrome and other disabilities. When I am not working as a teacher's aide, I am working at our non-profit organization. I earn money for our programs by giving talks and workshops all over the country.

When I was taking classes in early childhood development at Portland Community College, I was very surprised to learn that children with developmental disabilities were not even allowed into regular schools. I was very lucky that many families, before I was even born, worked together to change all that. I owe those families a great deal because by the time I was born, early intervention programs were set up to help children like me get a head start on learning and overcoming our limitations. Laws had been passed to make sure students like me were allowed to go to school with everyone else!

I started school when I was 3 months old, and I have been learning ever since. I was ready for the first grade when it was time for me to go, but some of my teachers weren't ready for me. It was not an easy road for me, but at least I have had the opportunity to try. I had that opportunity because of all those people who worked hard to change minds, to pass laws, and to open doors. I am very grateful to those who have done that for me.

I have had the opportunity to give talks and present workshops to audiences all around the country, where I usually talk about overcoming limitations and what can be accomplished with positive expectations. I happen to have a lot of personal experience with that! Sometimes, I talk about the keys to success for inclusion in the classroom and the kinds of things that helped me along the way.

I also give workshops on physical fitness for other young people like me with disabilities. I talk about the importance of regular exercise and how to set up a regular exercise program. You see, I am a long-distance swimmer. A really long, long-distance swimmer.

I started swimming when I was 9 MONTHS old, and I have been swimming ever since. I usually swim about 2 miles every day, and I work out on weights, too. A few years ago, I became the first person with Down syndrome to swim a relay across the English Channel. I was the first, but I don't want to be the only person with Down syndrome to have made that kind of swim. So, I keep trying to recruit other swimmers to share that experience with me. You know, it's not so bad swimming the English Channel. You really do get used to the cold water, after a mile or two!

I love talking to audiences about my English Channel swim and all the challenges we faced. But, when I talk to the students in the schools, I usually talk about one of the biggest challenges I faced while I was growing up. It was not the long summers I spent in body casts, recovering from five different hip surgeries. It was not all the extra time I spent studying, just to keep up with others in my class; it was not all the homework or the tests. It was having friends.

I had to work hard to keep up with everyone else in school, and I still do now. Sometimes, I can't hear everything that the others are saying. Sometimes, I can't see people clearly unless they are right in front of me. I can't see everything on the board or bulletin boards. I don't always understand things right away. But, with a lot of hard work and effort, I get there.

Many people like me may have some of these same difficulties. But I know, just like me, they want to learn, they want to understand what is going on around them, and even more importantly, they want to belong—and they are probably working very hard in ways others can't see to do just that!!

School playgrounds and gyms, school hallways, and cafeterias can be pretty lonely places for people like me . . . students that everyone considers different from them. Behind the color of our skin, the shape of our eyes, the sizes of our bodies or our abilities to learn, we are all people first. We ALL want to feel like we belong, like we are INCLUDED.

Something that may have helped me would have been talking more openly about the acceptance of people with differences in the schools. Everyone has them. It's just that most people can hide their differences better than I can. I think we all need to work together to help students talk about these things more openly. We need to help pave the way for acceptance for those who are different. And I am trying to do just that in some of the schools in my community.

I am working with some of the high schools in our area on a new program that we think will make a huge difference! We call this program, the "Friends First Network!" It is a new club for all students. We are working with the schools to get the Friends First programs started—where students with disabilities will meet up with students without disabilities—they come together, they form a club, and they work together on social service projects. In the process, they will all learn more about each other and what it takes to just be a friend. It is my dream to have a network of Friends First clubs all over the country, making a difference every single day!

I am trying to do my best to make the most of what others have done for me, and I am trying to use my experiences to help others reach out and achieve as well. I know that many people with Down syndrome have faced challenges that are much more difficult than swimming a relay across the English Channel, or giving a talk in front a huge group of people. And we face those challenges every single day.

And we overcome them. We CAN do it. We CAN go the distance. With high expectations and support from our families and others, we will do our part to reach our highest potential.

You can read more about my experiences and my work by visiting my website at http://www.karengaffneyfoundation.com. Thank you for giving me the opportunity to share my experiences and my story with you.

... 19 ...

Contribution and Community Life

Fostering Social Relationships,
Community Participation, and Full Inclusion

Angela Novak Amado and K. Charlie Lakin

Since the 1970s, there has been a substantial change in the inclusion and active participation of people with disabilities in social, economic, political, spiritual, and other aspects of American society. For people with Down syndrome and other developmental disabilities, changing social values and expectations, increased acceptance, and effective advocacy manifested in social service systems have all contributed to this increased inclusion. Other chapters in this book describe some of these influences, including the dramatic growth in the self-advocacy movement; increased consumer control over service funding; and new laws, regulations, and funding streams that have influenced service-system design. This chapter addresses several aspects of the inclusion of individuals with Down syndrome and other developmental disabilities in the larger community, including both physical and social inclusion. Numerous changes in recent decades will be reviewed, as well as current status and anticipated future directions and challenges.

The nation's commitment to achievement of community inclusion for adults with developmental disabilities has a number of aspects. It is possible to consider inclusion as having four levels, all of which are important in achieving the highest and most satisfying levels of inclusion. They are 1) *physical inclusion,* or presence in the community; 2) *social inclusion,* or having interactions and meaningful relationships with others in the community; 3) *cultural inclusion,* or having valued roles and opportunities to contribute to the community; and 4) *full citizenship,* or living life on the same terms, with the same freedom and self-determination, as is typical of other community members. Each of these levels of inclusion is addressed in this chapter.

PHYSICAL INCLUSION

There are many aspects to physical inclusion, including where people live, where they work, their recreation, and opportunities to worship. This section addresses substantial changes in residential arrangements that allow for increased physical inclusion as well as national commitments that have dramatically altered the degree of physical inclusion of individuals with disabilities in the larger society.

Living in the Community

In approximately 25 years, publicly financed residential supports for individuals with intellectual disabilities and developmental disabilities (ID/DD) have been largely transformed from being an institutionally based system into a system of community- and home-based supports. In June 2003, of the estimated 437,289 individuals with ID/DD receiving residential and nursing facility services and supports, 75% (329,807) lived in community settings of 15 or fewer residents. Of those, 84% (275,461) lived in settings of 6 or fewer residents, and 54% (177,260) lived in settings of 3 or fewer residents (Lakin, Prouty, Polister, & Coucouvanis, 2003). These statistics do not include the estimated 500,000 individuals who received various support services, in addition to education, while living in the homes of birth or adoptive family members. Figure 19.1 summarizes the changes between 1982 and 2003 in the number of people in various sizes and types of residential settings in which people with ID/DD lived outside their family homes.

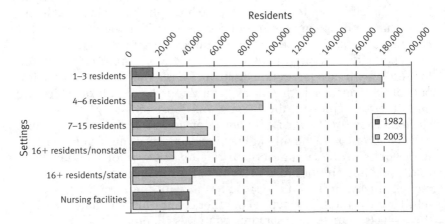

Figure 19.1. Changes in populations of individuals with intellectual and developmental disabilities in different sizes and types of residential settings.

At the same time, as has always been the case, most people with ID/DD were not living away from their family home. According to estimates from the National Health Interview Survey–Disability Supplement (Larson, Lakin, Anderson, & Kwak, 2001), in 2003 there were an estimated 4.2 million individuals with ID/DD in the United States, about 1.5% of the total population. Approximately 462,000 of these individuals were in residential support arrangements other than homes shared with natural or adoptive family members. Of this number, an estimated 401,300 were adults with ID/DD receiving residential supports away from family homes. As shown in Figure 19.2, approximately 79% of all adults with developmental disabilities were living in family homes or in their own homes without formal residential services.

National Commitments to Inclusion

There can be no doubt that the United States has made firm commitments to the inclusion of individuals with Down syndrome and other developmental disabilities; however, fulfilling the national commitment to inclusion remains a challenge, one that cannot be met solely through policy. Professional consensus of desired goals is necessary. In 2003, a group of representatives of 40 professional organizations met to establish national goals for service and research concerning individuals with ID/DD (The Arc of the United States, 2003). A key foundation of all the established goals reflected the commitment to inclusion in every aspect of life and throughout every aspect of the services system.

Increasing Physical Inclusion

Clearly, physical inclusion is an absolute prerequisite to any level of inclusion. One cannot have relationships, be valued, or live as a full

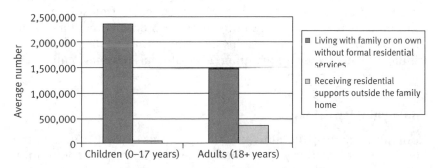

Figure 19.2. Estimated number of children and adults with intellectual and developmental disabilities living with families or receiving out-of-family home residential or nursing services.

citizen without being included within the community. Despite the substantial progress since the 1980s, large numbers of people with developmental disabilities remain institutionalized.

One of the major challenges in assuring physical access is to secure not only national commitment but commitments in all of the states as well. There are notable variations among states in the achievement of physical inclusion. In June 2003, in nine states more than 90% of all recipients of residential supports lived in settings of 6 or fewer residents, whereas in seven states more than one third of all individuals receiving residential supports in developmental disabilities facilities lived in institutions of 16 or more residents. When nursing facilities are included, this number increases to 11 states.

Many people who are not living in institutions are also waiting for community services such as residential and in-home support—an estimated 75,300 in June 2003, based on reports from 36 states. Residential service systems need to be expanded by 19% to serve all individuals currently receiving or waiting for services. Access to services is one of the most visible and important ethical issues in human service delivery. States are attempting to address the crisis of people waiting for service, despite budgetary difficulties. Many states have found family support for children and adults living with family members as an important aspect of doing so. Such support provides essential assistance to families with members with developmental disabilities, while at the same time delaying demand for much more costly out-of-home residential services.

SOCIAL INCLUSION

Simply being physically included is not enough. For people with Down syndrome to experience true community inclusion, social inclusion is also necessary. Social relationships and community participation are cornerstones of community life and are generally acknowledged aspects of a quality life. Therefore, they are a goal of most home and community-based services for individuals with developmental disabilities. Although social relationships and community participation contribute in many ways to each other, each also has unique components that deserve independent attention.

Community Participation

Community participation includes many aspects of participating in the life of the community, including whether and how community resources are used and the amount and degree of use of community activities, such as recreation and leisure opportunities. In the 1970s, the first major studies of the community participation of individuals with developmental disabilities compared the lives of people who lived in institutions with those of people who lived in community homes. Many research studies have shown that there were, and continue to be, major and significant differences between the community participation of people living in community settings and that of people who live in institutions (Conroy, 1996; Horner, Stoner, & Ferguson, 1988; Stancliffe & Lakin, 1998). In more recent years, studies have compared the community lives of people who live with their families with people in agency-supported homes, the quantity and types of social relationships of people in different kinds of residential settings, and many other facets of community participation and both physical and social inclusion.

In analyzing just the single topic of how community resources are used, there are many differences between people who live in the community and those who live in institutions. People who live in the community go to more movies, restaurants, stores, and sporting events. They go on more walks away from their homes and have more visits to friends away from their homes. They are more likely to participate in organized sports, have friendships with people without disabilities, go places with their families, and attend community churches.

At the same time, despite the personal, cultural, and habilitative values of community participation, it has been noted that many individuals living in community settings participate in their communities less than might be expected or desired (Abery & Fahnestock, 1994; Hill et al., 1989). In addition, not all community resources are readily available for those who live in community settings. When people with disabilities are asked to identify areas where they need support but are not receiving it, the most frequently reported needs are for: physicians and dentists, transportation for both work and leisure activities, social and recreational services, service management services, and income assistance (Ittenbach, Larson, Speigel, Abery, & Prouty, 1993).

Recreation/Leisure Participation

If a person participates in community leisure and recreation activities, it could be assumed that these participatory activities would help lead to increased social relationships and valued social roles (Ittenbach et al., 1993; Putnam, Werder, & Schleien, 1985). However, many leisure and recreation programs are aimed at activities, not relationships, and there are not many examples of programs intentionally designed to use those activities to develop and support people's social relationships.

In fact, one study documented an unusual aspect of the lives of people with disabilities who receive paid, professional services. This study examined the formal recreation and leisure opportunities of people with developmental disabilities who lived in residences with six or fewer residents. The recreation lives of these individuals were compared with recreation lives of 100 adults without disabilities in the general population. People with disabilities were found to use *more* community resources for recreation and leisure than people without disabilities (Hill et al., 1989). That is, people with disabilities had a more "programmed" life than citizens without disabilities.

A national survey of individuals with developmental disabilities indicated that one third of all people with intellectual disabilities have needs for recreational/leisure services that are unfulfilled (Temple University Developmental Disabilities Center, 1990). The major barriers to social and recreational inclusion that were identified include a lack of companionship, friends, or advocates; lack of finances, transportation, available activities, needed assistance, time, and specific skills; interference of challenging behaviors; and the need for a support group (Ittenbach, Abery, Larson, Spiegel, & Prouty, 1994). A Minnesota study found that 61% of 400 interviewees with developmental disabilities were unable to select their own leisure activities because of limitations of staff support, information, and transportation (Hewitt, Larson, & Lakin, 2000). Families report that one of their biggest challenges is engaging family members in social, leisure, and recreation activities matching their interests (Hayden & Heller, 1997). Overcoming these barriers requires systematic support to improve skills, identification of and facilitation of linkages with available resources, and development of new resources.

One of the recurring findings in research on community resource use and recreation/leisure participation is that the more severe the degree of a person's impairment, the less likely he or she is to engage in community activities (Dalgleish, 1983; Lakin, Burwell, Hayden, & Jackson, 1992). The development of social opportunities for people with more severe impairments is particularly challenging.

Social Relationships

Many compelling arguments have been made about the importance of social relationships in the lives of people with Down syndrome (O'Brien, 1987; Strully & Strully, 1985; Taylor, Biklen, & Knoll, 1987). When the community participation and social relationships of a person with Down syndrome are enhanced, there are numerous results that directly affect quality of life. For all people, social networks and community participation have been shown to be directly related to numerous social, psychological, and physical outcomes, directly affecting a relatively higher or lower quality of life. People with increased social participation and relationships are less likely to experience depression and psychological distress, and these people are also less likely to abuse their children. They are more likely to experience reduced stress, greater job satisfaction, more effective coping, and enhanced mental well-being (Abery & Fahnestock, 1994; Cohen & Syme, 1985; Cohen & Willis, 1985; Gottlieb, 1985; Kessler & Wethington, 1986; Rosen, Simon, & McKinsey, 1995).

In the general population, it has been documented that the quality of a person's relationships is the number one reason for the degree of happiness in the person's life (Myers, 1993). People who have closer relationships are less lonely, are healthier, and live longer (House, Landis, & Umberson, 1988). Much attention has been given to the nature and importance of people's support networks, which significantly affect quality of life (Abery & Fahnestock, 1994; Rosen & Burchard, 1990). Professional practice should treat social relationships and community participation as desired outcomes of a well-supported community life.

Much of the impetus for developing community services was derived from the logical presumption that if people were physically located within the community, this would naturally lead to increased participation in community activities, increased utilization of community resources, and enhanced individual community membership. Although there is significant evidence of physical inclusion of individuals with disabilities into local communities, there is little evidence that physical inclusion automatically translates into social inclusion. This phenomenon has been described as the fact that although people might be *in* their community, they are not *of* their community. Contrary to earlier beliefs, people with disabilities who are living and working in community settings often remain socially isolated from that larger community and remain socially segregated in a "disability world" in which they continue to be primarily surrounded by paid staff and other people with disabilities.

Adults who have disabilities typically do not have rich and meaningful relationships with adults without disabilities (Abery & Fahnestock, 1994). Although people might be physically included, simply being physically included in community settings does not guarantee that adults with disabilities will establish desired social and interpersonal relationships with typical community members (Rosen & Burchard, 1990). Limited community participation and social isolation are themes common in the lives of many adolescents, young adults, and adults with disabilities (Bogdan & Taylor, 1987; Calkins et al., 1985; Ittenbach, et al., 1994). Some research even indicates that some people who have been deinstitutionalized appear as socially isolated in the community as they were when they were living in institutions (Bercovici, 1983). Current service systems are often not sufficiently responsive to the social needs of people with Down syndrome and other developmental disabilities. These findings point to the fact that the development and maintenance of social relationships is a major challenge in supporting the community lives of individuals with developmental disabilities (Walker, 1999).

Relationships with Family Members

Most of the research regarding social relationships is about people with developmental disabilities who are living in out-of-home settings, such as group homes or apartment programs; however, as indicated previously, more than three fourths of all individuals with developmental disabilities live with their natural or foster families, a far greater number than those in out-of-home settings. The social lives of individuals in family settings often differ markedly from those in out-of-home placements.

In comparison to individuals who live in formal residential settings, adults with developmental disabilities who live in their family homes have smaller social networks and spent most of their leisure time with family members. Krauss, Seltzer, and Goodman (1992) found that sons were more socially isolated than daughters, and if a child had more severe intellectual disabilities, then he or she was usually more isolated. In general, the most common aspect of the social networks of adults living at home is that the majority of people in their social networks are family members. Nearly half of the adults living at home have no friends (peers) in their social networks, and paid professionals are seldom viewed as having a social relationship or role in the lives of the people living at home. It has also been observed that families have very little formal (paid) support for activities that might extend social support, and the social lives of the adults living at home are highly dependent on the social relationships of their parents.

The social networks of individuals living with their families often contrast sharply to the social networks of people living in residential settings. For example, most friends of individuals living in residential settings are peers who live in the same settings, and the social activities of individuals in residential settings generally involve, and are dependent on, paid staff. In addition, people living in community residential settings have been found to engage in a much higher number of community activities, and, in this regard, have lives that are very different from adults living in their family home.

Efforts continue to understand how to sustain and support constructive family involvement in the lives of individuals with developmental disabilities who are living away from their families. Many trends in service delivery have greatly increased the opportunities for family involvement. For instance, person-centered planning approaches, such as Personal Futures Planning (Mount, 1997) and Essential Lifestyle Planning (Smull & Burke Harrison, 1992), highlight the role of family members in understanding what is important to the person (see Chapter 7). Several approaches to *outcome-based performance measures*, such as the Council on Quality and Leadership's (2000) quality outcomes, also emphasize that the family has significant input to understanding what a quality outcome is for an individual. The entire direction of more consumer control, such as individually managed service budgets and individual-controlled housing (owned or rented), usually requires and benefits from enhanced participation and commitment from family members.

There are also more individualized service approaches, such as the establishment of *microboards,* which are individualized nonprofit agencies organized around one person. In these microboard arrangements, family members usually play a critical role as board members. The same family involvement also usually applies to individualized entrepreneurial agencies in which the individual with disabilities is self-employed.

Research on parent attitudes and experiences with deinstitutionalization and community placement provides many suggestions from families about how family involvement can be supported and sustained: 1) attending and responding to the perceptions, needs, and concerns of family members regarding program change; 2) facilitating the participation of the individual and family in decision making about changes (e.g., where, when, with whom); 3) arranging opportunities for family members to learn about and visit potential residential and work sites and service providers; 4) providing real choices for individuals and their families in selecting residential settings and service providers; and 5) establishing and maintaining effective communication and promoting family participation between community service providers and family members after placement (Larson & Lakin, 1991).

Relationships with Other People with Disabilities

Many people with Down syndrome view other people with disabilities as their primary friends. Like other members of society, they tend to draw friendships from their immediate surroundings (e.g., place of residence, place of work or other significant activities). Over the years, inadequate valuing of these relationships has often failed to support and assist such friendships, sometimes even separating individuals from their key friends as they are moved from program to program within the community. Approaches to service planning and support based on honoring people's preferences and their own definitions of quality of life can have important effects on such perceptions.

For instance, when assisting a person with Down syndrome in selecting and securing an apartment or home, planning methods should include identifying with the individual whom he or she considers a friend and whom he or she might like to live with, regardless of whether that potential roommate has disabilities. Such trends will surely continue as a part of the generally increasing respect for personal preferences and the right to maximum self-determination. While continuing to enhance relationships with other community members, it is important to appreciate the value of a person's relationships with his or her closest peers, including those of the opposite sex.

At the same time, however, it is also important to recognize that many people with Down syndrome do not prefer the company of others with disabilities. Many individuals with Down syndrome have been grouped with others with disabilities their whole life, starting with their preschool program, through their special education programs, on into their adult life of group homes and day programs. Many do not realize that any other choice is available. Often, having been forced by unconscious cultural assumptions ("they belong with their own kind") and service system designs to be congregated with other people with disabilities, many people with Down syndrome, their families, and service providers simply become used to these congregated options. Individuals often live in an isolated "disability world" without the opportunity for other options. When they are really listened to and given concrete choices and opportunities, many individuals with Down syndrome express preferences for living with and socializing with others who do not have disabilities.

For example, sometimes individuals with severe behavior problems have been grouped in homes and day programs with others with similar challenges. Sometimes they do not get along with their peers, and they engage in aggressive behaviors toward staff, housemates, or fellow workshop employees. When these individuals are moved to their own apartment or home or assisted to have a community job, these behaviors often decrease dramatically.

Relationships with Community Members without Disabilities

Regardless of whether adults with Down syndrome live with their own families or in residential settings, relationships with nonpaid community members are much less common than those with people with disabilities and with family members (Abery & Fahnestock, 1994; Rosen & Burchard, 1990). Such friendships with typical community citizens are not only important for obvious social reasons but are key to community inclusion. In 1967, Edgerton conducted a classic study of former institution residents who had moved to the community. He found that the presence of a *benefactor* (a personal advocate and friend) was a key predictor of an individual's success and degree of inclusion in the community.

Horner and his colleagues (1988) analyzed the social networks of 67 people who had been deinstitutionalized. They found that, on average, participants had 12.25 socially important people in their lives. Of these, 5.5 were paid providers, 2.4 were family, 2.0 were other friends with disabilities from their group homes, 1.9 were co-worker friends (with disabilities), and only .45 were neighbors. Hayden, Lakin, Hill, Bruininks, and Copher (1992) asked about the "best friends" of people living in community residential settings and found that only 4% were community members without disabilities. Furthermore, 60% of the people in those settings did not have even one friend who was a community member without disabilities. Hewitt and colleagues (2000) found that of Minnesotans receiving support through the Medicaid waiver program, 25% did not have any best friend or regular friend— even another person with disabilities—to talk or do things with.

Some studies have found that even if individuals with ID/DD had social relationships with community members, those relationships were often few, shallow, and short lived (Clegg & Standen, 1991; Kennedy, Horner, & Newton, 1989). Other research indicates that when long-term friendships/benefactor relationships with community members are present, those friends tend to be individuals who at some point in the past provided professional services (Abery & Fahnestock, 1994; Newton, Olson, & Horner, 1995).

Although reciprocal, mutually satisfying relationships between people with Down syndrome and other community members might not be present for a majority of people, there is a large body of research that shows the value and importance of these relationships, when they do exist, for both members of the friendship (Bogdan & Taylor, 1987). Adults with Down syndrome value and treasure the true friendship of people who are not paid to, or required to, be with them, but who are with them simply because they like them. Community members benefit from the unique gifts and contributions of individuals with Down syndrome, and they may report getting more out of the relationship than their counterparts with Down syndrome. Such friendships and relationships are critical for true community inclusion.

Often, such relationships between people with Down syndrome and community citizens without disabilities evolve, not because of intentional efforts to develop them, but because people "find each other" (Taylor, Bogdan & Lutfiyya, 1995). More recently, consistent efforts have been applied by community services agencies to assist in promoting and developing such relationships and to increase community belonging, both for individuals living in their family homes and for those living in residential settings (Amado, 1993). Efforts in this area continue to focus on increasing the number of such relationships, expanding their depth, and lengthening their duration.

The problem of the social isolation of people with developmental disabilities and the associated lack of skills in developing, accessing, or using interpersonal contacts, relationships, and networks have many facets and contributing factors. In the past, research in the area of interpersonal relationships focused on the "deficiencies" of individuals themselves in social skills and other areas of adaptive behavior (Craig & McCarver, 1984; Gollay, Freedman, Wyngaarden, & Kurtz, 1978; Holman & Bruininks, 1985). It was thought, for instance, that if an individual had too severe a level of disability, he or she could not have friendships; however, other studies have shown that it is not that simple.

The attitudes and efforts of staff are often a bigger influence on social relationships than a person's level of disability. Relationships have a contextual nature, and often contextual interventions that deal with the complexity of interactions in a given environment can result in more effective changes (Hunt, Farron-Davis, Wrenn, Hirose-Hatae, & Goetz, 1997). For instance, Willer and Intagliata (1980) found that the social interactions of individuals in community residential settings were affected not only by the characteristics of the residents but also by the characteristics of their residential environment. Social interactions were significantly more frequent among individuals living in homes that were smaller, had fewer residents, and taught practical social skills. For example, going to a restaurant at 4:00 P.M., when it is almost empty, is often more convenient for staff but is significantly less likely to result in interactions between individuals with developmental disabilities and members of the general public than going at a more typical, later dinner time when more interactions could occur.

Other research suggests that social networks that include community members without disabilities are most frequent among individuals with disabilities who live in environments in which care providers also live, that is, foster, natural, or adoptive families (Hayden et al., 1992; Krauss & Erickson, 1988). In large measure, it appears that individuals in family or foster care are included in the social networks of the families with which they live and that relationships of the individuals with developmental disabilities tend to derive directly from the personal, social, and neighborhood associations of their care providers.

Promoting the Development of
Social Relationships with Community Members

An important variable influencing the development of social relationships among individuals with Down syndrome and other developmental disabilities is the extent to which community support systems provide opportunities for and promote such relationship development. A significant danger in the approach of many current services toward community inclusion is that programs equate "community inclusion" with "community activities." Although most agencies support activities in community life, such as shopping or eating in restaurants, these activities do not necessarily result in relationships with community members.

Although some agencies work at social inclusion, many remain both overtly and subtly segregating and isolating (Council on Quality and Leadership, 2000). Agencies may get positive scores on the Council on Quality and Leadership's (2003) outcome goal of "People participate in community activities," but few get positive scores on the outcomes of "People have friends" and "People have social roles." In some agencies, the social activities of individuals living in group homes consist of dances, bowling, or other social events with large groups of people with disabilities.

When people do go out "into the community," a typical pattern is that they are merely "visiting" places. Lutfiyya (1996) described this phenomenon as people with disabilities "being tourists in their own home town." Few agencies organize around the social and emotional attachments and connections that constitute "community" as a sense of belonging (Walker, 1999).

At the same time, there are numerous demonstration activities and studies of connecting individuals, agencies, and communities that have shown how much can be accomplished in expanding people's social networks of valued relationships (Andrews, 1995; Center on Human Policy, 1998; Ducharme, Beeman, DeMarasse, & Ludlum, 1994; Gomez, 2001; Schleien, Ray, & Green, 1997). Given that social relationships with friends and neighbors are important to everyone, specialized and generic community service providers will increasingly be expected to assist people with developmental disabilities to form friendships and to become involved in the social activities of community associations and organizations. Professional and popular literature has noted numerous successful efforts to establish friendships through

1) community leisure/recreation programs and agencies; 2) casual contact with community members; and 3) participation in typical social institutions such as churches, community arts groups, and community associations (Gretz & Ploof, 1999; Reidy, 1993; Taylor & Bogdan, 1989).

One of the most powerful contributors to the establishment of friendships for individuals with and without disabilities is regular, ongoing social contact (Abery & Fahnestock, 1994; Abery, Thurlow, Johnson, & Bruininks, 1990). More specifically, if adults with developmental disabilities are to develop friendships with community members, residential providers and family members need to ensure that these individuals participate in activities that are likely to result in social interaction and to take place frequently. For example, facilitating a person's joining a club whose members play cards or work together on community projects on a weekly basis is much more likely to result in the development of social relationships than taking that same individual to a baseball game, movie theater, restaurant, or other settings in which interpersonal interactions do not regularly occur with the same community members. Thus, many authors have documented the effectiveness of people with developmental disabilities joining community associations and groups (Center on Human Policy, 1990; Gretz & Ploof, 1999; Reidy, 1993). Other excellent avenues for such regular and meaningful involvement are the ongoing activities in faith communities (Gaventa, Simon, Norman-McNaney, & Amado, 2001). Promoting relationships and belonging means agencies supporting individuals not only to simply attend services but also to join the groups and membership activities of that faith community in order to get to know others.

Stable relationships between individuals with and without disabilities can grow regardless of whether the person with disabilities is supported by a formal program. At the same time, if the person does receive formal supports, certain environments tend to foster social relationships more readily than others. For example, smaller community homes can foster such relationships more readily than larger community facilities or institutions. Numerous strategies have been effective in fostering successful and satisfying social relationships, and these can be integrated into community service programs (Amado, 1993). For example, person-centered planning has been widely used to assist in the development and expansion of social networks (see Chapter 7).

Other approaches that have been used include the use of *social inclusion facilitators,* or people who have in-depth knowledge of and connections with the community and who have been recruited and trained to facilitate an individual making connections with other people of his or her choosing in the community (Abery & Fahnestock, 1994). *Community mapping* has been used to gain an understanding of the people, places, and associations that provide an individual with a sense of belonging. In community mapping, the person provides the inclusion facilitator with a guided tour of his or her community so that facilitators can concentrate their efforts on promoting the development of relationships with specific individuals within these environments (Carlson, 2000). These and other strategies (see Amado, 1993) look to the broader community for natural sources of relationships that 1) promote continued use of the family and child's social network after a child leaves home; 2) recognize the value of friends and neighbors and take them into consideration when contemplating a move; 3) involve individuals with disabilities in organizations that are typical sources of friendship (e.g., churches, recreation organizations, Boy or Girl Scouts, other dedicated civic organizations); and 4) continue movement toward employment in typical inclusive job settings.

Community inclusion is not only dependent on individuals with Down syndrome or on human services agencies but also on communities and community members who can play a more direct and substantial role in and be accountable for building inclusive communities. Kretzmann and McKnight (1993) showed that neighborhood organizations could be used to promote such accountability, and the City of Seattle's Department of Neighborhoods organized neighborhood efforts to be inclusive of people with disabilities (Carlson, 2000). Amado and Victorian-Blaney (2000) documented an approach of holding Community Member Forums to solicit communitywide commitment to inclusion. In several Model Communities projects funded by the Center for Medicaid & Medicare Services, community entities such as city councils and chambers of commerce were integrally involved in planning inclusion efforts. Such approaches hold great promise for an even more effective realization of the goal of inclusive communities.

CULTURAL INCLUSION

Although individuals with Down syndrome and other developmental disabilities can have significant and meaningful social relationships with community members, it is also important for them to be seen as valued contributors by the larger community. A valued identity in community life, wherein people are recognized as a *normal* part of the community, is increasingly sought by and for people with Down syndrome and other individuals with developmental disabilities. Although being part of the community begins with using the resources and participating in the typical activities of community organizations and settings, it is also much more than that. As people with disabilities have been increasingly provided with opportunities to live in ordinary communities, they have naturally, or by design, taken on many of the ordinary social roles of a typical community member, such as neighbor, shopper, and bus rider, among others. At the same time, it is important to go beyond these ordinary roles and to strive for more visible and highly valued social roles.

The development of such goals has been influenced by the principle of *normalization*, a key cornerstone concept in the evolution of human services. This concept proposes that people with disabilities and other marginalized or devalued people should be assisted to live lives as normal as possible, as much as possible like those of other citizens. Furthermore, not only should people have lives as normal as possible but they should also have social status that is enhanced as much as possible.

The principle of normalization posits that people's status is enhanced by engaging in activities associated with one's age in the settings in which those activities normally take place; participating in typical social/cultural and economic roles of the community; and having friends, associates, and social roles that are valued in the community. Community participation, then, becomes an essential aspect of one of normalization's primary goals: "the establishment, enhancement, or defense of the social role(s) of a person or a group by the enhancement of people's social images and personal competencies" (Wolfensberger, 1983). The ideas from the original formulation of the principle of normalization were later expanded in the development of the principle of *social role valorization*, which stressed even more the importance of valued social roles as the cornerstone of truly inclusive community lives. Supporting people with disabilities to have roles that allow them to be seen and valued in the eyes of community members alters the role of individuals with disabilities in society and affects larger social issues of discrimination in every arena of life, including housing, employment, schooling, medical care, and neighborhood life. Social role valorization seeks to overcome the sometimes unconscious devaluation of individuals with disabilities.

There are numerous examples of valued social roles that have been held by individuals with Down syndrome (e.g., film and television actors). Kingsley and Levitz, two young men with Down syndrome, have written a book called *Count Us In* (1994) about their lives growing up in families in which they were highly valued. Levitz has shared about his job working in a bank and wearing a suit every day. A young woman in New Mexico with Down syndrome ran for a representative position in her state legislature and was believed to be the first person with Down syndrome in the nation to do so (National Down Syndrome Society, 1998). Popular magazines such as *People* often feature individuals with Down syndrome or other disabilities who are artists or entrepreneurs with their own businesses. A Minneapolis trio of singers called the Down Beats have performed their original song "Too Many Chromosomes to Drive a Car" to hundreds of people in audiences throughout North America and Europe. All of these social roles—television actor, author, bank employee, state representative, artist, performer, self-employed entrepreneur—are roles highly valued in the common culture. Increasing these examples will change the nature of services and community inclusion in the future.

FULL CITIZENSHIP

Passage of the Americans with Disabilities Act (ADA) of 1990 (PL 101-336) was a significant event for individuals with disabilities, as were the Rehabilitation Act of 1973 (PL 93-112), the Developmental Disabilities Assistance and Bill of Rights Act of 1975 (PL 94-103), and the *Olmstead* (1999) decision. As these laws and Supreme Court decisions continue to be implemented, greater perspective and understanding continue to be gained on their effects and implications. For example, under ADA, public places and worksites have implemented accommodations for people with disabilities, in many cases with minimal difficulty and expense. Efforts to encourage voluntary compliance through education and negotiation have generally been successful. A Harris Poll of 200 corporate executives (senior vice presidents or higher) and 204 equal-opportunity officers found substantial support for ADA: 1) more than 90% supported the provisions of ADA prohibiting discrimination in employment and public accommodations; 2) 80% reported no change or only a "little" change in the costs of accommodating people with disabilities, even though 81% of the companies reported workplace modifications for employees with disabilities; and 3) 75% reported they were "somewhat" or "very" likely to increase efforts to hire people with disabilities in the future (Harris, 1995).

Although many aspects of ADA have resulted in positive benefits for many people with disabilities in the larger population, such as those with physical disabilities, there remain questions about its benefits for those who have intellectual disabilities. Such individuals typically have functional disabilities in areas such as oral language, judgment, memory, interpersonal interactions, reading, and writing. These disabilities typically require accommodations that are very different from those required by people who use wheelchairs or who have hearing or visual impairments. Successful accommodations for individuals with intellectual disabilities include 1) increased public education about these disabilities and appropriate job accommodations related to the functional disabilities associated with ID/DD; 2) development and promotion of a variety of employment and other inclusive opportunities for individuals with intellectual disabilities to reduce stereotype-driven work, including improved education and training of job developers; 3) development of a variety of inclusive recreation opportunities to expand beyond typical role limitations; and 4) education of individuals with disabilities to advocate for themselves.

The effects of these national commitments for inclusion are seen not only in employment situations but also in many other public and private arenas. Personnel in such diverse areas as transportation, recreation, and service settings must permit equal opportunity for individuals with disabilities to participate in or benefit from a service or activity as it is offered to the general public. For example, a person with developmental disabilities may not be denied access to an aerobics class simply because he or she cannot keep pace or complete the entire workout.

Many cities still struggle with the physical accommodations of their public transportation systems, limiting the community participation of many individuals with developmental disabilities. Realizing the *Olmstead* mandate that people receive services in "the most integrated setting appropriate" remains a daunting challenge. The full implementation of these national commitments will continue to affect the full citizenship of individuals with Down syndrome.

One of the most significant contributors to full citizenship is, and will continue to be, the growing self-advocacy and self-determination movements. Chapter 24 describes the growth and development of this movement and how the significance of speaking for oneself is a critical component of citizenship. As people with disabilities increase their political identity, they also have the opportunity to grow as a political force and further influence the realization of full citizenship for all.

SUMMARY

As the service system for individuals with Down syndrome continues to shift toward individual-directed services, and if restrictions on service budgets continue, acknowledgment and respect for the importance of family relationships can only continue to grow. Families are not only the most basic and enduring relationships that most people know but they also offer emotional commitment to the well-being of members that is critical to people who depend on the support of others. That support and associated advocacy is extremely difficult to replace by paid or unpaid advocates.

Many families who have raised their children in the past generation of increased publicly supported educational opportunities are far more experienced than their counterparts of previous generations with regard to active involvement in service planning and delivery for their children. It can be expected that these parents will maintain a central role in the lives of their adult children as they grow up and eventually leave the family home. In the evolving service system, ever-increasing numbers of families will be involved in more significant and sustained roles, acting as service managers, securing housing with or on behalf of their sons or daughters, helping adult children find jobs, managing public resources to purchase services for their children, and other roles that are quite different from the passive acceptance of whatever services were offered in the past. If parents are prepared and appropriately supported, these relationships will not only enhance the overall quality of life for their children but also will help sustain the quality and frequency of family relationships and the support derived from them.

If family members are expected to participate effectively in such advocacy roles, then they must be prepared and supported to collaborate with professionals, and professionals must value and know how to collaborate with families. There is a strong association between families' empowerment and their degree of collaboration (Turnbull & Turnbull, 1996). Often, this sense of empowerment can be nurtured throughout the years of special education and other planning systems, starting from their children's earliest years and continuing throughout the adult years.

One of the great future challenges for providers of community services will remain that of providing opportunities for adults with Down syndrome to meet and develop relationships with other community members. For individuals who live in agency-supported programs, planning and organizational investment is needed to enhance the quantity and quality of community participation and social relationships. Effective service providers make efforts to ensure that individuals are engaging in activities that have a greater potential than others to promote belonging within the community. No matter how severe the disability of a given individual, the agency culture and the provision of concrete opportunities are important in meeting the person's social needs and preferences.

Opportunities are expanding for people with Down syndrome to enjoy greater participation in valued ways in the community. An important contribution to the increasing acceptance by community entities and agencies is their recognition of the rightful place of citizens with developmental disabilities in their environments and programs. Each year, greater numbers of public and private community organizations, employers, and programs include people with Down syndrome and other disabilities. These outcomes derive from a number of factors, including the increased presence of people with disabilities within communities; advocacy for the participation of individuals; increased responsibility by service providers to deliver such outcomes; society's growing commitment to nondiscrimination; increased expectations for and purchase of services from agencies that deliver such outcomes; and training, technical assistance, and monitoring of services for community inclusion efforts.

The changes that have taken place since the 1980s are extraordinary. For instance, just the longer life span of many people with Down syndrome challenges thinking about what is possible for people's lives and their role in community life. The rising expectations provided by school programs, employment possibilities, self-advocacy, and increased valued contributions of people with disabilities can only continue to alter the ways in which people with disabilities are an integral part of the larger society.

REFERENCES

Abery, B.H., & Fahnestock, M. (1994). Enhancing the social inclusion of persons with developmental disabilities. In M.F. Hayden & B.H. Abery (Eds.), *Challenges for a service system in transition: Ensuring quality community experiences for persons with developmental disabilities* (pp. 83–119). Baltimore: Paul H. Brookes Publishing Co.

Abery, B.H., Thurlow, M.T., Johnson, D.R., & Bruininks, R.H. (1990, May). *The social networks of adults with developmental disabilities residing in community settings.* Paper presented at the annual meeting of the American Association on Mental Retardation, Washington, DC.

Amado, A.N. (1993). *Friendships and community connections between people with and without developmental disabilities.* Baltimore: Paul H. Brookes Publishing Co.

Amado, A., & Victorian-Blaney, J. (2000). Requesting inclusion from the community: The necessity of asking. *TASH Newsletter, 26*(5), 15–17.

Americans with Disabilities Act of 1990, PL 101-336, 42 U.S.C. §§ 12101 *et seq.*

Andrews, S.S. (1995). Life in Mendocino: A young man with Down Syndrome in a small town in Northern California. In S.J. Taylor, R. Bogdan, & Z.M. Lutfiyya (Eds.), *The variety of community experience: Qualitative studies of family and community life* (pp. 79–100). Baltimore: Paul H. Brookes Publishing Co.

Arc of the United States, The. (2003). *Keeping the promises: Finding and recommendations: January 2003 invitational conference, national goals, state of knowledge and research agenda for persons with intellectual and developmental disabilities.* Washington, DC: Author.

Bercovici, S.M. (1983). *Barriers to normalization: The restrictive management of mentally retarded persons.* Baltimore: University Park Press.

Bogdan, R., & Taylor, S.J. (1987). Toward a sociology of acceptance: The other side of the study of deviance. *Social Policy, 18*(2), 34–39.

Calkins, C., Walker, H., Bacon-Prue, A., Gibson, B., Martinson, M., & Offner, R. (1985). *The learning adjustment process: Implications of a national profile of adult development.* Logan: Utah State University, Developmental Center for Handicapped Persons.

Carlson, C. (2000). *Involving all neighbors: Building inclusive communities in Seattle.* Seattle: Seattle Department of Neighborhoods.

Center on Human Policy. (1990). *A guide to knowing your community.* Syracuse, NY: Author.

Center on Human Policy. (1998). *Resources and reports on community integration.* Syracuse, NY: Author.

Clegg, J.A., & Standen, P.J. (1991). Friendship among adults who have developmental disabilities. *American Journal on Mental Retardation, 94,* 663–671.

Cohen, S., & Syme, L.S. (1985). *Social support and health.* San Diego: Academic Press.

Cohen, S., & Willis, T.A. (1985). Stress, social support, and the buffering hypothesis. *Psychological Bulletin, 97,* 310–357

Conroy, J.W. (1996). The small ICF/MR program: Dimensions of quality and cost. *Mental Retardation, 34,* 13–26.

Council on Quality and Leadership. (2000). *The Council's national outcomes database.* Towson, MD: Author.

Council on Quality and Leadership. (2003, July). *Attaining outcomes.* Workshop presented at the Reinventing Quality Conference, Minneapolis, MN.

Craig, E.M., & McCarver, R. (1984). Community placement and adjustment of deinstitutionalized clients: Issues and findings. In N.W. Bray & N. Ellis (Eds.), *International review of research in mental retardation.* San Diego: Academic Press.

Dalgleish, M. (1983). Assessments of residential environments for mentally retarded adults in Britain. *Mental Retardation, 21,* 275–281.

Developmental Disabilities Assistance and Bill of Rights Act of 1975, PL 94-103, 100 Stat. 840, 42 U.S.C. §§ 6000 *et seq.*

Ducharme, G., Beeman, P., DeMarasse, R., & Ludlum, C. (1994). Building community one person at a time: One candle power. In V.J. Bradley, J.W. Ashbaugh & B.C. Blaney (Eds.), *Creating individual supports for people with developmental disabilities: A mandate for change at many levels* (pp. 347–360). Baltimore: Paul H. Brookes Publishing Co.

Edgerton, R.B. (1967). *The cloak of competence: Stigma in the lives of the mentally retarded.* Berkeley: University of California.

Gaventa, W., Simon, S.R., Norman-McNaney, R., & Amado, A.N. (2001). Feature issue on faith community and persons with developmental disabilities. *IMPACT, 14*(3).

Gollay, E., Freedman, R., Wyngaarden, M., & Kurtz, N.R. (1978). *Coming back: The community experiences of deinstitutionalized mentally retarded people.* Cambridge, MA: Abt Books.

Gomez, O. (2001). *Facilitating social interactions of adults with developmental disabilities in the community.* Doctoral dissertation, Lehigh University.

Gottlieb, B. (1985). Social support and community mental health. In S. Cohen & S.L. Syme (Eds.), *Social support and health* (pp. 303–326). San Diego: Academic Press.

Gretz, S., & Ploof, D. (Eds.). (1999). *The common thread: A collection of writings about friendships, relationships and community life.* Harrisburg: Pennsylvania Developmental Disabilities Council.

Harris, L. (1995). *The N.O.D./Harris survey on employment of people with disabilities* (No. 951401). Washington, DC: National Organization on Disability/Louis Harris and Associates.

Hayden, M., & Heller, T. (1997). Support services, coping strategies and burden of younger and older caregivers. *Mental Retardation, 35,* 338–346.

Hayden, M.F., Lakin, K.C., Hill, B.K., Bruininks, R.H., & Copher, J.I. (1992). Social and leisure integration of people with mental retardation who reside in foster homes and small group homes. *Education and Training in Mental Retardation, 27*(1), 187–199.

Hewitt, A., Larson, S.A., & Lakin, K.C. (2000). *An independent evaluation of the quality of services and system performance of Minnesota's Medicaid Home and Community-Based Services for persons with mental retardation and related conditions.* Minneapolis: University of Minnesota, Research and Training Center on Community Living.

Hill, B.K., Lakin, K.C., Bruininks, R.H., Amado, A.N., Anderson, D.J., & Copher, J.L. (1989). *Living in the community: A comparative study of foster homes and small group homes for people with mental retardation.* Minneapolis: University of Minnesota, Center for Residential and Community Services.

Holman, J., & Bruininks, R. (1985). Assessing and training adaptive behaviors. In K.C. Lakin & R.H. Bruininks (Eds.), *Strategies for achieving community integration of developmentally disabled citizens* (pp. 73–104). Baltimore: Paul H. Brookes Publishing Co.

Horner, R.H., Stoner, S.K., & Ferguson, D.L. (1988). *An activity-based analysis of deinstitutionalization: The effects of community re-entry on the lives of residents leaving Oregon's Fairview Training Center.* Eugene: University of Oregon, Specialized Training Program, Center on Human Development.

House, J.S., Landis, K.R., & Umberson, D. (1988). Social relationships and health. *Science, 241,* 540–545.

Hunt, P., Farron-Davis, F., Wrenn, M., Hirose-Hatae, A., & Goetz, L (1997). Promoting interactive partnerships in inclusive settings. *Journal of The Association for Persons with Severe Handicaps, 22,* 127–137.

Ittenbach, R.F., Abery, B.H., Larson, S.A., Spiegel, A.N., & Prouty, R.W. (1994). Community adjustment of young adults with mental retardation: Overcoming barriers to inclusion. *Palaestra, 10*(2), 32–42.

Ittenbach, R.F., Larson, S.A., Speigel, A.N., Abery, B.H., & Prouty, R.W. (1993). Community adjustment of young adults with mental retardation: A developmental perspective. *Palaestra, 9*(4), 19–24.

Kennedy, C., Horner, R., & Newton, J. (1989). Social contacts of adults with severe disabilities living in the community. *Journal of The Association for Persons with Severe Handicaps, 14,* 190–196.

Kessler, R.C., & Wethington, E. (1986). Perceived support, received support, and adjustment to stressful life events. *Journal of Health and Social Behavior, 27*, 78–89.

Kingsley, J., & Levitz, M. (1994). *Count us in: Growing up with Down syndrome.* Orlando, FL: Harcourt, Brace, & Co.

Krauss, M.W., & Erickson, M.E. (1988). Informal support networks among aging mentally retarded persons: Results from a pilot study. *Mental Retardation, 26*(4), 197–201.

Krauss, M.W., Seltzer, M.M., & Goodman, S. (1992). Social support networks for adults with retardation who live at home. *American Journal on Mental Retardation, 96*(4), 432–441.

Kretzmann, J., & McKnight, J. (1993). *Building communities from the inside out.* Evanston, IL: Northwestern University, Institute for Policy Research.

Lakin, K.C., Burwell, B.O., Hayden, M.F., & Jackson, M.E. (1992). *An independent assessment of Minnesota's Medicaid Home and Community-Based Services Waiver program* (Project Report No. 37). Minneapolis: University of Minnesota, Center on Residential Services and Community Living.

Lakin, K.C., Prouty, R.W., Polister, B., & Coucouvanis, K. (2003). Selected changes in residential services over a quarter century, 1977–2002. *Mental Retardation, 41*(4), 303–303.

Larson, S.A., & Lakin, K.C. (1991). Parental attitudes about residential placement before and after deinstitutionalization: A research synthesis. *Journal of The Association for Persons with Severe Handicaps, 16*, 25–38.

Larson, S.A., Lakin, K.C., Anderson, L., & Kwak, N. (2001). Characteristics of and service use by persons with MR/DD living in their own homes or with family members: NHIS-D analysis. *MR/DD Data Brief, 3*(1).

Lutfiyya, Z.M. (1996, October). *Tourists in their own hometown: Community living for people with disabilities.* Address at the annual St. Amant Conference, Winnipeg, Manitoba, Canada.

Mount, B. (1997). *Person-centered planning: Finding directions for change using personal futures planning.* New York: Graphic Futures.

Myers, D. (1993). *The pursuit of happiness.* New York: Harper Collins.

National Down Syndrome Society. (1998, Summer). Nannie Sanchez wants to change her corner of the world. *Update, 14*(2), 1.

Newton, J., Olson, D., & Horner, R. (1995). Factors contributing to the stability of relationships between individuals with mental retardation and other community members. *Mental Retardation, 33*(6), 383–393.

O'Brien, J. (1987). A guide to life-style planning: Using *The Activities Catalog* to integrate services and natural support systems. In B. Wilcox & G.T. Bellamy (Eds.), *The activities catalog: An alternative curriculum for youth and adults with severe disabilities* (pp. 175–190). Baltimore: Paul H. Brookes Publishing Co.

Olmstead et al. v. L.C. et al., 527 U.S. 581 (1999).

Putnam, J.W., Werder, J.K., & Schleien, S.J. (1985). Leisure and recreation services for handicapped persons. In K.C. Lakin & R.H. Bruininks (Eds.), *Strategies for achieving community integration of developmentally disabled citizens* (pp. 253–274). Baltimore: Paul H. Brookes Publishing Co.

Rehabilitation Act of 1973, PL 93-112, 29 U.S.C. §§ 701 *et seq.*

Reidy, D. (1993). Friendships and community associations. In A.N. Amado (Ed.), *Friendships and community connections between persons with and without developmental disabilities* (pp. 351–372). Baltimore: Paul H. Brookes Publishing Co.

Rosen, J.W., & Burchard, S.N. (1990). Community activities and social support networks: A social comparison of adults with and without mental retardation. *Education and Training in Mental Retardation, 25* 193–202.

Rosen, M., Simon, E.W., & McKinsey, L. (1995). Subjective measure of quality of life. *Mental Retardation, 33*(1), 31–34.

Schleien, S.J., Ray, M.T., & Green, F.R. (1997). *Community recreation and people with disabilities: Strategies for inclusion.* Baltimore: Paul H. Brookes Publishing Co.

Smull, M., & Burke Harrison, S. (1992). *Supporting people with severe reputations in the community.* Alexandria, VA: National Association of State Directors of Developmental Disabilities Services.

Stancliffe, R.J., & Lakin, K.C. (1998). Analysis of expenditures and outcomes of residential alternatives for persons with developmental disabilities. *American Journal on Mental Retardation, 102,* 552–568.

Strully, J., & Strully, C. (1985). Friendship and our children. *Journal of The Association for Persons with Severe Handicaps, 10*(4), 224–227.

Taylor, S., Biklen, D., & Knoll, J. (1987). *Community integration of people with severe disabilities.* New York: Teachers College Press.

Taylor, S.J., & Bogdan, R. (1989). On accepting relationships between people with disabilities and non-disabled people: Toward understanding of acceptance. *Disability, Handicap and Society, 4*(1), 21–36.

Taylor, S.J., Bogdan, R., & Lutfiyya, Z.M. (Eds.). (1995). *The variety of community experience: Qualitative studies of family and community life.* Baltimore: Paul H. Brookes Publishing Co.

Temple University Developmental Disabilities Center. (1990). *The final report on the 1990 National Consumer Survey of people with developmental disabilities and their families.* Philadelphia: Author.

Turnbull, R., & Turnbull, A. (1996). *Families, professionals and exceptionality* (3rd ed.). Columbus, OH: Merrill/Prentice Hall.

Walker, P. (1999, September 24–25) *National Program Office on Self-Determination Proceedings of the Annual Project Director's Meeting, Baltimore.* Available from http://www.self-determination.org/publications1251

Willer, B., & Intagliata, J. (1980). *Deinstitutionalization of mentally retarded persons in New York State.* Buffalo: State University of New York at Buffalo, Research Foundation.

Wolfensberger, W. (1983). Social role valorization: A proposed new term for the principle of normalization. *Mental Retardation, 21*(6), 234–239.

20

My Life So Far

STEVEN WILLIAM SAUTER

My name is Steven William Sauter, and I am a 2004 graduate of Canton Central District Hugh C. Williams High School in the town of Canton, in Upstate New York. I have four family members. They are a brother who is 17 named Michael Sauter, a father named Robert Sauter, a mother named Jackie Sauter, and a cat named Shadow.

I am a 19-year-old native of Canton, and I was born in Potsdam-Canton Hospital in the town of Potsdam. I like to go swimming, walking, and riding bikes. I like the musical *Titanic* and like to read about the ship, too. I like listening to Broadway musicals, and I am a history buff (this means that I know a lot of history). I love computers a lot. I like to take pictures, too. I like to read books about history, folklore, and legends and mystery novels like *Murder, She Wrote*.

On June 2, 2004, on Wednesday night at 7:00 P.M. I was inducted in the International Thespian Society in Troupe 259 at my high school. Thespians are actors and actresses who have performed in a play and a musical, and they have rehearsals so they can get better for Opening Night. I was in my first musical named *Crazy for You*, written by two American composers named George and Ira Gershwin. I was the head banker, which means that I was in charge of the bank. This was my Broadway debut on stage! For this spring, I am thinking to be in another musical named *Bye Bye Birdie*.

I am a member of a club in Canton. This club is called Saturday Club, and we go to places in Canada, Canton, Potsdam, Alexandria

Bay on Lake Ontario, and the St. Lawrence River. This club is organized by St. Lawrence NYSARC. It is for people with disabilities and their friends. My best part of this club is to go to Dodge Pond, which is a camp in the Adirondacks, and have fun there like watching movies and playing games, baking pastries, and having a sleepover.

I graduated from high school in 2004. I got my diploma. Then, after graduation I went to a local restaurant in town and had a party there with my family and friends. I participated in a program in high school that teaches you about volunteering and helping people, and that's what I did. I took classes like English, American history, social studies, math, and speech. I also sing in chorus, and I am a tenor, and we performed concerts. Now, I am a postgrad, and I am learning about different jobs and how to succeed in the community. I have worked at the Historical Society, the United Cerebral Palsy Office, Family Dollar store, Aubuchon Hardware store, NYSARC, St. Lawrence County Clerk's Office, and the District Attorney's Office in the courthouse.

My dreams for the future are to be an office worker and, for a hobby, a baker. And I will marry a girl, and I will stay in Canton for the rest of my life. I'm very interested in politics, and I hope our divided nation will come to love each other in the future.

I think that it's great to have Down syndrome. My advice to all mothers and fathers and nonsyndrome brothers and sisters is go to the library and bookstore to find books about kids with Down syndrome. Every year, there is a Down Syndrome National Conference Program, and I like to go with my parents. I have been to conferences in different major cities like Nashville; Philadelphia; Washington, D.C.; and Chicago. I like to go because I learn more about Down syndrome and how I can overcome my disability.

Sometimes, I am sad because sometimes people don't understand me. Most of the time, I am happy because I am proud that I have so many accomplishments and I love my life.

21
■ ■ ■

Life Is Good

JOEL C. PETERSON

■ ■ ■

My life is good. My family helps me. Lots of friends help me. I feel comfortable with them—friends at Shaw's (where I work), at the library, at dancing school, Mom and Dad's friends, friends in the community and at church. Now, I am beginning with new friends at school.

I have friends that are boys and friends that are girls, but only one is my girlfriend. We both like to dance (especially tap dance), swim, and go to the Boston Pops, and we both play Special Olympics golf. We don't drive, so our parents help us to get together once in a while, sometimes for shows or dinner or a movie.

When I was growing up, I tried out lots of different jobs—paper delivery, mailings for a doctor's office, pizza store helper, library volunteer, and then, a big job at the supermarket, Shaw's, getting carriages and singing while I work, and I became a steady paid worker. I still work when I am on school break.

I have had fun trying all kinds of activities: inclusive softball, bowling, tennis, karate, swimming, horseback riding, kayaking, and now golf. My brothers are swimmers and golfers, and I still do lots of these. I still like to be an altar server and to go hiking and do yoga.

Listening to music, especially Broadway shows, is something I like to do a lot. Some other favorite things are tobogganing at night with my sister, cross country skiing, being an altar server, acting, dancing, singing while I get carriages at Shaw's and dancing at the Shaw's Christmas party, putting music on tapes when I make a theme tape, showing my nieces and nephews how to dance to show tunes, washing dishes on my dish night, and trying new food and Mom's good food. I like going to different places like museums and the Boston Pops and the symphony, Thomas Jefferson's home in Virginia, Universal and MGM Studios in Florida, but I don't like some of the amusement park rides and scary stuff.

I feel good about being able to walk to my activities around town—to my job, to my dentist's office, to church, to get a haircut, and to the bank—and I am proud of knowing how to choose healthy foods in restaurants and stores.

It was a great day when my girlfriend and I were able to try out for the high school musical. No one from the special class had ever done it. We made it! We were sailors in *Anything Goes,* and I was a knight in *Once Upon a Mattress* in our senior year.

I have danced all my life because I like music. We went to many shows, and I saw my sister dance. I know all the names of the musicals and the names of the writers of the musicals. When we found the Peggy McGlone Dance Studio, I was 20 years old. I was thrilled to have two dance classes every week including tap, jazz, and ballroom routines. The recitals were exciting, especially when I was allowed to be part of the finale and dance with the teachers. I feel that my dancing is a gift.

I really like acting, too. When I saw *I'm Special, You're Special,* I said, "I could do that." So I tried out, got the part, and for 8 years I played the part of David. We performed in schools, mostly in Rhode Island. I really like learning to act, and it was great getting paid for the performances. I also got a part in *The Wizard of Oz* at Wheelock Theater in Boston, I performed in a community theater program in Everett two summers, and I played in *Oliver* in Melrose. Even small parts are fun.

My new stage work is really making me happy. I am learning liturgical dance, which I do in church and also in a production called *A Dancer's Christmas* at Boston College. One of my favorite parts is when I dance with the choreographer, Fr. Bob VerEecke. I am very busy in December at rehearsals and productions.

Now that I have graduated from Berkshire Hills Music Academy (BHMA), I am performing very often in different places. This is different because I perform with other people like me. We all live in a house near the school campus. We are graduates of BHMA and are learning living skills as we perform and earn money for our expenses.

It is good to dream and to reach for the stars. It feels right and makes me happy.

22

...

My Story

SUJEET S. DESAI

...

Hello, I am Sujeet Desai. My nickname is "Suj." I am a musician and self-advocate. I give music performances and do workshops. I would like to share my story with you.

I am 23 years old. I was born with Down syndrome. Today, I am who I am because my parents believed in me and helped me with my dreams. I have a brother "Ninad" who is 2 years older than me and lives in Buffalo, NY. My parents took me everywhere they took Ninad. He became my role model. We did many things together. I miss him a lot.

I graduated from Fayetteville Manlius High School (in New York) in 2001 with honors. I was the first student to be included in Oak Chapter of National Honor Society in our school. I had *A* grades in my music classes and exams. School was fun with my friends and all the music, but it was not easy to keep up.

The middle school was the hardest. Teasing by other classmates made me sad. I was shy to talk, and mom said I could not defend for myself when other students told lies and got me in trouble. However, my mom believed in inclusion and kept working with my teachers. She had to advocate hard for me as I was the first music student with a disability in my school. Also, my brother was in the same school and used to look over me. That was a big help. My brother's friends became my friends more than my own classmates.

The high school years were better. I was already doing music well. I had taken many Piano Guild auditions and NYSSMA (New York State

School Music Association) exams for clarinet and violin like other music students. I was in school orchestra, different bands, and all-year-round music concerts and competitions. I was on the varsity swim team. I had a black belt in Tae Kwon Do.

While attending high school, I also went to Onondaga Community College and Syracuse University for extra credits. My teachers said I had a very busy and hard-to-keep schedule than any other students in my school, but I managed that well. I got better speaking for myself and started performing my own concerts. I was in many newspaper articles and on TV and radio shows. My abilities made other students respect me and like me.

My parents always gave me every chance to learn different things. My mom would look for good teachers who had patience and believed in me. I loved music since I was very young. I play six instruments. For my solo performances, I play clarinet, violin, piano, and bass clarinet. Recently, I started playing alto saxophone and drums.

I started performing over 6 years ago. It makes me happy to see people like my music and enjoy it and cheer for me. I do small events like birthday parties to annual banquets, Buddy Walks, to very large conferences. The largest crowd I ever played was over 5,000 for a baseball game where I played the national anthem.

I play different styles of music like classical, Broadway popular, movie and TV themes or jazz, and pop music as needed for the theme of the event. My mom makes all the programs and works with the inviting party, and my dad manages my sound, video, and computers. We three in the family are a great team.

I had my own band in 2000 with 12 musicians. It was at my home in our basement. It was very hard work to get going with band rehearsals and to book gigs. My parents helped me a lot. I have been a member of many community bands for the last 7 years. I enjoy playing in ensembles. I was a member of Young Actors Workshop in Syracuse University for over 5 years. We did 3 musical shows every year. I have been a member of Potential Unlimited Production for the last 3 years. With them, I do musicals and summer music camps.

I also love to do duets and trios. I did many of those when I was in the academy. My band rehearsals, ensembles, solo performances, and different sports keep my evenings and weekends very busy. Performing in front of a crowd gave me confidence to speak.

I started doing musical and fun workshops for young children. First, my mom used to join me for workshops. My audience loved it. I was encouraged. Now, I do workshops on my own with PowerPoint.

We have traveled many places to do concerts in the U.S. and other countries like Singapore, Malaysia, Canada, and India. During my travel, I have made many friends with other self-advocates like Chris

Burke, Mia Peterson, Karen Gaffney, Carrie Bergeron, pianist Tony Dubois, and many more. I love to travel around the world and meet people from different cultures.

I have won many awards. While in high school, I won a community award for my work in different music stores, Syracuse University band library, and volunteer entertainment in the community. I have won four International Awards. In April 2004, I received an "Honor & Pride" award given by the World Down Syndrome Congress for Most Outstanding Individual with Down Syndrome. Over 35 countries had participated.

My other three awards are from the President and Minister of the Community Development of Singapore in 2001, "Yes I can" award from the Council for Exceptional Children in the year 2000, and "2004 Christian Pueschel Memorial Citizen Award." My honor was it was given to me by his father, Dr. Pueschel, himself at the NDSC (National Down Syndrome Congress) 2004 conference. In 2004, I was selected as "Our Heroes" by AADMD (American Academy of Developmental Medicine and Dentistry) and posted on their web site along with Mrs. Eunice Kennedy Shriver.

I wanted to go to college just like my brother. My parents supported me. I joined the Berkshire Hills Music Academy in Massachusetts for 2-year residential postsecondary study in music and human services. My parents were worried about me leaving home. But I enjoyed living on the campus with a roommate. I learned many living skills like cooking, laundry, and banking.

I graduated from the academy in 2003. I met many famous musicians in the academy. I had the 2 best years with my classmates who were all musicians with different music skills. They are my friends forever. I miss them a lot. We continue to call and write e-mail to each other.

In 2003, I moved back home to live in Cleveland, NY, with my parents. I work for OMRDD (Office of Mental Retardation and Developmental Disabilities). I am also a member of the national organization AmeriCorps and do self-advocacy workshops. I work part time as a teacher's aide in an elementary school music department and part time in a library where I also play music. From work, I go to different senior centers, nursing homes, and Day-Hab centers to entertain them, and, a couple evenings, I play music in a restaurant.

In September 2004, I moved in a house with a couple roommates to Rome, NY. Now, I am very close to my work. I enjoy living on my own. I still visit my parents on weekends.

In addition to music, my parents involved me in different sports. In 1999, I received a black belt in Tae Kwon Do. I worked very hard for it over 6 years. My brother did Tae Kwon Do with me 'til he moved to Buffalo. He was a gold medalist in the national tournament. We traveled all over the U.S. for his tournaments. I also won medals in two state tournaments.

I am a very good swimmer and an Alpine skier. I participated with Special Olympics since I was 9 years old. I have won many awards. My most memorable award was Special Olympics World Games 1999 for Aquatics. All these sports kept me strong and healthy during both summer and winter.

Two documentaries are done on my life story. I have my own web page, "Suj's Site," http://www.sujeet.com. I started this when I was in computer graphics class in tenth grade. My teachers and brother helped me. Now, it is very big, and my dad manages it. Over 59,000 people around the world have visited my web page to read my story. Many parents send me e-mails saying that I am a role model and bring hope to their children with disabilities. I am glad to read those e-mails from all around the world and hear that my story brings hope to parents of new babies born with disabilities. I work very hard without giving up. If I can do it, you can do it, too. Believe in what you can do. Believe in your abilities and work hard at it. Then, you will have a bright tomorrow.

My mom says when I was born, the hospital staff did not give her any information about Down syndrome babies and how to raise them at home. She was sad and discouraged as she did not get the support she needed from the hospital and also from the community, doctors, and my schools. She had to struggle to get me things that I needed. She says the only people she felt were friends and helped her were the services that work for people with disabilities. Therefore, now she does workshops to help other parents of children with disabilities.

One of her workshops is titled "Improvising Disability with Music." She believes that music and different sports help me to learn other things that are hard for me. It helped me in school with my studies. She talks about how music can be used for people with disabilities to do better in life. Music, arts, dance, massages, and yoga relieves your stress and improves your memory to help you learn new skills. This is called "improvising disability."

I know I am slow and have a hard time to understand many things, especially when they get complicated, like money matters and business skills, but I still manage with someone's help. I live a busier and happier life than many people without disabilities. I bring joy to others. I get happy when I hear my parents saying they are proud of me. My mom says I am the "sunshine of her life." I feel sad when I hear my mom talking to her friends that she worries about me when I get older and she is not around me to take care of me. She says only the parents of children with disabilities can understand the pain and hardship they go through to raise their child in the real world.

I don't understand everything about Down syndrome or why God makes one child normal and one with disabilities. I hate when people don't respect persons with disabilities. People with disabilities have feelings like anyone else.

They may not do well in the studies. Their skills may be hidden because they are not always able to self-advocate and not able to speak for themselves. But if people give them a chance, take time get to know them, then they sure can show their hidden talents. People without disabilities should understand this and respect persons with disabilities.

Together, I and my mom do workshops, and we travel around the world to encourage and help people with disabilities, their parents, and the people who work with them. This is our mission and my dream. My music is not only for entertainment, but it is for inspiration. My workshops are educational to send my message "Improvise Your Disability" and " Make It Happen." My dream is to find a beautiful girl who enjoys music and likes to swim, ski, bowl, and golf. When I find such a girl, I want to marry her and live with her in my own apartment. I know my mom won't be worried about me then as I will have someone to share my life with, love me, and take care of me after my parents.

(As I am finishing my story, I think I have met the girl of my dreams. She has a beautiful smile. She is full of love and joy. When we are together, we enjoy talking and sharing a lot of things. I miss her when she leaves. I wish I could spend more time with her.)

... 23 ...

Guardianship and Its Alternatives

Robert D. Dinerstein

One of the most important aspects of adulthood for any person is the recognition of that person as someone who is not only capable of making decisions but also is treated by society as such. For many people, turning 16, 18, or 21 years of age (depending on the decision in question) is a rite of passage that brings with it the ability to make such important decisions as whom to vote for, where to live, whom to marry, how to spend one's money, and what medical procedures to undergo. The ability to make such decisions—with or without the assistance of others—is a critical component of the self-determination and autonomy that society values so dearly.

Adults of typical intelligence are presumed to value self-determination. Moreover, they are presumed to have the capacity to make decisions in their own way. Even if individuals disagree with the decision an adult makes—such as whether to forgo a recommended medical procedure—they cannot legitimately override the person's decision (though, of course, they can try to persuade the person to make a different decision). The right to self-determination is so basic that society rarely needs to invoke it for most citizens; it is simply understood.

Historically, people with Down syndrome and other intellectual disabilities have not benefited from these presumptions. Rather, they have been subjected to institutionalization, where the need to make decisions was rarely in evidence, and overprotective, if well-meaning, policies resulted in others (family members, staff) making decisions for them in what was thought to be "their best interest." Regardless of whether these decisions were objectively "good ones," they were plainly not the decisions of the individuals with disabilities themselves. Moreover, even where statutes provided explicitly to the contrary, people with Down syndrome and other intellectual disabilities were presumed to *lack* capacity rather than possess it. Once one determines (or assumes) that another human being lacks decision-making capacity, it is a short step to make decisions for the person without even considering what his or her wants, desires, or needs might be.

Dating back to the 14th century in Anglo-Saxon jurisprudence, guardianship has been the most popular form of legal intervention in the decision-making rights of adults deemed to lack capacity for reasons of mental illness, dementia, intellectual disability, or age. Guardianship of the estate (i.e., the financial affairs of the individual) or the person (other aspects of the individual, e.g., caring for oneself, determining residence, and making medical decisions) are the formal mechanisms by which an individual (the *guardian*) steps into the shoes of the individual (the *ward,* now often called the incapacitated person) and is empowered to make decisions for that person.

Historically, guardians acted as plenary or complete guardians with complete decision-making rights in the sphere (financial or personal, or both) in which a court appointed them. Although guardianships (sometimes called *conservatorships* in some states) were designed to protect a person (or his or her property) from harm, they often failed to function as positive interventions (American Bar Association, 1989; Associated Press, 1987; House Subcommittee on Health and Long-Term Care, 1987; Knauer, 2003; Mental Disability Rights International, 1997; O'Sullivan, 2002; Winick, 2005). Even when they did function as intended, guardianships exacted a heavy price on the allegedly incapacitated person by denying his or her right to make any decisions and, therefore, consigned the individual to a form of civil death.

As in many areas affecting the lives of adults with Down syndrome, the legal landscape is changing regarding decision-making capacity and guardianship. The civil and human rights revolutions for people with disabilities, reflected in such U.S. statutes as Section 504 of the Rehabilitation Act of 1973 (PL 93-112) and the Americans with Disabilities Act (ADA) of 1990 (PL 101-336) and in such international forums as the United Nations, where efforts are proceeding to draft a convention to protect the rights of people with disabilities, represent a new paradigm in which people with disabilities are considered to be citizens with rights and not people to be abused, ignored, or overprotected (ADA; Kanter, 2003; PL 93-112; United Nations, 2001).

The presumptions about capacity for decision making that apply to people without disabilities can and should be applied to people with all kinds of disabilities, including Down syndrome (Montreal Pan American Health Organization, 2004). Where those presumptions are properly overcome—for people who truly lack decision-making capacity—society is increasingly insisting on intervening in the least restrictive manner possible. Plenary guardianship is no longer the only answer to the question posed by an adult who lacks decision-making capacity. Rather, guardianship is simply one form of surrogate decision making and the most restrictive one at that.

This chapter explores the nature of guardianship and its alternatives for adults with Down syndrome. It argues that many adults with Down syndrome either have, or can be trained to have, capacity for decision making in numerous areas of their lives. It urges the adoption of various forms of assisted decision making that are less intrusive and less formal than court-ordered guardianship. In those cases where guardianship is the appropriate form of decision-making intervention, the chapter advocates use of a full range of due-process safeguards before guardianship may be imposed. It further concludes that concepts such as the least restrictive alternative, substituted judgment, and periodic review must be applied to the entire guardianship system. Consistent with the presumption of decision-making capacity, provision for surrogate decision making has its place, so long as one does not assume that surrogate decision making always means guardianship or that once a guardian is appointed, no further focus on the guardian or the incapacitated person is necessary. In the final analysis, a thoughtful system of surrogate decision making, including, where necessary, guardianship, can assist adults with Down syndrome in making their own decisions to the extent of their capacity while providing protection in those areas where they truly need it.

ROLE OF CAPACITY IN DECISION MAKING

Adults, including adults with Down syndrome, are presumed to have the capacity to make decisions. *Capacity* (a term preferred to the alternative *competency*, which implies more of an all-or-nothing determination) is one of three components underlying consent, along with information and voluntariness (Dinerstein, Herr, & O'Sullivan, 1999; Ellis, 1992). That is, before an individual can consent (or withhold consent) to a decision, he or she must have the capacity to make the decision, must have adequate information regarding the decision in question, and must make the decision voluntarily and free from coercion. Only when all three elements are present can one assume that a decision is the free, knowledgeable, and intelligent expression of a person's will.

Each of these elements of informed decision making for adults with Down syndrome requires further elaboration. For example, many adults with Down syndrome may be in situations in which they are unable to make voluntary decisions free of coercion. Institutional settings are the most obvious example of this circumstance, but it is also possible that people with Down syndrome are in community-based programs or enmeshed in family relationships in which they are not really free to make their own decisions (with or without assistance). Also, for a decision to be informed, the information provided (e.g., by a physician who seeks to perform a medical procedure on a patient) must be clear and understandable to the person receiving it. So, for example, one would expect a physician proposing a medication to a patient to identify the risks and benefits of the medication in question, as well as any alternatives that may be available (e.g., nonmedication alternatives, another medication). There is nothing about the mere diagnosis of Down syndrome that renders the person unable to understand information presented to him or her, though the person's level of functioning may dictate the manner in which the information is conveyed.

It is in the area of decision-making capacity, however, that people with Down syndrome and other disabilities have faced the greatest challenges. As noted previously, these individuals are often wrongly presumed to be incapable rather than capable. Once one reverses that presumption, however, one still must ask some very basic questions:

- Is capacity a legal or medical determination?

- Is capacity an all-or-nothing proposition?

- Is there one standard for capacity, and, if so, what is it?

- Can one have capacity to make some decisions and not others?

- Can one's capacity vary over time?

Modern answers to these questions reflect a developing consensus. First, it is clear that capacity is a legal and not a medical decision. (Anderer, 1990). That is, only a legally appointed official, such as a judge, can make a determination that an individual lacks capacity. Although individuals who come into contact with the adult with Down syndrome may act as if the person lacks capacity, such behavior does not establish the legal status of incapacity. Of course, the judge must make his or her determination of capacity based on evidence, and typically a portion of that evidence will be provided by a clinical professional (who may, but need not be, a medical professional), who will be asked to make an assessment of the person's capacity. Too often in the past, judges called on to make capacity determinations have deferred reflexively and excessively to the medical professional (without adequate challenge by the allegedly incapacitated person's legal representative, if he or she has one). Professional evidence of capacity, or its absence, is important, but it is not necessarily dispositive.

Second, capacity is not an all-or-nothing proposition. Nor is it a concept that can be determined in the abstract. That is, one has (or lacks) capacity to do something in particular (e.g., write a will, drive a car, make a medical decision) (Buchanan & Brock, 1989). Experts increasingly recognize that global determinations of capacity (or incapacity) are of dubious value and do not reflect the wide variations in human experience for people with and without disabilities (Knauer, 2003). People possess a range of capacities (Minow, 1990). An intellectually gifted person may thrive as a university professor (he or she may have the capacity to make the kinds of decisions professors are called on to make) but may be totally unable to fix mechanical problems on his or her motor vehicle (he or she lacks the capacity to make sound mechanical decisions). That one does not tend to use this kind of vocabulary when discussing the capabilities of mechanically challenged university professors does not detract from the essential point that everyone, including people with disabilities, can understand some concepts and take steps to implement those understandings better than other concepts.

The role that guardianship or another surrogate decision-making arrangement plays in the life of an adult with Down syndrome is premised on whether the individual can make decisions on his or her own (or with some form of assistance). Thus, the focus is specifically on the person's capacity to make a decision. Whether an individual can make a decision depends not only on his or her decision-making capacity, but also on the particular decision in question and the circumstances under which it is made (Buchanan & Brock, 1989). Put differently, decision-making capacity is inherently a contextual determination and represents an interaction between a person and his or her environment (Anderer, 1990).

If capacity is context specific, then it is also true that capacity can vary over time (especially for people with serious mental disorders). It can also be developed over time with the right kinds of interventions and training. So, if an adult with Down syndrome is deemed not to have capacity currently to handle money matters, then it is possible that with the right kinds of habilitative programs he or she might be trained to develop that capacity.

Commentators stress the need to focus on functional impairment in determining decisional incapacity. For example, the influential Uniform Guardianship and Protective Proceedings Act of 1997[1] defines an incapacitated person as:

---

[1]Guardianship is a state law function, which means that each state has its own laws on the subject. However, the National Conference of Commissioners on Uniform State Laws (1997) drafts model statutes, such as the Uniform Guardianship and Protective Proceedings Act of 1997, that many states adopt in whole or in part as their own legislation.

> An individual who, for reasons other than being a minor, is unable to receive and evaluate information or make or communicate decisions to such an extent that the individual lacks the ability to meet essential requirements for physical health, safety or self-care, even with appropriate technological assistance. (National Conference of Commissioners on Uniform State Laws, 1997)

In assessing functional impairment, it is important, among other things, to identify with some precision the needs the person can and cannot meet, the harm to person or property that could result from this failure to meet one's needs, and the nexus between the impairment in the person's decision-making process and his or her ability to make the decisions necessary to avoid the harm in question (Anderer, 1990).

One would expect that if capacity is such a crucial concept in determining an individual's ability to make decisions, then a clear definition of capacity and established methods of determining its presence or absence would be available. Unfortunately, although research is proceeding, these elements are far from solidly established. Historically, statutory definitions of capacity typically have been conclusory in nature—the person "lacks sufficient understanding or capacity to make or communicate responsible decisions" (Anderer, 1990, p. 7).

Moreover, the focus on "responsible" decisions can import a substantive standard that is fraught with the possibilities of abuse. It is too easy to construe a proposed decision as irresponsible and thus as proof that a person lacks capacity when the decision is merely inconsistent with the decision *others* think the person should make (Herr, 1989–1990). The more stringent the adopted standard for capacity, the easier it is to find that a person lacks capacity in whole or in part, subjecting the person to possibly unnecessary surrogate intervention, such as guardianship. And yet, if the definition of capacity is too loose, it may subject the person to decisions that expose him or her to an unacceptable risk of personal and/or financial harm or perpetuate the fiction that the individual can make the decision in question when he or she clearly cannot do so in any meaningful sense.

Remarkably little research has been done on assessing the specific decision-making capacity of people with intellectual disabilities, and there are no clear standards for its determination (Cea & Fisher, 2003). Accordingly, researchers and commentators have looked to the mental health field, where researchers have identified four potential components of decision-making capacity when determining whether a person can consent to treatment. These are the ability to express a choice, understand relevant information, appreciate the importance of the information for one's situation, and rationally manipulate the information to weigh pros and cons (Appelbaum & Grisso, 1995;

Grisso & Appelbaum, 1998). These standards are not free from controversy, especially with regard to the last two elements of the definition, which may set too high a standard for capacity determinations (Saks, 2002; Slobogin, 1996), but at least this definition focuses on the process of decision making rather than on the resultant decision the person purports to make as a measure of decision-making capacity (Buchanan & Brock, 1989).

CONSEQUENCES OF DETERMINING A LACK OF CAPACITY

Some adults with Down syndrome will not have adequate capacity to make at least some decisions, but a determination that such individuals lack capacity to make certain decisions does not mean that they need to have a guardian appointed. There are some decisions that are so minor that even if a person were properly deemed to lack capacity, the appointment of a guardian or other surrogate decision maker would be inappropriate. Consider asking a person with Down syndrome whether he or she wants to go to the movies or to a baseball game. Even if the person lacked capacity to make the decision—because he or she did not understand the nature of the activities or could not weigh the pros and cons of each—one would not think of appointing a guardian to make the decision for him or her. The risk of a "wrong" decision is minor. No one, including the person with Down syndrome, is likely to be harmed by the decision one way or the other. To appoint a guardian or other surrogate in such a situation would not only be overly costly and administratively inconvenient but also lead to a loss of rights (the ability to make a wide range of decisions) that would be greatly disproportionate to the supposed gains of making a good decision in this particular instance.

The person in this example might well have people in his or her life—family members, staff, others with whom he or she lives—who would be able to assist the person informally in making the decision. As the field of intellectual disabilities increasingly embraces the use of natural supports, such assistance can and should play a role in the life of the person with Down syndrome. The closer the person providing assistance is to the individual in need of decision-making assistance, the more likely the decision will reflect the values of the latter. If a staff member in the group home in which a person with Down syndrome resides knows that the person reacts very badly to crowds, he or she might reasonably conclude that the person would prefer to attend a movie in a small theater rather than a baseball game at a sold-out stadium.

To pursue our example further, if the person with Down syndrome has never attended a baseball game, he or she might have difficulty in making a decision about whether to go to one. That difficulty might well be less related to intellectual capacity and more a product of an impoverishment of life experiences. People involved in the person's life can help him or her develop greater decision-making capacity by exposing the person to more of what life has to offer and devising creative alternatives for presenting the information needed to make an informed choice about the activity in question.

Society also must be careful not to impose a model of decision making that fails to appreciate the manner in which people *without* disabilities make decisions. In the previous example, if one asked a person with typical intelligence if he or she wanted to attend a baseball game and the person indicated that he or she would do "whatever Joe wanted to do," then one would not think of telling the person that such a basis for decision making reflected a lack of capacity. In this case, one might say that the decision-maker cares more about camaraderie with another than about the specific activity proposed. At the other end of the decision-making spectrum, people with typical intelligence faced with highly important decisions (e.g., whether to purchase a home) are unlikely to make the decision without consulting with others. It should not be a measure of incapacity when a person with Down syndrome or other intellectual disability similarly consults with, or even defers to, others before making a decision.

As noted in the beginning of this chapter, an individual's interest in autonomy and self-determination is of great importance and provides the rationale for erring on the side of finding that a person has decision-making capacity. But autonomy is not an absolute value, regardless of whether an individual has a disability. For people with disabilities, the interest must be balanced against what has variously been described as the principle of beneficence or the *parens patriae* power (Kapp, 1999). This principle means that under some circumstances it may be appropriate to intervene to protect an individual from the consequences of a decision. This "paternalistic power" has been the subject of much controversy within the disability field, as it has often been employed in an overprotective fashion that denies the person's right to take risks and that may serve the interests of others over that of the person with disabilities. If carefully limited, however, there is an important role for this protective concern. If the decision in question exposes the person to a greater physical or psychological risk or is perceived to be at odds with the person's known values and interests, then there is greater justification for closely scrutinizing the person's capacity to make the decision (Dinerstein et al., 1999; Sundram, 1994).

Close scrutiny, however, does not necessarily mean appointing someone else, including a guardian, to make the decision for the allegedly incapacitated person. Rather, it means that the person's capacity for making a decision may need to meet the more rigorous version of the capacity standard discussed in the previous section. If the person cannot meet that standard, then one must explore alternatives to the person's unconstrained decision making. Some of those alternatives are the subject of the next section.

ALTERNATIVES TO INDEPENDENT DECISION MAKING

Some adults with Down syndrome "will not always have the cognitive, communicative, or educational capacity to make autonomous decisions, nor to give valid consent" (Dinerstein et al., 1999; Ellis, 1992). Even though some advocates argue that every person has legal capacity (Canadian Association for Community Living, 1992; United Nations, 2004), the level of "assistance" in decision making that some people need is such that to claim they have "legal capacity" or that they have in some sense "chosen" to receive assistance would appear to be a semantic fiction. Whether one conceptualizes the following alternatives as assistance to the person's decision making or substitutes for it, the practical effects are quite similar. Assistance in decision making lies on a continuum from informal, relatively nonintrusive arrangements to plenary guardianship. Consistent with the principle of the least restrictive alternative, the more informal and focused alternatives should first be exhausted before turning to the more intrusive and formal arrangements (Montreal Pan American Health Organization, 2004).

A number of alternative forms of decision making require that a person has capacity at one time even if he or she loses capacity at a later time. A *durable power of attorney* is a written instrument in which an individual designates an agent to make decisions (frequently financial decisions) on his or her behalf at some later time (O'Sullivan, 1999). The power is considered durable in that it survives any later incapacity that the individual may experience. The agent stands in the shoes of the principal and can act in most ways that the principal could have acted if he or she retained the capacity to act. The durable power of attorney should set out clearly those areas in which the principal authorizes the agent to act so that there is limited ambiguity about the principal's intentions and the agent's powers. Durable powers of attorney can be very useful for those individuals who have capacity but fear they may lose it later, or for those who have periods of alternating capacity and incapacity. Many adults with Down syndrome have sufficient capacity to be able to execute a durable power of attorney; however, individuals with Down syndrome who need pervasive supports in a number of areas (see American Association on Mental

Retardation, 1992) may not be able to use a durable power of attorney if they never had capacity in the first place.

Although state laws differ on the precise format of the durable power of attorney, many states and the District of Columbia have adopted a version of the Uniform Statutory Form Power of Attorney Act of 1988 (National Conference of Commissioners on Uniform State Laws, 1988). In the District of Columbia's version, the individual executing the power of attorney (the *principal*) appoints an agent (called the *attorney-in-fact*) "to act for [him or her] in any lawful way with respect to…initialed subjects"; initials those powers he or she wants the agent to exercise (e.g., power to enter into "banking and other financial transactions" or "benefits from social security, Medicare, Medicaid, or other governmental programs, or military service") or else indicates that the attorney-in-fact may exercise all financial powers; provides any special instructions to the attorney-in-fact; and provides that "this power of attorney will continue to be effective even though I become disabled, incapacitated, or incompetent" (D.C. Code §21-2101 [a], 2005).

For individuals whose only needed assistance is in handling money and who receive income from discrete governmental sources such as Supplemental Security Income, a *representative payee* may provide adequate assistance (O'Sullivan, 1999; Skoler & Allbright, 2000). A representative payee is someone who has the authority to receive and cash checks for an individual and use the funds to pay the person's bills or for other legitimate purposes that serve the interests and needs of the person. It is critical that the person appointed representative payee not have a conflict of interest with the individual, which can happen when, for example, a provider or institution uses the funds from the person to "pay" itself for expenses allegedly incurred, or takes a fee from the funds the person receives. There are legal requirements that must be met if one is to become a representative payee for another individual. Both durable powers of attorney and representative payees present certain risks to the individual whose decision making is supplanted, but a major advantage of each alternative is that its scope is relatively limited and does not entail additional legal disabilities that can affect the individual more generally.

For many adults with Down syndrome, the major area in which they will need assistance in decision making is concerning health care. Here, too, there are a number of potential alternatives to guardianships that can adequately serve a person's interests and needs.

Some individuals with Down syndrome can execute a *health care power of attorney*, similar to the durable power of attorney described previously but limited to health issues. If the person with Down syndrome has capacity, he or she can designate an individual to serve as his or her *proxy decision maker* at a later time. The proxy functions as an agent empowered to make health care decisions for the individual, though there are some decisions that the proxy would be unable to make without some additional (court-ordered) approval. As with the durable power of attorney, an adult with Down syndrome needs to have enough capacity to designate the proxy, even if later he or she loses capacity. But certainly, some individuals who might be unable to handle financial affairs might be able to make health care decisions, or at least name a trusted person who could do so for them.

As with durable powers of attorney in general, the precise nature of health care powers of attorney differs from state to state. In the District of Columbia, for example, the health care agent (called the *attorney-in-fact*) has the

> Authority to grant, refuse, or withdraw consent to the provision of any health-care service, treatment or procedure; the right to review the health care records of the principal; the right to be provided with all information necessary to make informed health-care decisions; the authority to select and discharge health-care professionals; and the authority to make decisions regarding admission to or discharge from health-care facilities and to take any lawful actions that may be necessary to carry out these decisions (D.C. Code § 21–2206 [a] [1]–[5], 2005).

The *principal* (the person with a disability appointing the attorney-in-fact) nevertheless retains the right to give or withhold informed consent with regard to any particular health care decision if he or she is able to do so (D.C. Code, § 21-2206 [b] [2], 2005).

In addition to designating someone as a health care proxy, an adult with Down syndrome can execute an *advance directive* or *advance medical directive* (again, assuming he or she has the level of capacity needed to do so) (Hurley & O'Sullivan, 1999). The advance directive is similar to the health care proxy but may be more specific in its focus on what the person wants done (or not done) rather than on naming a person to make those decisions for him or her (though an advance directive can also name an individual to be an agent to implement elements of the directive). A *living will* is another form of advance directive but is more limited in that it does not become effective until a person reaches a predetermined point in an illness (e.g., having a terminal illness, entering into a persistent vegetative state) and generally entails the person indicating that he or she does not want extraordinary treatment measures employed if the anticipated stage of illness occurs (Fraleigh, 1999).

A number of states have enacted legislation to provide for *health care surrogate decision making* for individuals without capacity who do not have (or need) guardians but need medical care (Herr & Hopkins, 1994; O'Connor, 1996). Although the statutes differ from state to state (as of 1996, 34 states and the District of Columbia had statutory provisions covering surrogate health care), many provide for family members or, in their absence, others to serve as surrogate health care decision makers when a patient who lacks capacity has not previously designated a health care decision maker. Under specific circumstances, these surrogates can make health care decisions for the incapacitated person, even in the absence of written instruments.

Although family members are frequently the preferred surrogate decision makers, many statutes provide for others to serve as surrogates in the absence of interested and available family members. Some states, such as New York, have developed innovative systems of providing panels of individuals to serve as health care surrogates in the absence of available family members (Herr & Hopkins, 1994). The statutes differ in important ways regarding the standard of decision making the surrogate should employ (substituted judgment or best interest); the determination of who, other than family members, can serve as surrogates (including whether physicians can do so) or otherwise make health care decisions on behalf of the incapacitated person; the issue of whether the person's incapacity alone is sufficient to permit a surrogate to act, or whether some additional qualifying condition is necessary; and the procedural requirements that must be observed once surrogate decision making is implemented (O'Connor, 1996). The Uniform Health-Care Decisions Act (National Conference of Commissioners on Uniform State Laws, 1994) provides an important resource for states seeking to update their health care surrogate laws, or enact new legislation altogether.

In addition to the previously mentioned forms of intervention, some states also permit individuals without capacity to conduct one-time transactions with the assistance of another person. Such arrangements do not require the appointment of a permanent guardian and can be a relatively informal and nonintrusive way to permit these individuals to take care of important business matters (O'Sullivan, 1999). For example, if an individual with Down syndrome who lacks decision-making capacity inherits money from a relative (e.g., proceeds from the sale of a house that his or her parent owned), he or she could have an individual appointed on a one-time basis (either as a temporary guardian or under some other designation) to approve the investment of the proceeds in a pooled trust that would be managed by a professional organization. Once the initial investment is made, the temporary guardian's role ceases.

There are also much less formal arrangements that can serve to protect the interests of the person with Down syndrome without the need of appointing a guardian. In appropriate circumstances, relatives, lay advocates, or advocacy groups, such as local protection and advocacy organizations, can assist individuals in making decisions even without formal statutory or court-ordered designations.

These alternatives by no means exhaust the wide range of alternatives to guardianship that are available to assist, and, where necessary, serve as forms of surrogate decision making for people who lack decision-making capacity in some area or other. The availability of more formal alternatives will vary from state to state, and one may want to consult a lawyer to learn which alternatives are possible in a particular state. The more informal alternatives are likely to be available almost everywhere, and one can contact a local social service agency or conduct research on the Internet (being careful to evaluate the results critically) to learn how to take advantage of these alternatives. Although each modality has its own pros and cons and should be evaluated in the context of the particular needs and circumstances of the individual with Down syndrome who lacks decision-making capacity, the increasing proliferation of these alternatives is a recognition of society's changing conceptions of how to deal with decisional incapacity in a manner that does not unduly deny people the capacities that they in fact retain.

GUARDIANSHIP

There will be some adults with Down syndrome for whom guardianship indeed will be the appropriate form of surrogate intervention. For these individuals, it is critically important that guardianship be used in a manner that provides the necessary level of protection without excessive denial of the person's civil rights. Although guardianship is a function of state law and thus subject to many variations, there is an increasing consensus on a set of best practices regarding guardianship that should inform the use of this form of intervention.

Limited Guardianships

As a starting point, even where some form of guardianship is appropriate, the least restrictive alternative principle must still be operative. That is, the guardianship must provide only that form of intervention, and only in those areas where the individual with Down syndrome needs surrogate decision making that cannot be satisfied through the kinds of nonguardianship alternatives described in the preceding section. In the context of guardianship proper, the least restrictive alternative principle means that limited guardianships that precisely identify the areas in which the guardian has authority to make decisions, as well as those in which he or she does not, are to be preferred over plenary or complete guardianships. Currently, most state guardianship statutes provide for limited guardianships, and many of these provide explicitly that limited guardianships are preferred over plenary guardianships (Frolik, 2002).

The notion of limited guardianships is not new (Frolik, 1981; Kindred, 1971) and the capacity of limited guardianships to function as a less restrictive alternative to plenary guardianships seems obvious; however, for a variety of reasons, the legal system makes insufficient use of this alternative. Many judges, court clerks, families, service providers, and even lawyers for the allegedly incapacitated person seem to view limited guardianships as inconvenient, potentially costly (if the individual needs to come to court for adjustments in the areas in which limited guardianship is needed), and ultimately unnecessary (Rogers, 1984). The persistence of this view is troubling in light of the important interests of autonomy and self-determination served by limiting guardianship to only those areas where it is truly needed. Moreover, this view is inconsistent with any notion that capacity can change over time, that a person can learn to develop capacity with the right forms of training, and that not all decision-making situations can be anticipated at the time a specific order for guardianship is sought. If the paradigm in the field of intellectual disabilities (including Down syndrome) has truly shifted toward self-determination, person-centered planning, recognition of people's strengths as well as weaknesses, and reliance on natural supports, then advocates for adults with Down syndrome who lack decision-making capacity must insist on the use of limited guardianship where statutes provide and argue for statutory amendments where they do not.

An order of limited guardianship can provide, for example, that the allegedly incapacitated person lacks capacity to make decisions and needs a limited guardian (assuming nonguardian alternatives have been exhausted) for financial matters only, but retains decision-making capacity in other areas, such as health care decision making and decisions about residence. One advantage of a limited guardianship is that it may permit an individual under guardianship to exercise his or her right to vote, a right that in a majority of jurisdictions would be extinguished under plenary guardianship (O'Sullivan, 2002).

Limited guardians would be required to consult with the partially incapacitated person even on matters considered within the purview of the guardianship. That a court deems an individual to lack full decision-making capacity does not mean that the individual does not retain some preferences and desires that can be expressed (in whatever form of communication is available to the individual) to his or her guardian.

Due Process Guarantees in Guardianship Proceedings

Even a limited guardian should not be appointed before a court of competent jurisdiction holds a hearing at which full due process safeguards are made available (O'Sullivan, 1999, 2002). Because these due process safeguards are the same for both plenary and limited guardianship, they are discussed together.

A guardianship proceeding begins when an individual (the *petitioner*) files a petition requesting that a guardianship be established over an allegedly incapacitated person (the *respondent* in the proceeding). Each state will have its own statutes setting out the standards for filing the petition. In many states, the statutes will contain a statutory form that a petitioner can fill out. In other states, one can go to the clerk's office in the courthouse and ask whether there are any forms available for filing the petition. Some of these forms may be available from court system sites on the Internet. Although it is not necessary to have the assistance of a lawyer in filing the petition, if the matter is to be contested it is a good idea to have legal representation. Under most state statutes, the petitioner is a family member or otherwise "interested person." The petitioner alleges the ways in which he or she believes the allegedly incapacitated person lacks capacity and why a guardianship (whether limited or plenary) is believed to be the least restrictive alternative. Once the petition is submitted to a court of competent jurisdiction (often a state probate court), the court sets in motion a process in which a hearing is held before a judge or magistrate of the court.

The allegedly incapacitated person, as well as other specified individuals, must receive adequate notice of the hearing. The court may also appoint a visitor or guardian *ad litem* (for the purposes of the legal action only) to make additional inquiries of the need for guardianship. The court will also provide that a professional with the appropriate expertise be appointed to assess the basis for the person's alleged incapacity. For an individual with Down syndrome, that professional would presumably be someone from a discipline, and with professional training, related to Down syndrome or intellectual disabilities in general, such as a psychologist or special educator. If the alleged incapacity related to an individual with Down syndrome's ability to make health care decisions, a health care professional with a background in intellectual disabilities might be the appropriate professional.

It is highly desirable that the allegedly incapacitated person have an attorney appointed to represent him or her. Almost all jurisdictions permit an allegedly incapacitated person to be represented by counsel, and many provide for court appointment of counsel for individuals who cannot afford an attorney (O'Sullivan, 2002). A number of commentators have called for counsel to be provided as a matter of right for the allegedly incapacitated person in light of the serious individual interests implicated in a finding of guardianship. The individual's attorney should function as a "typical" attorney in advocating zealously for the interests of his or her client rather than functioning more as a guardian *ad litem* or otherwise acting in what the attorney believes is in the client's best interest (O'Sullivan, 1999). The American legal system is premised on dispute resolution based on an adversarial model designed to produce the best result when each side has every incentive to pursue its position as it sees fit. There is no justification for questioning this premise for people with Down syndrome in guardianship proceedings (or in any other proceedings for that matter).

If the allegedly incapacitated person clearly objects to the appointment of a guardian (whether limited or plenary), the attorney's role is plain: to present evidence and make arguments against the guardianship. If the allegedly incapacitated person appears to go along with the appointment of a guardian, the attorney's role is to make sure the client understands all of the implications and ramifications of the appointment, advise the client of his or her options (including advising the client that it is legitimate to oppose the guardianship even if a family member or other trusted person is proposing it), and then argue the client's position at the hearing. The results of such counseling could transform the client's position from acquiescing to a plenary guardianship to advocating for a limited guardianship that preserves some decision-making authority for the client. Where the client does not or cannot express an opinion regarding the appointment of a guardian, the attorney may take the position of opposing guardianship (or arguing for an alternative, including limited guardianship) to ensure that the court is presented with arguments for and against the proposed intervention.

At the guardianship hearing, the allegedly incapacitated person must be able to present (through the attorney) his or her own witnesses and other evidence, as well as cross-examine the witnesses (and challenge the evidence) presented by the petitioner or the evidence from any court-appointed professional who has evaluated the person. Although many statutes permit the allegedly incapacitated person not to attend the hearing, the importance of the interests at stake strongly argues for the person's attendance unless he or she truly is too ill to attend. Indeed, absence from the hearing might make it much more difficult for the allegedly incapacitated person to understand that a guardian has been appointed (if that is the court's decision) and what it means than if he or she attended the hearing, even if the person does not understand the proceedings completely. Certainly, the petitioner(s)' reluctance to confront the allegedly incapacitated person directly with uncomfortable evidence of the person's alleged incapacity is insufficient reason for that person's nonattendance.

The burden of persuasion for appointing a guardian is on the petitioner(s). Because of the important decision-making and liberty interests involved, the court should not grant the petition for guardianship unless the petitioner establishes the need for one by clear and convincing evidence, the highest standard of proof in noncriminal cases. The allegedly incapacitated person is also entitled to have the judge or magistrate make specific findings of fact regarding the need for a guardianship. Those findings, which should be written, should include a formal determination that 1) the allegedly incapacitated person lacks the capacity to make specific decisions (with those decisions specifically identified); 2) that because of this lack of capacity to make specific decisions the person is likely to suffer significant physical or psychological harm or substantial financial harm; and 3) that there are no less restrictive alternatives, including assisted decision making and other alternatives discussed previously, or limited guardianship (if the petitioner's request is for a plenary guardianship), that would address the person's functional limitations adequately. If the court approves a limited guardianship, the court's order should set out clearly what powers the guardian has, as well as what rights the partially incapacitated person retains. The order should set out those kinds of decisions (e.g., sterilization, abortion, consent to participate in experiments that pose more than minimal risk) that even a plenary guardian cannot make on behalf of the incapacitated person at all, or without an additional court order. Finally, the allegedly incapacitated person must have the right to appeal an adverse judgment to an appellate court.

The court order creating the guardianship needs to set out the specific obligations of the guardian, including the guardian's requirements to report to the court periodically. These requirements can be quite detailed, and a full discussion of them is beyond the scope of this chapter (see Hurme, 1991). But a critical element of the order is that it should set out a clear standard of decision making to which the guardian must abide. The standard most protective of the residual liberty interests of the allegedly incapacitated person is the substituted judgment standard, whereby the guardian is to make the decisions that the individual would make if he or she had the capacity to do so (Superintendent of Belchertown State School v. Saikewicz, 1977). This standard is to be contrasted to the best interests standard, in which the guardian acts in the manner that he or she thinks is best for the individual, even if the individual is likely to have chosen to act otherwise.

When the individual with Down syndrome or other intellectual disabilities has never expressed a preference regarding the decision in question, and in cases in which he or she truly lacks the present capacity to communicate any kind of preference, the substituted judgment standard essentially collapses into the best interest standard, but it is important to retain the conceptual distinction between the two standards so as not to overuse the latter when the former is legitimately possible to use.

Because it has been all too easy for guardians to fail to carry out their duties fully (for reasons of neglect or conscious exploitation), the court must exercise continued supervision over the guardianship. In addition to receiving the reports mentioned previously, the court should conduct a periodic review of the guardianship to assure that it is meeting its intended purposes and to confirm that the guardianship is still needed. At least one jurisdiction restricts limited guardianships to a period of time (5 years), at which time a party seeking to retain the guardianship would bear the burden of establishing the continued need for it (Michigan Compiled Laws §330.1626, 2004).

Not every person with Down syndrome who needs a guardian will have a responsible family person or other interested person available to serve in that capacity. In many states, there is some form of public guardianship system in place in which trained state employees are available to serve as guardians if a court deems a guardianship is appropriate (Siemon, Hurme, & Sabatino, 1993). Although there is no general listing of states that have public guardianship systems, research by Siemon et al. determined that, as of 1993, 42 states have some form of public guardianship system in effect. All states have private professionals or corporations (both for profit and nonprofit) that are available, for a fee, to provide guardianship services if there is no available family member to do so (Barnes, 2002). Individuals seeking information about private guardianships, including those that are certified by the National Guardianship Foundation, can go to the Internet to find relevant information (The Arc of the United States, 1999; National Guardianship Association, 2005; National Guardianship Foundation Registered Guardians, 2005). A discussion of this form of guardianship is beyond the scope of this chapter, but in both kinds of guardianships it is critical that the guardians be adequately trained and have manageable caseloads that would permit the kind of individualized attention that the incapacitated person needs. As in all other forms of assisted decision making for people with Down syndrome, public or professional guardians, no less than family guardians, need to interact with the incapacitated person regularly and continue efforts to ascertain the person's decisional interests and preferences when making decisions for him or her.

WHEN GUARDIANSHIP CAN PROTECT THE INDIVIDUAL'S RIGHTS

The thrust of this chapter has been to demonstrate that guardianship, while frequently well-intentioned, is often an unnecessary intervention in the lives of people with Down syndrome and other intellectual disabilities. Our focus must be on maximizing the decision-making capacity of adults with Down syndrome and minimizing the nature of any surrogate interventions that become necessary when those individuals legitimately lack capacity. When guardianship is an appropriate form of surrogate intervention, the serious nature of the intervention requires a full panoply of due process safeguards before it may be imposed.

But there are circumstances in which the appointment of a guardian can actually enhance the autonomy and self-determination of the individual with Down syndrome. Probably the most famous instance of guardianship functioning in such a manner was the case of Phillip Becker, a young man from California with Down syndrome (Guardianship of Phillip B., 1983). Phillip's parents placed him at birth in a licensed board and care facility where he received few developmental or educational programs. After an initial period in which they visited him often, Phillip's parents decreased the frequency of their visits and became emotionally detached from him. When Phillip was almost 5 years old, his parents moved him to a licensed residential facility for children with developmental disabilities after they became aware that the original board and care home, which was under new management, had significantly deteriorated, was unclean, and was seriously neglecting Phillip. In the new facility, the parents remained emotionally detached from Phillip, but a couple that volunteered at the new facility worked closely with him and developed a personal relationship with him.

Phillip had a congenital heart defect (relatively common in individuals with Down syndrome) that could have been addressed through open heart surgery performed when he was 6 years old, but his parents neither approved the surgery nor explored alternatives to it. Later, they refused to give permission for a low-risk heart catheterization procedure recommended by a pediatric cardiologist that would have addressed a ventricular septal defect in Phillip's heart (also commonly found in people with Down syndrome), even though the doctor informed them that without the surgery Phillip would probably not live beyond the age of 30. The parents apparently were concerned that they would not be able to care for Phillip in his later years. The parents were not helpful in the facility's efforts to place Phillip in a special education school program, though they eventually consented to his placement in one for "trainable mentally retarded" children.

Phillip, who later was tested with an IQ of 57, which placed him in the mild range of mental retardation based on the pre-1992 definition, would have benefited from classes for "educable mentally retarded" children.

When Phillip's father became aware of the close relationship the volunteer couple had developed with Phillip (which included their having Phillip over to their home on weekends), he refused permission for him to leave the facility, except to attend school or for medical purposes, and tried to limit all private contact between the couple and Phillip. Phillip did not understand why he could no longer visit with the couple; his behavior deteriorated, and he showed clear signs of depression.

The volunteer couple filed a petition to be declared guardians for Phillip, and thus to supersede the role of his parents. After a complicated series of court hearings and other procedural steps, a California appellate court upheld their appointment as guardians, concluding that the couple functioned as Phillip's psychological, or de facto, parents while the original biological parents were guilty of a pattern of emotional, physical, and medical neglect of their child. The couple eventually adopted Phillip after he reached adulthood, approved his open-heart surgery, which was concluded successfully, and welcomed him into their home on a full-time basis (Mnookin, 1988). As important, they were able to provide the emotional nourishment and support and educational input that Phillip needed but did not receive from his biological parents.

In the case of Phillip Becker, guardianship provided a means to open up possibilities for him, to increase his opportunities for self-determination and autonomy. Although the facts of the case are somewhat unusual, there are other instances in which individuals have petitioned for guardianship as a way to permit the allegedly incapacitated person to experience more freedom than an existing guardian or family member was prepared to permit (Herr & Weber, 1999.) Thus, for some people who lack decision-making capacity, guardianship can serve as an enhancement to, rather than detraction from, self-determination and autonomy.

SUMMARY

This chapter has attempted to answer a common question in the field of intellectual disabilities, "When does an adult with Down syndrome need a guardianship?" by posing a different, more nuanced question, "Under which circumstances does an adult with Down syndrome lack capacity for decision making to such an extent that he or she needs the intervention of a surrogate decision maker (and possibly a guardian)?"

One hopes that what the revised question loses in terseness is more than made up for by its emphasis on guardianship as an extraordinary intervention in the lives of adults with Down syndrome. It is a form of intervention that has achieved good things for many but also has been subject to numerous abuses. It is the blunderbuss that has been deployed to kill the proverbial fly of supposed incapacity. It is time to use a much wider range of alternatives to guardianship to solve the "problem" of incapacity, while at the same time recognizing that the concern for individual autonomy militates strongly against easy findings of global incapacity. A decent respect for the fundamental rights of adults with Down syndrome demands no less.

REFERENCES

American Association on Mental Retardation. (1992). *Mental retardation: Definition, classification, and systems of supports* (9th ed.). Washington, DC: Author.

American Bar Association. (1989). *Guardianship: An agenda for reform.* Washington, DC: Author.

Americans with Disabilities Act (ADA) of 1990, PL 101-336, 42 U.S.C. §§ 12101 *et seq.*

Anderer, S.J. (1990). *Determining competency in guardianship proceedings.* Washington, DC: American Bar Association.

Appelbaum, P.S., & Grisso, T. (1995). The MacArthur Treatment Competence Study. *Law and Human Behavior, 19,* 105–126.

Arc of the United States, The. (1999). *Future planning: Guardianship and people with mental retardation.* Retrieved December 2, 2005, from http://thearc.org/faqs/guard.html

Associated Press. (1987). Guardians of the elderly: An ailing system. In the U.S. Congress House of Representatives Select Committee on Aging, Subcommittee on Health and Long Term Care, *Abuses in guardianship of the elderly and the infirm: A national disgrace.* Washington, DC: U.S. Government Printing Office.

Barnes, A. (2002). The virtues of corporate and professional guardians. *Stetson Law Review, 31,* 941–1026.

Buchanan, A.E., & Brock, D.W. (1989). *Deciding for others: The ethics of surrogate decision making.* Cambridge, England: Cambridge University Press.

Canadian Association for Community Living. (1992). Supported decision making—Statement of principles. In *Task force on alternatives to guardianship.* Alberta, Canada: Author.

Cea, C.D., & Fisher, C.B. (2003). Health care decision-making by adults with mental retardation. *Mental Retardation, 41,* 78–87.

Dinerstein, R.D., Herr, S.S., & O'Sullivan, J.L. (Eds.). (1999). *A guide to consent.* Washington, DC: American Association on Mental Retardation.

Ellis, J.W. (1992). Decisions by and for people with mental retardation: Balancing considerations of autonomy and protection. *Villanova Law Review, 37,* 1779–1809.

Fraleigh, A.S. (1999). Note: An alternative to guardianship: Should Michigan statutorily allow acute-care hospitals to make medical treatment decisions for incompetent patients who have neither identifiable surrogates nor advance directives? *University of Detroit Mercy Law Review, 76,* 1079–1134.

Frolik, L.A. (1981). Plenary guardianship: An analysis, a critique and a proposal for reform. *Arizona Law Review, 23,* 599–660.

Frolik, L.A. (2002). Promoting judicial acceptance and use of limited guardianship. *Stetson Law Review, 31,* 735–755.

Grisso, T., & Appelbaum, P.S. (1998). *Assessing competence to consent to treatment: A guide for physicians and other health professionals.* Oxford: Oxford University Press.

Guardianship of Philip B., 139 Cal. App. 3d 407 (1983).

Herr, S.S. (1989–1990). Representation of clients with disabilities: Issues of ethics and control. *New York University Review of Law and Social Change, 17,* 609, 621.

Herr, S.S., & Hopkins, B.L. (1994). Health care decision making for persons with disabilities. *Journal of the American Medical Association, 271*(13), 1017–1022.

Herr, S.S., & Weber, G. (1999). Prospects for ensuring rights, quality supports, and a good old age. In S.S. Herr & G. Weber (Eds.), *Aging, rights, and quality of life: Prospects for older people with developmental disabilities* (pp. 343–370). Baltimore: Paul H. Brookes Publishing Co.

House Subcommittee on Health and Long Term Care of the Select Committee on Aging. (1987). *Abuses of the guardianship of the elderly and the infirm: A national disgrace.* (H.R. Doc. No. 639, 100th Congress, 1st Session)

Hurley, A.D.N., & O'Sullivan, J.L. (1999). Informed consent for health care. In R.D. Dinerstein, S.S. Herr, & J.L. O'Sullivan (Eds.), *A guide to consent* (pp. 39–55). Washington, DC: American Association on Mental Retardation.

Hurme, S.B. (1991). *Steps to enhance guardianship monitoring.* Washington, DC: American Bar Association.

Kanter, A.S. (2003). The globalization of disability rights law. *Syracuse Journal of International Law and Commerce, 30,* 242–267.

Kapp, M.B. (1999). Health care decision making: Legal and financial considerations. In S.S. Herr & G. Weber (Eds.), *Aging, rights, and quality of life: Prospects for older people with developmental disabilities* (pp. 45–58). Baltimore: Paul H. Brookes Publishing Co.

Kindred, M. (1971). Guardianship and limitations upon capacity. In M. Kindred, J. Cohen, D. Penrod, & T. Shaffer (Eds.), *The mentally retarded citizen and the law* (pp. 71–80). New York: Free Press.

Knauer, N.J. (2003). Defining capacity: Balancing the competing interests of autonomy and need. *Temple Political and Civil Rights Law Review, 12,* 322–331.

Mental Disability Rights International. (1997). *Human rights and mental health: Hungary* (pp. 58–64). Washington, DC: Author.

Minow, M. (1990). *Making all the difference: Inclusion, exclusion, and American law.* Ithaca, NY: Cornell University Press.

Mnookin, R.H. (1988). The guardianship of Philip B.: Jay Spears' achievement. *Stanford Law Review, 40*, 841–855.

Montreal Pan American Health Organization (PAHO)/World Health Organization (WHO) Conference on Intellectual Disability and Montreal WHO/PAHO Collaborating Center. (2004). *Montreal Declaration on Intellectual Disabilities: Article 6.* Lachine, Canada: Lisette-Dupras Readaption Centre & West Montreal Readaption Centre.

National Conference of Commissioners on Uniform State Laws. (1988). *Uniform Statutory Form Power of Attorney Act.* Retrieved December 2, 2005, from http://www.law.upenn.edu/bll/ulc/fnact99/1980s/usfpaa88.pdf

National Conference of Commissioners on Uniform State Laws. (1994). *Uniform Health-Care Decisions Act.* Charleston, SC: Author.

National Conference of Commissioners on Uniform State Laws. (1997). *Uniform Guardianship and Protective Proceedings Act of 1997.* Retrieved October 26, 2005, from http://www.law.upenn.edu/bll/ulc/fnact99/1990s/ugppa97.htm

National Guardianship Association. (2005). *Guardianship resources.* Retrieved October 26, 2005, from http://www.guardianship.org/displayassocicationlinks.cfm

National Guardianship Foundation Registered Guardians. (2005). *State listing of NGF registered guardians and phone numbers.* Retrieved October 26, 2005, from http://guardianship.org/associations/2543/files/NewRGs505.pdf

O'Connor, C.M. (1996). Statutory surrogate consent provisions: An overview and analysis. *Mental and Physical Disability Law Reporter, 20*, 128–132.

O'Sullivan, J.L. (1999). Adult guardianship and its alternatives. In R.D. Dinerstein, S.S. Herr, & J.L. O'Sullivan (Eds.), *A guide to consent* (pp. 7–34). Washington, DC: American Association on Mental Retardation.

O'Sullivan, J.L. (2002). Role of the attorney for the alleged incapacitated person. *Stetson Law Review, 31*, 687–698.

Rehabilitation Act of 1973, PL 93-112, 29 U.S.C. §§ 701 *et seq.*

Rogers, P.R. (1984). Understanding the legal concept of guardianship. In T. Apolloni & T.P. Cooke (Eds.), *A new look at guardianship: Protective services that support personalized living* (pp. 35–48). Baltimore: Paul H. Brookes Publishing Co.

Saks, E.R. (2002). *Refusing care: Forced treatment and the rights of the mentally ill.* Chicago: University of Chicago Press.

Siemon, D., Hurme, S.B., & Sabatino, C.P. (1993). Public guardianship: Where is it and what does it need? *Clearinghouse Review, 27*, 588–599.

Skoler, D.L., & Allbright, A.L. (2000). Judicial oversight of the nation's largest guardianship system: Caselaw on social security administration representative payee issues. *Mental and Physical Disability Law Reporter, 24*, 169–174.

Slobogin, C. (1996). "Appreciation" as a measure of competency: Some thoughts about the MacArthur group's approach. *Psychology, Public Policy, and Law, 2*(18), 18–30.

Sundram, C.J. (1994). A framework for thinking about choice and responsibility. In C.J. Sundram (Ed.), *Choice and responsibility: Legal and ethical dilemmas in services for persons with mental disabilities* (pp. 11–16). Albany: New York State Commission on Quality of Care for the Mentally Disabled.

Superintendent of Belchertown State School v. Saikewicz, 370 NE 2d 417 (Mass. 1977).

United Nations, Economic and Social Council. (2001). *Draft resolution II: Comprehensive and integral convention to protect and promote the rights and dignity of persons with disabilities.* Retrieved December 2, 2005, from http://www.un.org/esa/socdev/enable/eres2003-26.htm

United Nations, Working Group to the Ad Hoc Committee on a Comprehensive and Integral International Convention on the Protection and Promotion of the Rights and Dignity of Persons with Disabilities. (2004, January). *Draft Article 9: Equal recognition as a person before the law.* Retrieved December 2, 2005, from http://www.un.org/esa/socdev/enable/rights/ahcwgreporta9.htm

Winick, B.J. (2005). *Civil commitment: A therapeutic jurisprudence model.* Durham, NC: Carolina Press.

··· 24 ···

Advocacy and Adults with Down Syndrome

Steven M. Eidelman

Perform an Internet search for the terms *advocacy, self-advocacy, legislative advocacy,* and *individual advocacy,* and you will get more than 1,000,000 hits, ranging from trade associations, to college courses, to lobbyists selling their wares. Clearly, advocacy is a popular topic today. *Advocacy* comes from a Latin root—*advocatus*—meaning to call or to summon. In modern times, it means that a person, group, or organization pleads the cause of another with him or her or on his or her behalf. Advocates experience or see a situation they feel is unjust, and they speak out or take action to right the wrongs. In a comic book analogy, advocates are the superheroes fighting to make the world a better place.

Adults with Down syndrome experience the same life events as other adults—education, higher education and/or job training, living outside of their family homes, love, marriage, family, and community—however, they may need specialized services and supports to enable them to accomplish all or some of these things. Advocacy—either by a person him- or herself, family members, advocacy groups, and/or legal advocacy organizations—is responsible and will play a continued part in his or her success. Whether individuals with Down syndrome or their families participate directly or not, advocacy looms large in their lives, whether visible to them or taking place in the background.

Advocacy for people specifically with Down syndrome frequently takes place through broader disability advocacy where, despite differences between groups and organizations, there are overarching themes of freedom; self-determination; the right to education and medical care; opportunities for employment; and the panoply of human, legal, and civil rights those without disabilities often take for granted. The key phrase, attributed to Florynce R. Kennedy (1976), an African

American civil and women's rights advocate, is, "Don't agonize. Organize." Advocacy is the work of all of us. Adults with Down syndrome and their families have something to contribute to that work.

HISTORY OF ADVOCACY

When I served as Executive Director of The Arc of the United States, (1999–2005), I witnessed daily the interactions of people with cognitive, intellectual, and developmental disabilities and their families with service and support systems, both specialized programs like special education and nonspecialized programs from housing to health care. At worst, these systems actively discriminate, and at best they may benignly ignore and overlook the unique needs of this subset of society. Writing this chapter from my perspective as having been part of an organization (The Arc of the United States) that in recent years has been reflecting a lot about advocacy and has tried to figure out where it has been and where it may be going, my conclusion is that there is not enough advocacy, especially considering that advocacy has the power to change the lives of all people with Down syndrome.

Advocacy in 2006 is different from how it was in 1950, when The Arc was founded. It is different from how it was in 1960, 1970, 1980, or 1990. Like everything else, it keeps changing. The role of people with Down syndrome and other disabilities has evolved from passive recipient of charity to active participant in the life of the community, including leadership roles, the responsibilities of citizenship, and the challenges of pursuing the American dream. Where once adults with Down syndrome were cared for in large congregate settings isolated from their communities or lived at home with their families, today most people with Down syndrome are choosing a life that is very different from their forebearers.

Even the concept of choice—each individual determining how to live as an adult—is a new and changing idea. Society thought (and many segments of society continue to think) that people with Down syndrome were not capable of making choices about their lives, exercising control, and making decisions that would never be questioned for people without an intellectual or developmental disability. Yet today, individually and sometimes collectively, adults with Down syndrome are organizing to make their needs known, to have society consider them as contributors in an increasingly diverse world.

From the period after World War II until the late 1970s, the goals of advocacy were clear: going from nothing to something, going from inhumane to humane, and going from unfair to fair. Today, the issues are in many ways the same, and yet, in many ways they are different. Although some people have adequate supports and others have a full range of services, most still have little or nothing. There are still inhumane situations, but for most people with Down syndrome and their families, things are better. Advocacy efforts are evolving, with the focus changing from what people have to what people want and need, from quantity to quality, from access to outcomes. People are no longer content with merely receiving services. Adults with Down syndrome have learned that the goal is not merely acquiring services for survival but pursuing a better life, not just living in the community but being a vital part of that community.

Advocacy for children with Down syndrome is something that family members and professionals must engage in if the child—or later, the adult—is to experience all of the benefits of life in the community. Advocacy is a lifelong pursuit, if not for the individual then for the collective of individuals similarly situated. For children who do not experience disabilities, the array of programs ranging from child care to elementary and secondary school, from preventative pediatric care to after-school activities, from religious education to scouting, all readily assist them in reaching a productive and independent adulthood. Family involvement is encouraged or at least tolerated, but it is the systems, and the people who work in them, that move children along from beginning to end.

Those same programs, while vastly improved—largely due to the efforts of parents and professionals advocating for change—frequently ignore or discriminate against those with disabilities. Sometimes it is active discrimination, and other times, it is passive and insidious. In any form, discrimination—whether it be bias, denial of services, or some other form of exclusion from the community—calls for advocacy.

To illustrate the point, here's a story from Donna Martinez, an advocate and Andy's mom, in Northern Virginia about the 2004 elections.

On that first Tuesday in November, after standing in line for more than 2 hours, 18-year-old Andy Martinez cast the first ballot of his adult life. Self-advocacy and his self-determined right to freedom of choice have always been an essential part of Andy's education and life. As he left the voting booth with his father, Jorge Martinez, ready at the side for support if needed, Andy exclaimed, "I voted for *my* candidate! I made *my* choice!" Andy knew whom he wanted, refusing to be swayed by the family debates held at the kitchen table. Rather, in the months leading up to the election, he studied the issues, charted the differences between the presidential candidates, read the newspaper, and listened to the candidates' speeches. In his government and reading courses, he learned new vocabulary using the sample ballot as his textbook. Andy was ready that November 2, 2004. He voted. (personal communication)

Who Andy chose is not relevant. The fact that he exercised his right is. And in the 1960s, before advocacy for young people like Andy, he could have been denied this right. Stories like Andy's were repeated thousands of times during the election of 2004. Voting, the most fundamental of American rights, is individual advocacy at its purest.

LEVELS OF ADVOCACY

Advocacy occurs at four levels: individual, systems, legislative, and legal. It takes place by individuals, groups, and organizations. All forms are necessary, interrelated, and important.

Individual Advocacy

Individual advocacy focuses on getting what one person wants or, at times, what others want for one person. Advocates can be family members, professionals, or volunteers. Ideally, the person with disabilities who is being represented agrees with the advocates. Individual advocacy works best when it's done *with* a person with disabilities, not *for* him or her.

Individual advocacy is about understanding the person, preparation, presentation, and use of power. Many adults with Down syndrome experience services that are not of their own design or choosing and live lives designed for them by others. Imagine getting up in the morning and dreading what you will do that day. Every day. What kind of an impact would this have on you as a person? Now imagine that you face challenges to change what you are experiencing. Others must voice what you want, but you know that their voices are not stating your true needs and wants.

There is always a gap between what a person with disabilities communicates and what advocates think the person wants. The more significant a person's intellectual disability, the greater the challenge for an advocate to understand what the person wants and the greater the temptation for the advocate to substitute his or her own judgment for the person's. Listening to and understanding what the person wants is vital.

Advocates must also be prepared. They must understand the rules and regulations, if they exist, for the situation they are trying to influence; understand the position of those they are trying to influence; and translate what the subject of advocacy—a real person—wants.

Presentation in advocacy is also an important skill, one worthy of preparation and rehearsal. Advocacy is not about being loud and angry, though there certainly are situations where being loud and angry is called for and works. Presentation is about forcefully explaining what is not right, what it takes to make it right, how it can be done, and getting an answer. It is in part a negotiation, in part a demand. In *Getting to Yes: Negotiating Agreement without Giving In,* Fisher and Ury (1991) talk about separating the relationship between the people involved from the substance of the issue. This book is a must read for anyone regularly engaging in advocacy. For many, it is hard to be forceful and polite, respectful and firm. Everyone wants to be liked, and advocating for an individual with disabilities may cause a person to be disliked.

Advocates must assess the situation they are advocating for, understanding the dynamics of those whom they are trying to influence and understanding what centers of power are available to them to help effectuate change, in order to get the outcome they want. Power need not be adversarial, and it need not be loud, but it is an important tool to understand as an advocate.

Systems Advocacy

Unlike individual advocacy, systems advocacy focuses on changing an organization, a set of practices, or an entire service-delivery system on behalf of many people. It requires a sustained and organized commitment and, as those organizations in the parent advocacy movement have learned over more than a half century, advocacy is most effective when done by people who are directly affected. Systems advocacy frequently involves multiple issues across a time span that is usually longer than the time span of issues affecting one person. It is both more work and different work from individual advocacy, though many of the core principles are the same. Systems advocacy is called for when an organization's or system's practices, laws, or policies cause the same problem or violate the rights of many individuals and when, without advocacy, a reasonable person might expect that these same problems would continue.

In systems advocacy, the basic principle of advocacy—effective communication of information—is the same, but how advocacy is implemented is quite different. For families, individuals with disabilities, and professionals, information is power. Communication styles and patterns are changing rapidly, and communication is the key to the future of advocacy. Advocates working at the systems level must communicate effectively in order to thrive and must disseminate information as needed. Leaders in systems advocacy must be viewed as those who are "in the know" in their communities.

The first task in a systems advocacy effort is much like an individual advocacy effort—defining the problem. Usually more than one family is involved, so systems advocacy presents multiple challenges to communicating a consistent message among those involved in advocacy. Many families looking to improve their children's elementary education, for example, will likely have different perspectives of what is called for. In these situations, there are most likely different perceptions of the problems and issues and perhaps disagreement that a problem actually exists. Building coalitions between individuals and groups calls for honest dialogue and communication about the issue, desired outcome, and strategies to reach that outcome.

After a problem has been defined, the Brain Injury Resource Center (http://www.headinjury.com/advosystem.html) offers the following advice:

1. Gather information—To do good systems advocacy it is important to understand the rules, laws, policies, and traditions of systems. You need to know who has the power and authority to make the changes you want.

2. Realize that organizations protect themselves—When you advocate with an organization, its first impulse may be to do nothing. You may need to find things that the organization wants in order to get what you want.

3. Understand the organization and how it works—Learn what you can about the organization, its governing structure, and its funding. This will help you create positive motivation for change.

4. Make sure your organization is considered by others to be informed, effective, and knowledgeable—It is important that others perceive you to be organized, focused, and informed.

In the field of services and supports for people with intellectual and developmental disabilities, the most prominent and, for many, the all-consuming target of systems advocacy since the 1970s has been to close state-run institutions and to support people living in the community. Since the 1980s, the population of people with intellectual and developmental disabilities living in large state-run facilities decreased by more than 67% (Prouty, Smith, & Lakin, 2004). The number of people in state-operated institutions peaked in 1975 and continues to decrease annually. This did not happen by accident, but rather as a result of long-term systems, legislative, and legal advocacy by groups of advocates, organized to accomplish the goal of eliminating institutional care in the United States. (For an in-depth account of one institutional closure, see Rothman & Rothman, 2005.)

The existence of public institutions today is a reminder that systems advocacy frequently takes place over a long period of time and that success requires a sustained effort on the part of many. Despite three decades of progress, more than 40,000 people (Prouty et al., 2004) remain in institutions today, decades after the field has proved successful in providing these same people with more effective support in the community.

Increasingly, systems advocacy is taking place in concert with organizations that have related missions and values but are not exclusively focused on people with intellectual and developmental disabilities. *Coalitions* are groups of organizations who choose to work together on a common goal or cause for a common purpose and to better utilize their own resources. A *collaboration,* however, is people or organizations working to accomplish a common objective. These concepts are related but not identical.

Working in coalitions and in collaboration with other organizations has benefits and challenges. A wise organizational executive once said, "Collaboration is an unnatural act by un-consenting adults!" Organizations collaborate due to the complex nature of problems, a scarcity of resources, and because it is more effective than working alone (Borden, Perkins, & Haas, 1998). They collaborate because multiple sources of input can help to solve complex problems easier than single sources of inputs. By definition, collaboration is an inclusive process. For adults with Down syndrome, collaboration with organizations not focused primarily on people with intellectual and developmental disabilities presents its own challenges.

As people with Down syndrome are regularly included in the fabric of community life, they will likely encounter individuals in organizations with preconceived and outdated notions about the ability of people with disabilities to effectively participate in community collaboration, especially in leadership roles. This can be a cause of tension. It is all too easy for individuals with disabilities to be either marginalized or relegated to roles that are supportive, rather than assuming leadership roles. People with Down syndrome have a great deal to contribute to the work of coalitions, and as a group can both receive benefit and contribute to the outcomes of these efforts. They do not deserve to be second-class citizens in their communities or in collaborations.

To avoid some of the downsides of collaborative efforts, it is important to plan in advance of collaborative efforts. Decisions about required outcomes and key values and principles—those things that cannot be compromised—must take place for collaborative efforts to be effective. People with Down syndrome can then enter into collaborative processes with a clear sense of what they want and need and what compromises they are willing to make in order to gain their objectives.

Working in collaborations or coalitions requires compromise. As an example, in most states the wages paid to those who directly support people with intellectual and developmental disabilities are inadequate. Bands of organizations that provide direct services are working to get increased funds from state legislatures to increase those wages. At the same time, there are waiting lists for services to adults, and there are an increasing number of adults with intellectual and developmental disabilities living in a household where one parent is older than 65 years of age. Those who are getting services or waiting for services are demanding increasing control of what is provided, how it is provided, and by whom it is provided. To get more funds for staff salaries, provider organizations are working with legislatures to address these issues.

Adults with Down syndrome are likely not opposed to increased staff salaries, but those in need of supports realize that if existing staff receive more funds, there are fewer funds for those waiting. Those with existing services are supportive of staff being paid a better wage, but they also want control of who those staff people are, as well as where they themselves live and what supports they get. In the mix of these issues, the possibilities for collaboration exist, and if managed carefully, multiple needs can be addressed at the same time. The compromises made in such situations are based on deciding between multiple issues that are all important and not dividing the issues between good and bad.

Legislative Advocacy

Because many of the programs and supports people need to function well in the community are governed by federal and state law, legislative advocacy is an important part of the equation for success. Although the systems in each state are somewhat different from one another and from the federal system, the basic rules for success are the same. Legislative advocacy through grassroots lobbying has affected how funds have been appropriated, how state laws enabling the implementation of federal laws and programs have been passed, and how advocates have accomplished a great many things, from closing state-run institutions to providing community-based supports and services in places of people's own choosing, to helping employment agencies do a better job of connecting people with disabilities to real jobs.

Working with state legislatures and Congress is foreign to most Americans and yet, to people with Down syndrome, it is close to becoming a survival skill. Programs and services that help people live a decent life in the community are affected by what goes on in each state capital and in Washington, D.C. There are enormous, almost unfathomable, amounts of money spent on lobbying on issues that affect the daily lives of people with Down syndrome, and organized groups representing people with intellectual and developmental disabilities cannot hope to compete with the sheer volume of paid lobbyists and financial support to politicians who work on those issues. There are dozens of programs for which the level of financial support for the program—and in the case of some legislation, even its mere existence—is dependent on advocacy by individuals, families, organized groups, and coalitions.

Government resources are, by definition, scarce, and as the population of the United States ages, the competition for those public resources will intensify. The current political climate also is dominated by calls for lower levels of taxation, and the courts have increasingly decided against individual rights in favor of states' rights.

To have an effective voice, legislative advocacy must be practiced year round and in an organized fashion. There are some basic principles to follow, whether dealing with one's county council, state legislature, or Congress. For people with Down syndrome—whether working as individuals, as part of an organized group, or in conjunction with their families and friends, or all of these—being an active participant in the political process has never been easier or more important.

Every legislature has three basic functions: 1) passing laws to address issues or solve problems of their jurisdiction and/or constituents; 2) appropriating funds for programs and services, based on the laws they pass; and 3) exercising oversight of the executive branch of the government of which they are a part. All legislators are elected to fulfill these basic functions. In some jurisdictions, they also confirm appointments made by the executive branch of government, such as judges or members of the mayor's, governor's, or president's cabinet. They are elected to represent their constituents and can be reelected only when the people in their area give them the most votes.

In 1993, Congress debated a plan to add a prescription drug benefit for those eligible for Medicare. The pharmaceutical companies had an enormous amount of money for lobbying. "In its budget for the fiscal year that begins on July 1, the pharmaceutical lobby earmarks $72.7 million for advocacy at the federal level, directed mainly at Congress; $4.9 million to lobby the Food and Drug Administration; and $48.7 million for advocacy at the state level" (Pear, 2003). People with Down syndrome, their families, and agencies and organizations that work with and for them cannot compete with this level of funding. To get an idea of how this plays out in your state, determine what percentage of the national population your state is (http://www.census.gov) and multiply that by $48.7 million. What kind of lobbying for resources, policies, and practices do you think this one industry favors in your state? Are their views necessarily in the best interest of individuals with Down syndrome? What happens when their views are heard but yours are not? Other industries, from hospitals and nursing homes, to providers of services for people with intellectual and developmental disabilities, to organizations representing teachers, school boards, employers, and transportation agencies, to name a few, also have a presence at the state and national levels.

So how does a person with Down syndrome compete? My advice to individuals with Down syndrome is this:

1. To have influence on elected officials, it is important that the officials hear from you. This means that you write (increasingly, it is better to e-mail and to fax than to send actual letters through regular mail to members of Congress due to screening precautions and procedures for mail, in place since September 11, 2001) and tell them of your support for or opposition to something they are considering or should be considering. It is important to be concise, brief, and never to use your vote as a threat when contacting an elected official. They know that you are interested in something, and they know that you may not vote for them if they do not support your position.

2. Be known to your elected officials. There are many ways to do this. One is to visit their local or district offices and to become known to their staff and to them. Follow-up your visit with a short letter repeating what you want. Elected officials, especially at the state and national levels, rely on staff to keep them informed of constituent concerns. So, even if you cannot regularly go to the state capitol or Washington, most district offices are convenient to people in that district. Do not go only when you want something, but go regularly. Make certain they know of your interest in a variety of issues, including issues specific to people with Down syndrome.

3. Volunteer for those elected officials who have a track record of supporting issues you favor. Except for U.S. senators who have a 6-year term, most elected officials are on a much shorter reelection cycle. Whether you volunteer on a campaign or in their office, they will recognize you and appreciate your efforts on their behalf. If you can, make contributions in whatever amount you can afford. Again, money is a big part of the elections process in all levels of government, and your contribution and support count.

4. When issues are in front of a legislative committee that affects people with intellectual and developmental disabilities, the most effective and important people to testify are not the paid profes-

sionals but rather families and people with intellectual and developmental disabilities themselves. Elected officials have difficult decisions to make, as there are never enough resources to go around. An effective presentation by people directly affected by their decisions makes an impression. Testimony should be genuine, concise, and to the point. It should be about the issues at hand and in the words of the person giving the testimony. If expert testimony on a particular aspect of legislation or policy is needed, there are ample experts available to give that testimony.

There are numerous guides on how to write to a member of Congress and how to testify. (See http://www.thearc.org/ga/trainmat. html.) Like anything else, there are rules and guidelines for being an effective legislative advocate. The late Justin Dart, Jr. (1930–2002), a person with a disability who served under President George H. W. Bush, who was awarded the Presidential Medal of Freedom by President Bill Clinton, and who advocated for 40 years for the rights of all people with disabilities, said, "Be involved in politics as if your life depended on it, because it does!" The interactions between people with intellectual and developmental disabilities and their government are crucial and, fortunately, the tools to be successful are readily available for those who use them. People with Down syndrome and their families, friends, neighbors, fellow congregants, and co-workers can be a powerful force for positive legislative change if they exercise their rights to vote and to participate in the political process.

I'm sure I'm not the first to tell you that the Internet is the future. It is ideally suited to advocacy; it's quick and it's cheap, and it reaches the entire world. Many systems and legislative advocates are using it daily, and others are joining in. Imagine how the movement for the rights and freedoms enjoyed today by people with all disabilities might have grown if the Internet had been around for the past half century. Advocates can use the Internet to communicate cheaply and rapidly with each other and with legislators and to find information to stay well-informed.

Legal Advocacy

Adults with Down syndrome sometimes take advantage of legal advocacy to assure rights, to receive or protect benefits, to get access to services, and to address wrongs. Legal advocacy is sometimes used in conjunction with individual advocacy, systems advocacy, and legislative advocacy. Legal advocacy is used to challenge a decision by an executive branch agency in a hearing and appeals process or in court; to challenge a trial court ruling on an issue related to services, rights, or benefits; to address discrimination or other harm done by a private or government agency; or to seek a ruling as to the interpretation of a statute.

In each state, there are multiple organizations that focus on legal rights, some specific to people with developmental disabilities (e.g., state Protection and Advocacy Agency), which are funded under a variety of statues, including the Developmental Disabilities Act (PL 106-402), and distributed to various rights centers for people who are poor, who have physical disabilities, or who live in a certain geographic region. In addition, there are attorneys in most states who have expertise and interest in disability law, both in private firms and in organizations focused on people with disabilities.

Legal advocacy is an important source of support for adults with Down syndrome. It can also be adversarial and be a long, drawn-out, and costly process to achieve the desired outcomes. Like other forms of advocacy, there are no guarantees with this process.

ADVOCACY THROUGHOUT THE LIFE SPAN

Being an adult with Down syndrome brings with it a recent (in terms of social history) sense of power and ability to control one's own life and to be a fully participating member of the community. Becoming an adult and living as part of the community successfully requires advocacy for the person with Down syndrome, for his or her family, and from both of them and others in the community. To fully understand some of the opportunities, obstacles, and challenges, this section presents issues ranging from early childhood to senior living in order to give the reader a more clear understanding of the transitions in advocacy at different stages in the life of a person with Down syndrome.

Childhood

Advocacy for children begins with the premise that a child's parents are experts on their own child. This does not mean that they know everything about their child; they are not expected to have the knowledge of a pediatrician, an educator, or a therapist. Yet, over time, parents acquire a lot of that sort of knowledge from professionals. A parent, more so than others, is the expert on his or her child's strengths and needs, likes and dislikes, moods, expressions, habits, and routines. All of these things contribute to making every child unique. Starting with that assumption, parents know that their child likes bright sunlight or a dim room, likes it cool or hot, likes food that is spicy or bland, and likes certain kinds of music. Stemming from a parent's knowledge of his or her child is the assumption that parents will do what they think is best for their child, which is typically the case.

Advocacy for children is somewhat different from advocacy for and by adults, as the social norms and laws for what a family does with and for their child are different from what adults, attaining or striving for independence, do for themselves and with their families. A family advocating for a child's inclusion in child care or preschool is a frequent situation, and the roles are clear. Parents make decisions for their infants and toddlers about such things. At the individual level, advocacy requires listening, helping a family to move from ideas to actions, and communicating options and choices. Families work to know and communicate what they want and learn to understand their power and ability to reach their goal of securing for their child good, inclusive child care. Most situations are not so clear and so easily resolved, but the principles apply regardless.

Adulthood

The goal of adult life for people with Down syndrome is the same as it is for people without disabilities: to do something productive to earn a living, to have a place to live they can call their own, to marry and raise a family, to be involved with friends, to take part in activities that they enjoy, and to participate in the fabric of the community in which they live, at levels that are of their own choosing. In the history of the United States, these goals are very recent for people with disabilities and came about because of the advocacy of family members and people with Down syndrome themselves.

The system for adults is different. Some programs have entitlements attached to them, whereas others are at the discretion of the state legislature. Advocating for a life in the community as an adult requires knowledge of the various systems available to help adults with Down syndrome live decently. What happens in Washington, in the state capital, and in the county courthouse has a greater impact on people with Down syndrome than on people who do not directly experience disabilities.

Services and Supports Most programs for adults with Down syndrome have both federal and state roots. Adults may need support from organizations providing vocational rehabilitation or employment services:

- Federal programs authorized by the U.S. Department of Education or the U.S. Department of Labor with implementation at state-operated or state-authorized agencies

- Health care services funded mostly by Medicaid or, for those eligible, Medicare

- Transportation services, either those used regularly by the general public or specialized services provided at the federal level as authorized by the U.S. Department of Transportation to a state, local, or regional transit agency

- Housing as provided through federal programs authorized through the U.S. Department of Housing and Urban Development (HUD) to state or local housing agencies

- Supplemental Security Income (SSI) from the Social Security Administration, with access through state Disability Determination Offices

- Home and community-based supports through Medicaid, a federal-state program with funds coming from both levels of government, the Centers for Medicare & Medicaid Services at the federal level, and a single state Medicaid agency in each state

- Technology services authorized through the U.S. Department of Education to state technology projects

There are many more programs that directly affect the lives of adults with intellectual and developmental disabilities, some specialized and others that benefit the general public as well. Increasingly, adults with Down syndrome are succeeding in the world with both specialized services and those programs available to the general public.

For adults with Down syndrome, the role of the family remains important. As a former federal official said, "When things for my son go to hell in a hand basket, who better than his father and I to make sure that things are fixed so he continues to have a good life?" (S. Swenson, personal communication). It is this unique relationship that is the source of strength as well as some challenges for adults with Down syndrome. As adults with Down syndrome are speaking out for themselves, what they want and what their families want are not always the same.

The system of services and supports for adults who need them is organized differently in each state. In addition to the differences between these systems and the public elementary and secondary education systems, they are also very different from one another. Although people with intellectual and developmental disabilities may be the reason such systems were created, the systems sometimes define themselves as entities that serve people with disabilities and don't consider the recipients of services as an integral part of those systems.

However, systems do not "own" people, and in too many places systems are still serving the dual function of limiting access to necessary supports and services and dictating what people receive, as opposed to what they may want and need.

In some states, a cabinet-level department funds and sometimes directly operates services for people. In other states, the primary agency for people with disabilities is contained in an agency that offers other human service programs and that is housed with agencies with a health and human service mandate. In many states, there is a local government or quasi-government entity between the state agency and the local provider of service, whether called a Regional Center (California), Community Services Board (Virginia), or County MH/MR Administrator (Pennsylvania). Sometimes, the regional entity is part of the same state department that funds, regulates, and operates the service. Regardless of the structure, no one has shown that there is relationship between those structures and the outcomes sought by adults with Down syndrome (R. Gettings, personal communication). To get a better understanding of the system in the state where you live, visit http://www.thearclink.org/system/index.asp.

Income Many people with Down syndrome can and do leave school and find ways to support themselves in their community, but the role of family and of the formal support system remains vital. Most adults with Down syndrome, even if working full time, earn a low income. In 2003, a single person in the lower 48 states earning below $8,980 per year was considered to be poor (U.S. Department of Health and Human Services, 2003). Only about 32% of all adults with disabilities work full time (National Organization on Disability, 1998, 2000), and the number of people with Down syndrome is suspected to be significantly lower than that. Therefore, interaction with public systems of support can be expected for some or all of a person's adult life.

SSI is an important program that makes monthly cash payments to people with disabilities to meet their basic needs. Although it is managed by the Social Security Administration, SSI is paid for with general tax dollars, not from Social Security Trust Funds. The basic federal amount is the same in all 50 states, though some states supplement the federal payment. In many states, people receiving SSI also automatically receive Medicaid, a health and long-term care program.

Although people on SSI can earn a small amount of money without losing eligibility for the cash benefit and Medicaid, the average person on SSI is by him- or herself below the poverty level and unable to afford his or her own housing. *Priced Out in 2002: Housing Crisis Worsens for People with Disabilities* (Cooper & O'Hara, 2003), a report on housing from the Technical Assistance Collaborative, found that by comparing SSI monthly income (equal to $545 in 2002) to the HUD fair market rents across the United States, in 2002, for the first time ever, the average national rent was greater than the amount of income received by Americans with disabilities from the SSI program. Specifically, the average rent for a modest one-bedroom rental unit in the United States was equal to 105% of federal SSI benefit amounts, up from 98% as reported in *Priced Out in 2000* (http://www.C-C-D.org//POin2000.html). In 2002, people with disabilities were priced out of every housing market area in the United States. Of the nation's 2,702 market areas, there was not a single area where modestly priced rents for efficiency or one-bedroom units were affordable for people with disabilities receiving SSI. People with disabilities continue to be the poorest people in the nation. As a national average, SSI benefits in 2002 were equal to only 18.8% of the one-person median household income.

SELF-ADVOCACY

Self-advocacy—people with disabilities advocating for themselves—is a growing and thriving movement. People who a generation ago were written off as noncontributing, as victims, as people without power or worth, are on a daily basis speaking for themselves; organizing and forming associations with others; and changing the way professionals, the media, and the three branches of government think about people with intellectual and developmental disabilities. The self-advocacy movement started in Scandinavia in the early 1960s, and the People First organization was formed in Oregon in the early 1970s (William & Shoultz, 1982). Self-advocacy is a natural outgrowth of the movements for educational rights (Individuals with Disabilities Education Act [IDEA] of 1990, PL 101-476), civil rights (Americans with Disabilities Act [ADA] of 1990, PL 101-336), and the move to close large segregated residential and school settings for people with intellectual and developmental disabilities.

Self-advocates today are organized in most states and have the vigor and passion often seen early in other social movements. Not content to have others speak for them, self-advocates have adopted the slogan "Nothing about us without us!" They want their voices and ideas to be heard and do not feel they need intermediaries to help them express their views. Their growth and successes are remarkable, and leaders are emerging from that movement in the same way leaders have emerged from other social movements.

Self-advocates face some unique challenges in conducting advocacy, mostly related to understanding of complex rules and regulations, most of which are not written to be easily understandable by nonprofessionals, let alone by those for whom reading may present some challenges. Yet, a generation of professional and family leaders readily acknowledge the leadership and contributions of self-advocates to the movement of inclusion and freedom for all people with disabilities. Self-advocates are beginning to take their place at the table when organizations are discussing and debating policy and legislative issues.

SUMMARY

For adults with Down syndrome, advocacy is moving from quantity and access to quality and outcomes. Services and supports are the means to an end, not the end itself. There is a difference between a high quality of services and supports and a high quality of life. Although it is easier to measure the effectiveness of services than the effectiveness of advocacy, both services and advocacy need to be done well. Just because a person advocates does not mean that he or she is good at it or that it achieves the desired outcome!

Over the course of more than a half century, organizations involved with people who have Down syndrome have been adapting to the changing needs of families and adults with Down syndrome. All organizations must modernize to meet future challenges facing people with Down syndrome. As a society, we have to develop both process and outcome standards and measurements for advocacy. We have to find sustainable financing vehicles for individual advocacy. We need to continue advocacy's transition from quantity/access to quality/outcomes. We must manage advocacy and self-advocacy so that they work together when necessary and separately when called for. All of these are wonderful challenges. As adults with Down syndrome continue to demand that they be part of their community and be treated as adults first and foremost, those of us interested in the well-being of people with intellectual and developmental disabilities must pay attention. Our roles are changing also, and people with Down syndrome and those who work with and for them will all be better off because of advocacy.

REFERENCES

Americans with Disabilities Act (ADA) of 1990, PL 101-336, 42 U.S.C. §§ 12101 et seq.

Borden, L., Perkins, D., & Haas, B.E. (1998, December 7). *Collaboration: The power of we the people.* Available from http://crs.uvm.edu/nnco/

Cooper, E., & O'Hara, A. (2003, May). Priced out in 2002: Housing crisis worsens for people with disabilities. *Opening Doors, 21.*

Developmental Disabilities Act, PL 106-402, 114 Stat. 1677, 42 U.S.C. 15001 *et seq.*

Fisher, R., & Ury, W., with Patton, B. (1991). *Getting to yes: Negotiating agreement without giving in* (2nd ed.). New York: Penguin Books.

Individuals with Disabilities Education Act (IDEA) of 1990, PL 101-476, 20 U.S.C. §§ 1400 *et seq.*

Kennedy, F.R. (1976). *Color me Flo: My hard life and good times.* Upper Saddle River, NJ: Prentice Hall.

National Organization on Disabilities. (1998, July 23). *NOD/Harris survey of Americans with disabilities.* Washington, DC: Louis Harris & Associates.

National Organization on Disability. (2000). *Employment rates of people with disabilities: N.O.D./Harris 2000 survey of Americans with disabilities.* Washington, DC: Louis Harris & Associates.

Pear, R. (2003, June 1). Drug companies increase spending to lobby congress and governments. *The New York Times,* p. 1.

Prouty, R.W., Smith, G., & Lakin, K.C. (2004, June). *Residential services for persons with developmental disabilities: Status and trends through 2003.* Minneapolis: University of Minnesota, Research and Training Center on Community Living, Institute on Community Integration.

Rothman, D.J., & Rothman, S.M. (2005). *The Willowbrook wars: Bringing the mentally disabled into the community.* New Brunswick, NJ: Aldine Transaction.

Silverstein, R. (2002). *A congressional insider's view: How to be an effective disability policy change agent.* Washington, DC: Center for the Study and Advancement of Disability Policy.

U.S. Department of Health and Human Services. (2003, February 7). Annual update of the HHS poverty guidelines. *Federal Register, 68*(26), 6456–6458.

William, P., & Shoultz, B. (1982). *We can speak for ourselves.* Boston: Brookline Books.

25

...

My Life

CHRISTINE D. MAXWELL

...

My name is Christine Maxwell. I live in Evanston, Illinois, with my roommate. My parents live in South Barrington, Illinois. It is about an hour away from me. I am 27 years old. I have two sisters, Becky and Suzy. They are 2 and 4 years older than me. I have two brothers in law, Michael and Dave. I also have three nieces and three nephews.

All of my life, I just wanted to do the same things as my sisters. When I finished high school, I wanted to live in a dorm at college, too. My mom worked hard to find just the right place for me. When I applied for college, they said I did not qualify for their academics, and no one with Down syndrome went there before, but my application looked interesting. So, I went for an interview and told them all about how I try really hard and I know about college from visiting my sisters in their dorms.

They decided to give me a chance. I proved to them I could do it, and I did it for 2 years. I graduated from National-Louis University PACE Program with a Prebaccalaureate Certificate. The program teaches career preparation, academics, life skills, and socialization.

I lived in the dorm for 2 years and have been in apartments for 4 years. My roommates are graduates of the PACE program, too. At first, I was in the Transition Program, having staff come by once a week to see everything was okay in the apartment and with my friends. Now, I graduated from that program and am completely independent.

I work at Century Theatre. I take tickets and tell people where to go for their movie. I sometimes work at the concession stand and make popcorn. I have been there 3 years. I had another job first at a dentist's office, but that didn't work out.

My favorite thing to do is being social with my friends. We go out for dinner, order carryout, or I cook. I take my friends to movies. That is a perk of my job—free movies—and I can bring a friend for free, too.

I live close to lots of stores, so I spend a lot of time shopping and just looking around and making lists of what I would like to have for my birthday and Christmas. I take a taxi, bus, train, or my friends drive me to get around. I have to pay close attention when I am out to keep safe from strangers and traffic and remember all the rules. When I am alone, I draw, paint, and play videogames. I take classes at Evanston Art Center, the YMCA, and Evanston adult continuing education classes. For vacations, I go with friends on planned trips with the Special Recreation Park District. Every day, I make lists to plan what I have to do.

I work hard to take my thyroid medicine. My biggest problem is my weight. It is hard. I work out on a treadmill a few times a week.

I go to the bank with my checks, pay bills, and keep my checkbook balanced. I also have a credit card that I have to be careful using. Doing laundry and keeping my apartment clean takes a lot of time, too.

The next decisions I am working on are I want to get married and have a wedding dress and wedding just like my sisters. I have a boyfriend. We know when you get married it is a big step and both people need to know how to live independently. I have made the decision I will not have children. It is not a good idea for me, and I decided it is too much work. I love being an aunt, and that is enough.

I have a wonderful life. It is okay with me having Down syndrome. I have been able to do a lot of things because of having it. I have always been very active with Special Olympics since I was 8 years old. I have been in almost every sport. In gymnastics, I went all the way to winning a Gold Medal at Special Olympic World Games. I have been able to fly to New York to tape a film for Special Olympics, give speeches, and have dinner at the White House with the President. I am on the board of NADS (National Association for Down Syndrome) and talk to a lot of parents with new babies with Down syndrome.

My life so far has kept me very busy. My big question to my family every day is what's next? What can I do now? I like to keep very busy.

26

■ ■ ■

My Life on the "UP"-side of My Down Syndrome disABILITY

ANN M. FORTS

■ ■ ■

Hi!!! My name is Ann Margaret Forts, and all my friends call me Annie. I was born with Down syndrome, and most people, except for my family, generally had very low expectations for me.

As most of you know, the doctor who discovered Down syndrome many years ago was named Dr. John Langdon Down, and that is why it is called Down syndrome. I prefer saying "UP" syndrome because Down syndrome always sounds too negative to me, and I have always been an "UP" person. Ever since I was 7 or 8 years old, I have changed the meaning of Down syndrome by crossing out the word "Down" and adding the word "UP," so that Down syndrome reads as "UP" syndrome instead.

I really wish that Dr. John Langdon Down, who discovered Down syndrome, was named Dr. Up instead. Then, Down syndrome would have been called "UP" syndrome and maybe more people would begin with a better attitude toward us as they begin to understand what we are all about and what we are really capable of doing.

People keep asking me how come I always seem to be so happy and satisfied with my life, even though I was born with Down syndrome. They seem to expect, just because my so-called *disABILITY* is Down syndrome, that I am not able to do the same things they do.

Well, based on my own personal experiences, I must say that those people who think that way, are definitely wrong. In fact, they are very wrong! I am leading a very happy and satisfying life mainly because I always try to be very positive, or have an "UP" attitude in everything I do.

I might not do some things as well as other people, but I certainly do enjoy myself because I am always willing to try something new—especially when people try to tell me that it is something they think that I cannot do. Sometimes, I really surprise them, and at times I surprise myself, too!

For someone like me, I feel it is very important to get involved in my community by working, volunteering, joining a service club, and being active in my church. Because of my community involvement in so many different areas, I am leading a very active, satisfying, and happy social life.

My family has always encouraged me to look for new challenges for me to try. I have had lots of fun competing in different Special Olympics events like swimming, track, and ski races. I have also taken lessons in ballet, horseback riding, piano, swimming, racquetball, exercise equipment, ice skating, water skiing, and snow skiing.

I hope you don't misunderstand me. I really am not an expert in everything. But, I do think I can swim and water ski pretty well. Also, my piano playing is not great, but I do play well enough to enjoy myself.

The things that I like most to do are reading, dancing, taking pictures with my camera, and working on my photo albums. I also enjoy writing letters and sending all kinds of greeting cards to family and friends, listening to country and western music, singing karaoke, and watching television. I love going to restaurants, plays, and music concerts. Most of all, I really enjoy traveling all over the United States for my motivational speaking engagements.

During the last 15 years, I have traveled from 5,000 to 20,000 miles each year speaking at local meetings and regional and national conferences and conventions. I have spoken to audiences of from 12 to 15 people, to over 2,000 people. I have enjoyed speaking to many different audiences like elementary and high school students and their teachers; college and med-school students and professors; parent support groups; professionals, including social workers, doctors, and nurses; federal, state, and local human services agencies; disability organizations; service clubs like the Lions and Rotary clubs; and many other clubs and church groups.

When I am not involved with one of my speaking engagements, I try to keep busy with my part-time jobs and volunteering in my community. My part-time jobs include working as a clerk in a video rental store, bagging groceries at a supermarket, and working at a farm stand. I volunteer at two local school districts, and I am a teacher's aide in a children's preschool program. I also work in the high school library and the school administration office.

During the summer months, I volunteer as an usher for a summer theater group. I have tried out for a part in a couple of plays but without any success. It was fun, and I guess that I will just have to keep trying.

I have also been kept busy with two separate fundraising projects that I started for the benefit of people with Down syndrome. I started *ANNIE'S "UP" FUND* over 10 years ago to help needy families in the National Down Syndrome Congress. I sold T-shirts, caps, sweatshirts, pins, and several other items that all use my own *"UP" Syndrome* logo design. I donated the profit of over $20,000 to the National Down Syndrome Congress.

I also started another fund about 7 years ago with a goal of at least $1,000,000 in donations. The fund is called *The Annie Forts "UP" Syndrome Fund.* Interest only is used to provide award opportunities for people with Down syndrome to enjoy new experiences and to encourage and help support individuals interested in careers in special education. So far, we have raised over $200,000 and have given out over $50,000 in awards and for special education scholarships. For more information, please check out my web site: http://www.anniefortsupfund.org.

As you can see, all of my interests, my successful community inclusion, my jobs, my volunteering, my motivational speaking career, my family, and lots of friends and acquaintances have made it possible for me to lead a very happy, satisfying, interesting, and rewarding life. I have been honored with many appointments to state and federal disability advisory committees and also have been recognized with many national, regional, and local awards.

From my experiences, I have learned that the four most important things that are needed to achieve a truly satisfying, happy, and meaningful life are

- To develop and maintain a positive, or an "UP," attitude

- To meet lots of new people and develop new friendships

- To learn how to be independent and not be afraid to try new experiences

- And finally, to dream and set goals for yourself!

Now let me tell you about some of my personal dreams and goals that I have for my future:

- To write a book about my life on the "UP"-side of Down syndrome

- To act in a movie or in a television series
- To continue with my "UP" syndrome motivational speaking career
- To continue to help my "UP" Syndrome Fund reach my goal of $1,000,000 in donations, so that the fund will be able to help more young people with Down syndrome reach their true potential and award more scholarships for special education
- And finally, I hope that I will always have the opportunity to keep meeting new people and developing lots of new friendships

Meeting new people and developing lots of new friendships always has been one of the most important items on my list of things that have had the greatest influence on my life. I strongly urge everyone to meet as many new people as possible. I am sure that I don't have to tell anyone that this world can be a very lonely place without friends, especially for someone with a *disABILITY.*

Speaking of friends reminds me of one of my favorite stories that I would like to tell you about. One summer night a couple of years ago, my dad and I were sitting on our boat dock looking up at the sky. It was a beautiful clear night filled with lots of blinking stars. While we were talking and waiting to see some shooting stars, I told my dad that someday I hope to have as many friends as the number of stars that we were looking at in the sky. Do you know that I really feel that I am getting very close to my wish of having as many friends as the number of stars that are in the sky!!!

I have a very special request for anyone who meets a person with a *disABILITY.* Please remember and always be guided by one of my favorite expressions . . .

"Please don't ever, ever prejudge the limits of a person's abilities, just because he happens to have a *disABILITY!!!*"

Now you all know all the reasons why I am so happy and satisfied with my life and why my favorite expression is:

"I LOVE MY LIFE!!!"

27

∎∎∎

My Wonderful Life

KAREN TOFF

∎∎∎

You may wonder what it's like to be a person with Down syndrome. My name is Karen Toff. Truthfully, I'm just like everyone else. I have the same feelings and emotions like everybody. Also, I can learn. It might take me a little longer, but I really can learn. I live a full life surrounded by my loving family and caring friends.

If you would ask me what I have done that I'm most proud of, I would say it is living independently. For the past 9 years, my roommate and I have shared a two-bedroom apartment in a small community outside of Philadelphia. We take turns doing the cooking, cleaning, and chores with the help of a support team that comes every weekday afternoon. The team also helps us with menu planning, shopping, and interpersonal relationships. I *love* living independently and have had to learn to make good choices and follow the rules for being a good roommate.

Another of my accomplishments is my volunteer job at Bryn Mawr Hospital for the last 3 years. In the past, I have volunteered at a nursing home, at a public library, and at a preschool summer camp. Working at the hospital is great because I get to be with people. Some of the things that I do are mailings, clerical work, filing, errands, transporting patients, and laundry. If you would come to my "job," you would see me in a royal blue lab coat just like the other volunteers. Every day, all by myself, I take the train from my apartment to the hospital and back.

My family is a big and important part of my life. My dad was my biggest fan and admirer, but he died 11 years ago. He always encouraged me to do my best, and he dreamed that I could work and live independently. And guess what, he was right. My mom worries about me all the time and reminds me about using appropriate behavior. Although she lives close by, I call her very often. She is my biggest supporter. We do lots of things together like shopping, sharing meals, traveling and watching movies. She takes really good care of me, and I try to take care of her whenever she needs me.

Even though I am 44 years old, I am the youngest child in the family with two brothers and a sister. I am proud that I graduated from high school and a vocational program at Elwyn Institute. One brother is a child psychiatrist, and the other is a pediatrician. My sister is a special education teacher. My mom thinks that I might have influenced them in their career choices.

My nephew, who is just starting his freshman year at the University of Pennsylvania, is pretty amazing. When he was in high school, he started PALS (Peers Assisting Learning Support), a club to help and support the students in the special education class. PALS did some cool events like bowling parties, pizza parties, board games, and dances. All the members of PALS have enjoyed making new friendships. There are even PALS groups in several other states besides Pennsylvania. My nephew even received a big award at the National Down Syndrome Congress Convention in August 2004.

Last, but not least, let me tell you about my social life. I am a member of a young adult group called the Association for Developmental Disabilities. We have activities every weekend such as movies, bowling, theater, holiday parties, and trips. We also have weekly rap sessions on Tuesday nights to plan social activities and to discuss topics like jobs, independent living, and relationships. In addition, on the weekends, I get together with friends and go to the movies or to a restaurant. Last spring, I received the "Member of the Year" award from my young adult group, and I was so proud and happy.

My hobbies are playing the piano, listening to music, doing aerobics, and doing word-find puzzles. You don't need a TV Guide when you're with me because I know when all my favorite shows come on. I'm also pretty good at telling you what movies are playing. As you can tell, I'm a very social person.

In conclusion, I feel thankful and fortunate that I have such great support. I don't think I would be where I am today without the help and support that I have had. My family is always there for me. I know I can call them whenever I need them. My friends make the weekends so special. My teachers and support team have always encouraged me along the way. I hope to continue to be successful in my apartment, at my work, and with my friends.

Index

Page numbers followed by *f* indicate figures; those followed by *t* indicate tables.